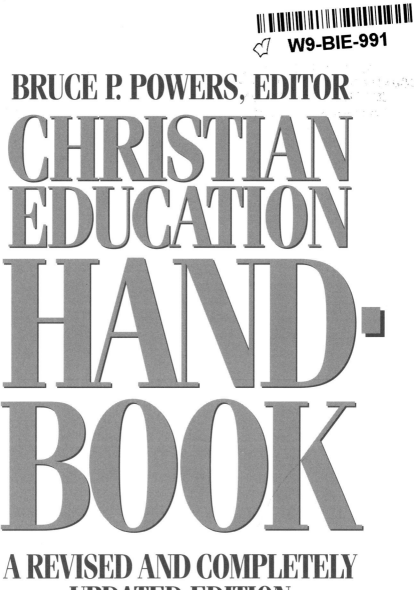

BRUCE P. POWERS, EDITOR

CHRISTIAN EDUCATION HANDBOOK

A REVISED AND COMPLETELY UPDATED EDITION

BROADMAN
& HOLMAN
PUBLISHERS

Nashville, Tennessee

To

Clara Langston and the memory of Perry Q. Langston,
friends and colleagues with a great vision
for the educational dimension of ministry.
Dr. Langston was professor of religious education
at Campbell University, Buies Creek,
North Carolina for more than thirty years.

© 1996
by Broadman & Holman
All rights reserved
Printed in the United States of America

4210–60
0-8054-1060-0

Dewey Decimal Classification: 268.1
Subject Heading: Religious Education—Administration
Library of Congress Card Catalog Number: 95–9335

Typography by TF Designs

Library of Congress Cataloging-in-Publication Data
Christian education handbook / Bruce P. Powers, editor.
    p. cm.
    "A revised and completely updated edition."
    Includes bibliographical references.
        ISBN 0-8054-1060-0 (pb)
        1.Christian education—Handbooks, manuals, etc. I. Powers, Bruce P.
    BV1471.2.C499   1996
    268'.1—dc20   95-9335
                                                                                          CIP

9 10 11   05 04 03 02

Contents

Section Three:
Educational Leadership in the Local Church

Preface

Time management is one of my biggest problems. As a church minister, as an educational administrator, and as a teacher with more than twenty years experience, I have found that keeping up with developments related to my work is a major drain on my time and energy.

The key problem as I have come to see it has always been *administrative overload*, related primarily to information, organizations, and administrative procedures.

As an educational leader, I always sought resources that would help me be more effective in my work by providing basic information and administrative guidelines. Being responsible for the total educational ministry of a church, however, I soon experienced *resource* overload. It was not that this information was unhelpful, but that each guidebook gave detailed instructions for administering a particular program or organization. This was excellent for directors of these activities, but it was an overload for me.

What about pastors, ministers of education, and other key church leaders who have major responsibility for administering the *entire* educational program? What is there to help leaders at this level of responsibility?

As I discussed this need with church leaders, I found that many of us shared similar concerns. One answer that emerged was the idea of a handbook that would bring together essential information and guidelines for administering the overall educational ministry in a local church: one resource piece combining the why and the how-to, with information and procedures appropriate for the key leader.

The result is this volume, written by persons who have served in churches, who know and love the educational dimension of ministry, and who have distinguished themselves as teachers and administrators.

In using this book, you will find that it can be read sequentially or that it can be consulted topically by referring to the expanded list of contents. Each chapter stands alone and references other portions as appropriate. Consequently, there is some overlap, but this is inherent in the design.

The book is divided into three sections: Foundations (chapters 1–3), Administration (chapters 4–12), and Leadership (chapters 13–15). Topics move from general theological and educational principles to specific administrative and leadership strategy. Each chapter focuses on practical ways to use the information presented.

The authors wish to express appreciation to Broadman and Holman Publishers for encouragement and insightful participation in planning for this new and enlarged edition; to the Sunday School Board (SBC) for supporting the project and providing access to pertinent resources; to more than thirty thousand church and denominational leaders, students, and professors who have used this resource; and to our students, who in their process of learning have helped us refine the concepts, values, and skills which we hope to impart.

I would like to express personal gratitude to the authors of this volume and to Mary Lou Stephens, my very helpful secretary.

Bruce P. Powers
Wake Forest, North Carolina

Contributors

Bob I. Johnson, Dean, Boyce Bible School, Louisville, Kentucky

Bruce P. Powers, Professor of Christian Education, Southeastern Seminary, Wake Forest, North Carolina, and visiting Langston Professor, Campbell University, Buies Creek, North Carolina.

Jerry M. Stubblefield, Professor of Christian Education, Golden Gate Seminary, Mill Valley, California

Edward A. Buchanan, Professor of Christian Education, Southeastern Seminary, Wake Forest, North Carolina

Daniel Aleshire, Associate Director, the Association of Theological Schools in the United States and Canada, Pittsburgh, Pennsylvania

James F. Hines, Academic Dean and Professor of Religious Education, Central Seminary, Kansas City, Kansas

C. Ferris Jordan, Professor of Christian Education and Adult Education, New Orleans Seminary, New Orleans, Louisiana

SECTION ONE:

Foundations for Administration and Leadership

1. Educational Ministry of the Church
2. Christian Education and Theology
3. The Christian Witness

Be imitators of God, as beloved children, and live in love, as Christ loved us and gave himself up for us.

Ephesians 5:1–2

CHAPTER 1

Educational Ministry of the Church

Bruce P. Powers

Although the church has always been a teaching institution, only since the early 1900s have churches identified their formal teaching activities as an educational ministry or program.

The Sunday school, largely an extrachurch, lay-directed organization during the nineteenth century, was later adopted by denominations as a means for teaching the Bible to the masses. This influence, along with increased public concern for education and moral development during the early twentieth century, exerted strong pressure on churches to devise educational organizations and programs to convey the content and values of their faith.

The first educational administrators came primarily out of the public school tradition. In larger churches, volunteers could no longer handle the time-consuming tasks of selecting and training teachers, organizing the Sunday school and other educational organizations, developing the curriculum, planning with leaders, and managing facilities. Thus, larger churches began to turn to their best-qualified volunteers and extended an invitation to broaden their responsibilities and opportunities in educational ministry.

From this modest beginning, a distinct area of church ministry has developed along with a corresponding administrative function—that of educational administration.

Education—along with worship, proclamation, ministry, and fellowship—is now recognized as one of the major functions of a church. Whereas the other functions have traditionally been administered by a pastor, educational responsibilities have been delegated in larger churches to a specialist and in smaller churches to several volunteer leaders. Although at first most educational specialists were not viewed as ministers, such leaders today usually are prepared theologically and educationally and serve on a church's ministerial staff.

In smaller churches, the pastor is usually the key educational administrator, assuming this responsibility along with other duties.

To some degree, however well or poorly done, educational ministry is provided in every church. The beginning point is found in the statement of purpose or objectives of a congregation, or if not formally recorded, in the people's hopes and dreams.

The purpose of a church has been encoded in certain formal and informal activities designed to perpetuate the institution. Formal activities such as Bible study classes and training groups make up a large part of the educational ministry or program, and informal teaching through congregational life and family nurture comprise a significant complementing influence.

It is the planned portion of activities under the direction and control of a church for which the educational administrator has primary responsibility. And it is these activities that comprise the structured, educational curriculum that enables a church to achieve its purpose.

WHAT ARE WE TRYING TO DO TO PEOPLE?

The answer to the question "What are we trying to do to people?" suggests a congregation's expectations about its educational ministry and the leader. If these expectations are clearly defined, appropriate structures and experiences can be provided. The alternative is to have unclear (or unsure) expectations, matched with structures and experiences which produce ambiguous results.

Teaching in the early church focused primarily on catechetical instruction, or *indoctrination*, which remained the major expression of Christian education until the development of the Sunday school in the eighteenth century.

Along with the idea of church school for laypersons came a renewed concern for *education*, dormant since the Reformation. An educated person could use the Bible and interpret God's message without depending on another. Commitments, freely chosen through personal study, could be the basis for one's Christian beliefs rather than adopting a set of beliefs passed down from others. Thus, education took its place alongside indoctrination as a means for passing on faith.

Revivalism, particularly in the United States during the eighteenth and nineteenth centuries, was a major influence in relating Sunday school and evangelism. The rapid growth of the Sunday school movement, the need for a way to teach converts, and the use of the Sunday school for *proclamation* (also called outreach and witnessing) contributed to an identity that has become an inseparable part of educational ministry in evangelical churches. Thus developed a general affirmation that Sunday school is responsible for Bible study *and* for proclamation, and that educational ministers/directors have a major responsibility for church growth.

Today the general view of a church educational ministry encompasses these three traditions: *indoctrination, education,* and *proclamation.* Each denomination, indeed every church, incorporates elements of each trying to answer the question, "What are we trying to do to people?" And, not surprisingly, each tradition provides a unique and necessary ingredient in effective Christian education.

THE TEACHING CHURCH

Whereas *teaching* encompasses any manner of imparting information, skills, and values so that others may learn, each of the above traditions embodies only a partial expression of the teaching church.

Indoctrination. Devoted to instruction in fundamental beliefs and practices, indoctrination is used to infuse learners with a partisan and distinctly sectarian point of view. This is necessary to maintain the beliefs passed from generation to generation and to provide a foundation for the young and for new Christians so that they can effectively move into the mainstream of congregational life.

Education. When this term became popular in churches during the early 1900s, the emphasis was on bringing out the latent, God-given capabilities of the young. As persons developed, they would be exposed to the history, beliefs, and practices of their faith appropriate for their level of readiness. This form of teaching would equip learners to pursue knowledge of their faith for themselves rather than relying only on instructors or tradition. Consequently, persons would become aware of and develop the capacity to interpret not only their own, but other faith traditions as well. Resulting religious convictions would be more personal than sectarian, and overall development would be consistent with each individual's ability.

Proclamation. Testifying or giving witness to that which one has experienced is the basis for proclamation as a third element of the teaching church. A desire to tell about and involve others in one's beliefs and practices gives evidence that commitment is strong. Two aspects of proclamation contribute to effective ministry: (1) giving testimony to one's beliefs and experiences, and (2) enlisting persons in the life and organizations of a church. Both are initiated by a believer in the hope that a convert and/or a new participant will result, thereby gaining the same benefits witnessed by the believers. Proclamation is necessary to spread the gospel message and to secure participation in the overt teaching activities of a congregation.

EDUCATIONAL MINISTRY TODAY

Most evangelical churches use the term *educational ministry* to identify the functions of a teaching church described above. It is important to recognize that all three traditions have a place and, in fact, contribute to the effectiveness of one another. Where one is weak or ignored, the others will suffer; and where one is emphasized to the neglect of others, there will be eventual decline in overall effectiveness.

What we are trying to do to people? Consider this as a possible answer: The purpose of educational ministry is to develop within persons an understanding of, commitment to, and ability to practice Christian teachings. Another way to view this is to describe Christian education as the ongoing effort of believers seeking to understand, practice, and propagate God's revelation.

Christianity may be viewed as the life of a community and educational ministry as the work of that community. The aim is not so much to promote the group as it is to contribute to the reconciling mission to which the community is called. Thus, from an overall perspective, educational ministry may be viewed as the effort "to introduce persons into the life and mission of the community of Christian faith."[1]

Many ministers have been influenced by the family image, especially related to the responsibility of parents and teachers. For example, the New Testament uses the figure of adoption to describe what happens to persons in Christian faith (Rom. 8:23; Gal. 4:5). In adoption children enter a family; the family becomes *their* family, and they become its children. They adopt the lifestyle of the family, its practice and ideas, its precious symbols, and its family jokes. The family receives the children in warmth, makes its resources available, and transmits to the young its habits and values. "In this educational process deliberate instruction plays an important part, but it is less significant than the teaching and learning that inevitably go with life. Thus, adoption is a suggestive metaphor for the educational ministry of the church."[2]

The response to the question "What are we trying to do to people?" is really a hope, an objective. It is central to our role as leaders and in today's ministry incorporates the best of the three traditions that make up our history.

UNDERSTANDING YOUR CHURCH
AND ITS EDUCATIONAL MINISTRY

Whatever form your educational ministry has assumed, it exists as it does because someone believed that the programs, facilities, organizational arrangements, curriculum, and other components were the best way to accomplish Christian education. These structures enable a church to do its work.

Teachers in the social sciences often refer to a life cycle through which organizations develop. By applying this theory to a church, we can gain an understanding of how structures develop, predict potential problems, and determine appropriate leadership strategy based on the needs of a particular situation.

Consider how a church moves through the phases of this life cycle, as illustrated in figure 1.

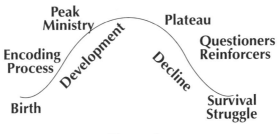

Figure 1

BIRTH

In the birth phase, the organization develops out of the hopes and dreams of a person or group. The initiators call others to join them in creating a church that will fulfill the original expectations of the founders, often called the *founding purpose*.

DEVELOPMENT

The second phase focuses on development of the institution. Considering the expectations of the charter members and available resources, structures are developed to help the church fulfill the dreams of its founders. A helpful term for this process is *encoding*. While an organization is born from ideas and dreams, how it fulfills its purpose is determined by the structures created to perpetuate the institution. This is the encoding process—development of the means to implement the founding purpose, such as programs, facilities, and curriculum. These are the ways in which a congregation does its work.

PEAK MINISTRY

In the peak ministry phase, the organization effectively meets congregational needs and also accomplishes its work in the community. This is a time characterized by cohesiveness and good feelings. The church experiences growth in membership, strong support and commitment among members, community appreciation, and relative ease in decision-making.

The church's mission and ministry are central to all activities and decisions.

PLATEAU

Inevitably, however, whatever has been encoded begins to lose effectiveness. In time, the situation and conditions which brought forth certain programs, organization, facilities, staff, and procedures change. There is a turnover in membership, resulting in new people who have no understanding of or appreciation for traditional forms or structures which have been encoded. Eventually, if adjustments and changes are not made, the means developed to help the church achieve its purpose begin to lose effectiveness.

The plateau phase often moves in subtly, when the desire for keeping things going as they have been gradually replaces a commitment to innovate and adapt. The desire to find security through familiar structures results in a congregation that resists change. The result is a gradual decrease in effectiveness.

Attendance and participation begin to level off, evangelistic concerns moderate, and the fervor associated with peak ministry disappears. There is a distinct emphasis on making the existing organization work and avoiding any major changes. Whereas mission and ministry previously guided the church, maintenance of a viable organization becomes equally important during this phase.

DECLINE

If the life cycle continues, decline sets in. This phase occurs when efforts to keep the system working are not adequate to maintain the plateau level. The congregation completes its shift from a primary focus on mission and ministry of the church to maintenance of the institution. Time and money formerly used in reaching and serving others are redirected to meet institutional and member needs.

The teaching ministry, formerly devoted to a balanced emphasis on instruction, nurture, and proclamation, usually emphasizes nurture and neglects the other areas. While attendance in Bible study, Christian development, and mission activities was strong during the development phase, participation in worship and other activities that require less personal responsibility often takes precedence during decline.

SURVIVAL STRUGGLE

The last phase, survival struggle, is faced by churches unable or unwilling to adapt to changing needs. For some congregations, existence will be an ongoing effort by those committed to the organization's survival. For others with inadequate resources or endurance, the life cycle ends.

QUESTIONERS AND REINFORCERS

An interesting development begins during the plateau phase and intensifies as a church begins to decline. One by one, members begin to polarize into questioners and reinforcers as they sense that all is not well.

QUESTIONERS

The initial response, usually among those not involved in the encoding phase, is an expression of doubt about the effectiveness of some aspect of church life. Questions and comments emerge such as "What is the matter with our church?" "Why do we have such difficulty enlisting workers?" "How can we improve the mission interest in our church?" "Why do we have to keep doing it this way?" "I think we need new leadership." "What should we be doing?"

REINFORCERS

In response to the unrest, persons committed to the church's heritage and traditions begin to doubt that the congregation is putting forth sufficient effort to get the job done. Questioners are viewed as troublemakers who do not understand that the organization has worked well in the past.

Reinforcers defend the existing structures, believing that renewal comes as members recommit and give of themselves unselfishly. They seek to conserve resources and to preserve the institution. Staff, facilities, programs, and such must effectively serve member needs; other concerns are secondary.

POTENTIAL RESULTS

If the reinforcers are strong enough to resist necessary change, questioners often will leave or develop a subgroup within the congregation. This can be observed when like-minded people begin to organize "renegade" Sunday school classes, prayer/share groups, and mission activities. Occasionally questioners simply accept the situation and become chronic complainers or passive participants. Without significant adjustments to meet the changed situation, decline will continue.

On the other hand, if questioners dominate, there is potential for radical and unfocused change that disrupts continuity in and operation of the organization. There is a loss of commitment to the institution and of problem-solving capacity normally gained from history and experience. Concern for studied, well-defined responses by the congregation gives way to expediency and immediate action.

Clearly, both questioners and reinforcers are needed for stability and initiative in problem-solving—but, either group can create problems that will foster further decline. Without significant adjustments to meet changing circumstances, the congregation will continue its downward path.

Fortunately, however, most churches do not reach the final phase. As decline begins and the questioners and reinforcers become prominent, there is an unusual development. The tension level builds as dissatisfaction increases, and leaders are faced with taking action. Some leaders choose this time to move to another church. Others become more assertive in seeking to resolve problems. Either way, leaders and congregation begin to address key issues such as:

- What are our problems?

- Why are we feeling as we do?

- What should we be doing?

- What are the best options for our circumstances?

It is this searching response that often creates opportunity for renewal, as persons find themselves involved in the same type of creative, problem-solving environment that birthed the original organization. Thus, the congregation has an opportunity to reencode what it is and how it does its work based on present needs and resources.

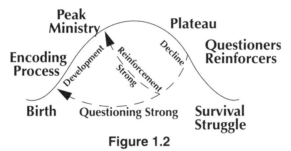

Figure 1.2

As shown in figure 1.2, this renewal might be extensive if questioning is strong, or it might be minor if reinforcement concerns are dominant. Regardless, a church recycles through the phases, with many of the same opportunities and problems to be faced again.

LEADERSHIP STRATEGY

Your church is in one of these phases. Consequently, the way in which you accomplish educational ministry must be viewed not only in the present perspective, but also in relation to the previous and the anticipated phases. Ideally, educational leaders will continually evaluate and adjust, avoiding decline. The questions such as "What should we be doing to fulfill our purpose?" and "What are the best options?" portray a leadership commitment that will encourage and assist a church in maintaining a viable organization and relevant ministries for the congregation as well as the world.[3]

A LEADER'S OBJECTIVES

Besides understanding the developmental pattern of your church and being committed to maintaining an effective organization, certain leader actions are necessary to be successful. As you administer the educational ministry of your church, seek the following objectives:

- Clarify and base all decisions on the church's mission statement.

- Lead members to establish, and help them in achieving, common goals.

- Involve in the decision-making process people who will be affected.

- Be flexible in meeting changing needs.

- Distribute leadership responsibilities widely among responsible people.

- Support group values when appropriate and question them when necessary.

- Learn from and do not be inhibited by the possibility of failure.

- Make decisions based on information rather than on emotion.

- Encourage the development and use of individual gifts.

- Maintain a healthy balance between caring for work and for people.

- Maintain a strong spiritual foundation in your personal life and in organizational life.

A LEADER'S COMMITMENT

During graduate study, I was deeply impressed by James Smart, an Old Testament scholar, who had a profound experience as he came to understand the role of Christian education in church ministry. Describing his experiences in *The Teaching Ministry of the Church*, Smart charged that our churches have missions, but the congregations do not see themselves as missionaries. Members prefer to be "ordinary Christians," with little personal involvement in the mission of Jesus Christ.

Reacting against the moralistic teaching of his day, he suggested that we redefine the purpose of Christian education so as to lead people to Christ and to develop believers who passionately live in obedience and response to the Word of God:

> Our Goal must be no lesser goal than that which Jesus and the apostles had before them. We teach so that through our teaching God may work in the hearts of those whom we teach to make of them disciples wholly committed to his gospel, with an understanding of it, and with a personal faith that will enable them to bear convincing witness to it in word and action in the midst of an unbelieving world. We teach so that through our teaching God may bring into being a Church . . . whose all-engrossing aim will be to serve Jesus Christ as an earthly body through which he may continue his redemption of the world.[4]

In essence, quality educational ministry demands commitment to reaching, teaching, developing, and involving persons in Christian service.

There is no greater need or opportunity facing educational leaders than to make disciples and bring them into the full life and faith of the church. Helping people find their life's fulfillment in being part of the body of Christ and sharers in his mission is a ministry that clearly embodies Jesus' teaching that effective leaders must be able servants (see Matt. 20:26).

CHAPTER 2

Christian Education and Theology

Daniel Aleshire

"Get on board, little children, get on board!" The words of this spiritual ranged through nineteenth-century church houses and rural camps. "Get on board, little children, get on board . . . the gospel train!" The song was a call to faith, a call to a new way of life. It was a call to board the good news and set out on the journey of what was, in the words of another early American hymn, "bound for the promised land." The image was of a joyful vehicle, rumbling through the countryside, picking up passengers along the way. The gospel train is a nineteenth-century vision of the Christian life. People became Christian, shared life and experiences together, and journeyed toward their heavenly reward.

This image of the church identifies a hope and a problem. The Christian life does have a beginning for any individual—a time to board the train. The problem is what do people do once on board? The gospel train is a good metaphor for the beginning and ending of the Christian life, but what about the long ride? What do Christians do on the journey?

The early church was born declaring the *kerygma*—the story of God's love and saving grace made available through Jesus Christ. It struggled with issues such as who was entitled to hear the good news (Acts 15:1–29) and how the missionary task should be staffed and undertaken (see Acts 15:36–41). As time passed, the issues confronting Christians expanded to include an increasing concern with the life and teaching of Jesus, as well as the church's understanding of the nature of faith and its implications for living faithful lives. The task of the *kerygma*, the proclamation of the gospel, never ended. But as believers began to live through whole lifetimes, the importance of the *didache*—the teaching about the work of God and the life of faith—increased.

"Get on board, little children, get on board." That is the call of the *kerygma*—to hear the call to faith and to respond. Boarding the train only begins the journey, however; continuing the journey requires instruction in the faith. The command to the early church was to teach, baptize, and make disciples (Matt. 28:19–20). It is never enough just to get the little children on board the train—though that is the undeniable beginning. They must also learn the profound truths of the Christian faith. They must come to understand the faith that breeds excitement for the coming of the kingdom and nurtures patience for the long days of the journey. Teaching, nurturing disciples, and dealing with life on the train are activities related to Christian education.

Education that leads to discipleship has several requirements, and this chapter is about four of them. First, education that is true to the grace of the gospel requires a vision of the church, its purpose, and mission. Christian education must emerge from the mission of the church and move its people toward authentic discipleship. Second, Christian education requires theologically informed goals and objectives. Third, the learning that results from Christian education requires some serious consideration. The learning must be of a special kind—the kind that provides knowledge, instills feeling, and leads to right living. Fourth, the processes and organizations that the church uses to educate people in faith require ongoing, thoughtful evaluation and renewal.

THE NATURE AND MISSION OF THE CHURCH

The gospel train is an "image" of the church. It is one picture of the church that accurately portrays the life of faith as a journey. But, like any image of the church, it does not describe the church in its fullness. W. O. Carver noted that "Since the New Testament nowhere has an explicit definition of the church, basic and determinative criteria must be reached by an inductive study of the New Testament books."[1] It is surprising, and sometimes puzzling, that the New Testament nowhere provides a definitive description of the church and its nature and mission.

Why, on such an important issue as the mission and nature of the church, does Scripture not provide a clear statement? As in many other issues of profound significance (i.e., the work of redemption, the quality of a disciple's life), no single image is adequate to capture the richness of meaning conveyed by the concept. Like the sounds that together form a symphony, faithful understanding often emerges from the sum of many parts.

The Bible speaks profusely on the nature of the church—but always in models and portraits, never in straightforward definitions. While images and models derived from the inductive study of Scripture lack precision, they are the best we have and, perhaps, the best way to understand the church and its mission. Consider three of them.

THE CHURCH AS THE PEOPLE OF GOD

The church is sometimes pictured as the "people of God." This concept of the church has its roots in the Old Testament. God made a covenant with the people of Israel, and they became God's own people. Through the people of God, the relationship between humankind and God—long ago broken by sin—could be restored. The idea of the "people of God" is that some people on earth are given the responsibility to share God's hope for reconciliation and redemption with all other people. This image does not mean that the people of God are God's favorite people. Rather, it means they have a special responsibility to share God's Word with the world.

Through the covenant with Abraham, Israel was chosen to be the people of God (see Gen. 12:1–3; Gen. 17:1–8). By keeping the covenant, Israel was called to be a blessing to all the world's people. Israel understood God's fair expectations of them, but had trouble abiding by them—just as Christians have had difficulty living faithfully by the teachings of Christ. In spite of the problems, God remained faithful to the covenant promises, and the Old Testament people of God were the means of God's most profound blessing to humanity: Jesus Christ, born of humble Jewish parents, in a small Jewish village. The martyr Stephen declared that the sons of Jacob had "received the law as delivered by angels and did not keep it" (see Acts 7:53, RSV). Jesus was absolutely faithful to the law, even to death, and through his faithfulness, the law was fulfilled. E. Glenn Hinson explains it this way: "Upon the faithfulness of Jesus of Nazareth, then, the first Christians declared, God made a new covenant in fulfillment of that foretold by Jeremiah (Rom. 11:27) and Joel (Acts 2:16–21). He was not calling a new people, but transacting a new covenant with his people. They were to be no longer Israel 'after the flesh' but Israel 'after the spirit'" (Rom. 9:6ff).[2]

Thus the followers of Jesus Christ, like Israel of the Old Testament, become the people of God: a people charged with the responsibility of sharing the Word that can restore the broken relationship between sinful humanity and a just, loving God.

THE CHURCH AS THE BODY OF CHRIST

Another image of the church frequently employed in Paul's letters is "body of Christ." This image or model of the church portrays Christ as the head, and individual believers, related to the body through the redemptive love of Christ, as other parts of the body. As members of the body, different persons are given different gifts, different abilities, and different functions. Together, the members accomplish the work of the body under the direction of Christ, the head. Though the body is characterized by diversity of function, it is unified in purpose and mission. Through the church, as the body of Christ, God continues the effort of incarnation, extending a physical presence of God's love and will in the midst of human life.

THE CHURCH AS THE NEW HUMANITY

Sometimes, the image of the church as the body of Christ is combined with the image of the church as the "new humanity." Both images are frequently found in the writings of Paul, and "new humanity" is especially present in Ephesians and Galatians. God has brought the new humanity into being through the redemptive mission of Jesus Christ. The old humanity consisted of persons who were dead in their trespasses and sins (see Eph. 2:1). But Christ has raised them up, and made them alive. "For we are [God's] workmanship, created in Christ Jesus for good works, which God prepared beforehand, that we should walk in them" (Eph. 2:10, RSV).

As the new humanity, the church is the evidence of God's continuing creative activity. It consists of people who have been made anew and are gifted with the ability to do what the old humanity could not accomplish. Hinson distinguishes the new humanity from the old humanity in several ways. While the old humanity is self-centered, the new humanity is God-centered. The old humanity expresses hatred toward both God and humankind, while the new humanity is characterized by unity and reconciliation. A high ethical sensitivity in the new humanity replaces the immorality or amorality of the old humanity.[3] The new humanity is God's new creation—made capable of righteousness and love.

The images of the people of God, the body of Christ, and the new humanity clearly emerge from the New Testament, but one must take care not to overinterpret any of these images. For example, while the church clearly is the body of Christ, it is not the incarnation in the same way that Christ was the incarnation of the *Logos* (see John 1:1–18). The body of Christ does not always do the will of the divine head, and it would be inaccurate for some to think that whatever the church did was clearly the same action that Christ himself would undertake if he were present in person.

Similarly, the church as the new humanity is an image that must be held with caution. While God has begun a new creative act in the new humanity and equipped people for love and righteousness, persons do not always live up to the endowment God has given them. It would be disastrous to think of some of the acts of church people as God's gift. Sometimes, the actions of the new humanity are nothing more than sin expressed in its most sinister form—the garb of piety. So each of these models of the church has limitations, and each must be assessed theologically.

CHURCH AS "SUBJECTIVE POLE"

As a way of affirming these cautions, theologians find ways to talk about the church that distinguish the church with its sometimes sinful expressions from the God who is unerringly good. One such theological definition describes the church as the "subjective pole of the objective rule of God."[4] It is not a very concrete image, but its power and meaning are not difficult to clarify. It suggests that whatever else the church may be, it is always the subject whose purpose is to point to the object: *God*. The clear, objective rule of God exists—but it exists in God, not in the church. The church tries to understand God's rule, but that understanding is always a subjective, editorialized version.

For example, faithful church members seek God's leadership in their decisions, and they will do what they think God is leading them to do. However, they must always realize that they are doing what *they think* God is leading them to do. There may be times when they misunderstand the nature of the gospel or the will of God in their lives. When this happens, the objective rule of God is not done through the church.

The church is the body of Christ; the church is the people of God; and the church is the new humanity. Yet it never completely functions as the body—members sometimes go against the command of the head. It is never wholly all the new humanity was created to be—because there are constant regressions to the behavior of the old humanity. The people of God continue to break and misrepresent the gospel because they do not yield to the will of God. *The church is this subjective pole of the objective rule of God.* Although the church seldom lives up to everything each model suggests, these models reflect what God intended when the church was brought into being.

WHAT IS THE PURPOSE OF THE CHURCH?

The church is to be a community of persons who are, wholeheartedly and overwhelmingly, committed to doing that which God longs to be accomplished on earth. What does God want? One summary statement of God's will for the human family is that God longs for "the increase of the love of God and the love of neighbor."[5] If the church accomplishes its purpose, the result will be more love for God and for humankind. Love of God results in prayer, devotion, commitment, a sense of piety, and growth in spiritual life. Love of neighbor results in caring, giving, confronting, admonishing, seeking justice, and working for the common good. The purpose of the church is to engage in those activities that increase the love of God and neighbor. What are these activities?

THE ACTIVITIES THE CHURCH USES
TO ACCOMPLISH ITS PURPOSE

First, the church gathers people together for the worship of God. In this gathering, the people of God are called upon to give themselves anew to the God of their salvation. The church gathers to seek God's leadership, to hear God's voice, and to respond to God's bidding as the body of Christ. The church gathers to confess the sins that have kept people from fulfilling God's call and to seek to become more truly God's handiwork. Worship is vital. It is a purpose of the church.

Second, the church seeks to increase love of God and neighbor by proclaiming God's Word to people who do not know Christ. Through evangelism, the church caringly distributes the good news of Jesus Christ. Evangelism is the process by which the people of God give love, hope, and glad tidings to people who do not know God.

Third, the church also engages in the work of missions. Missions is "what the church does to achieve her mission in areas of human need which are on the growing edge of the church's confrontation with the non-Christian world."[6] Missions involves taking the whole gospel of Jesus Christ to the world—including the gospel's call to salvation, social justice, physical healing, and wholeness. The task of missions is to see that the gospel's response to every human condition is implemented at the intersection where the Christian community meets the rest of the human family.

Fourth, the church seeks to increase the love of God and neighbor through fellowship. Christianity, unlike some religions of the world, calls believers into community. In some other religions, solitary worship is normative. By contrast, Christianity calls people into relationship with each other where they share their burdens and joys.

The church brings individuals into community, where they contribute to the common good and give encouragement, support, and discipline to one another. Christians cannot serve God and remain separated from each other. Jesus is emphatic about giving service to God by caring for one another (see Matt. 25:31–46). The church provides a community in which persons encounter each other, discover the meaning of love and care, and find fellowship.

Each purpose or task of the church is crucial; none is superior to the others. A church that only does evangelism is no more what God intended than the church that only does worship. The church that engages in worship and evangelism but does not take seriously the community of fellowship is only doing part of what God intended. Each task is necessary to the church fulfilling its purpose and claiming its identity as the people of God, the new humanity, and the body of Christ.

THE UNDERGIRDING ROLE OF CHRISTIAN EDUCATION

While no task is paramount, each task brings its distinctive contribution. The distinctive task of education is its undergirding of all the other tasks. Before people can worship in mature ways, they must understand what worship is and how believers engage in it. Before persons engage in missions, they must understand the task and methods of missions. People are more likely to engage in the efforts of evangelism if their own faith is growing, and faith grows as people are exposed to the practices of good Christian education. As people learn together, as they share ideas and burdens and discover new understandings, they grow together. Education, at its heart, leads to fellowship and community. Education informs and undergirds all the activities by which the church accomplishes its purpose.

This education must be wide-ranging, including the content of our faith, the patterns of faithful behavior, and the emotions of the faithful life. Persons must be educated in the content of the faith: the texts of Scripture, the doctrines that interpret these texts, and the ways by which the text becomes the authentic vehicle of God's Word and will in the world.

The church must teach the biblical ethics that will guide decision-making as well as personal and corporate behavior. Christians must be taught about right and wrong, both for individuals and for the social order. The content of faith is important, but believers must also be educated to live out their faith in meaningful discipleship. Knowing what is right is useless unless one has also been taught how to do the right. Scripture is full of stories of people who knew the right thing to do but failed to do it.

Christians must also be educated in the emotions that are part of faith. The God who has loved us and given an only-begotten Son for us evokes love and devotion. To love well is to learn not only how to think about faith and to respond in action, but also how to feel devotion, commitment, and surrender to the Source of life and hope.

Church is the new humanity, the body of Christ, the people of God. It gathers for worship, fellowship, mission, evangelism, and education. Through these tasks, the body of Christ is animated, the will of the divine Head is done, and the witness of a new humanity spreads.

THE OBJECTIVES OF CHRISTIAN EDUCATION

Christian education is a way to accomplish the purposes of the church; it is not a purpose itself. The church educates so it can accomplish its mission—but the mission of the church is not the education of its members. The educational task must be precisely understood, however. Education is fundamentally important for the church's work, and it should be conducted with understanding, integrity, and clarity. It is appropriate, even crucial, to ask the question: What should Christian education seek to accomplish in its service to the church? In short, what are the objectives of Christian education?

To answer this question, it is necessary to understand the nature of an objective. An objective provides a focus and serves as a magnet within an ongoing enterprise. For example, the objective of a construction project is, ultimately, to complete a building. The ultimate objective may have many other objectives as part of the total project. For example, completing the foundation for a building is crucial—but completing the foundation can never be substituted as the final objective. Objectives act as magnets, pulling an educational effort toward its ultimate purpose.

THE OBJECTIVES IN THE TEACHING MINISTRY OF JESUS

The identification of objectives of Christian education begins with an analysis of the objectives expressed in the teaching ministry of Jesus. James Smart, in *The Teaching Ministry of the Church*, has attempted such an analysis and concludes that Jesus' teaching was characterized by three primary objectives.

First, Jesus' teaching proclaimed the gospel of the coming of the kingdom. His teaching typically occurred in small group settings. To Jesus, the gospel was not just for the multitude on the mountainside. It was also for the few around the table who would hear and seek to understand. In fact, faithful teaching of the gospel requires a kind of interaction that is possible only in the small group settings.

Second, Jesus used his teaching—particularly the teaching of the disciples—as a means of instructing them fully in the nature of the gospel "so that they might leave behind their old inadequate understanding of God, of themselves, and of all the things in their world."[7]

A third objective in the teaching of Jesus was that the disciples would be able, both in mind and in heart, to carry on the ministry that Christ had done in their midst.

THE OBJECTIVES OF CONTEMPORARY
CHRISTIAN EDUCATION

These three objectives evident in Jesus' teaching provide the basis for determining faithful objectives for the contemporary practice of Christian education. Randolph Crump Miller writes: "The main task [of Christian education] is to teach the truth about God, with all the implications arising from God's nature and activity, in such a way that the learner will accept Jesus Christ as Lord and Savior, will become a member of the Body of Christ, and will live in the Christian way."[8] This statement identifies three objectives in Christian education that reflect Smart's summary of objectives in Jesus' teaching.

The first is that persons will seek to come into right relationship with Jesus Christ. There is disagreement among Christian educators about how this objective is accomplished. For example, some have argued that the role of Christian education is to help nurture children who are born to believing parents into the faith of their families. In this view, children are taught the gospel and grow up never knowing a time when they did not believe and accept the good news of Jesus Christ.

Others argue that persons can never be nurtured into Christian faith. Ultimately, becoming Christian is the consequence of conversion. John Westerhoff states that "The Christian faith by its very nature demands conversion. We cannot gradually educate persons through instruction in schools to be Christian. Of course, persons need to be and can be nurtured into a community's faith and life."[9]

At some point the individual must come to own the faith that has been taught. The language of the Baptist tradition is likely correct in saying that the individual "accepts" Christ and "professes his or her faith" in him. "Professing" is the act by which the individual claims the truth that has been taught. Westerhoff goes on to say that "Conversion, I believe, is best understood as this radical turning from 'faith given' (through nurture) to 'faith owned.'"[10] One objective of Christian education is teaching people about their need of a Savior and how they can affirm the faith of the community of believers as their own.

The second objective of Christian education is to help the converted grow into mature discipleship. Miller reminds us, in the image of Scripture, that the goal is a "maturity which feeds on the 'solid food' of the gospel, which is for the full-grown (Heb. 5:14). Strong meat is our goal, and we are to leave the milk which is for the babies behind."[11] The biblical image of "milk to solid food" suggests that faith matures and develops. True believers are forever relearning their faith. Concepts that were once useful (milk) must be supplemented by new vision (solid food). While the adult may still enjoy the milk of childhood, it no longer supplies all the needed spiritual food.

The believer does not necessarily abandon his or her first understandings of the gospel. Rather, those first understandings are supplemented by more mature appreciation for the magnitude of the God of the universe and the salvation God offers through Jesus Christ. Maturity in faith requires the continuing influence of education.

A third objective for Christian education is the equipping of disciples for the work of ministry. Competent ministry requires persons who are sensitized to the relevant issues, trained in appropriate skills, and motivated by their commitment to Christ.

These various objectives point to a consistent view of the role of Christian education: that persons become believers, mature as believers, and function as believers. As people learn these lessons, they enable the community of faith—the church—to become the effective body of Christ, the faithful new humanity, and the redemptive people of God.

Education, of course, in no way replaces the necessary presence of the Holy Spirit. Education alone cannot convict people of sin, preserve them in the hour of temptation, or comfort them at times of loss and grief. The ministry of the Spirit—power, boldness, comfort, presence—can never be replaced by an educational experience. But with the enabling presence of the Spirit, the word and work of faith come alive through the ministry of education.

THE KIND OF LEARNING
CHRISTIAN EDUCATION REQUIRES

If the objectives of Christian education are that people claim faith and mature in the faith they claim, what kind of learning does Christian education require?

Learning comes in many forms. Some learning, for example, results in the knowledge of facts—like learning state capitals or how to spell a word or the multiplication tables. This kind of knowledge is not subject to personal opinion.

Another kind of learning leads to the development of understanding. Understanding differs from factual knowledge because it does not deal with information that can be treated in simple right/wrong categories.

Then, there is a kind of learning that develops physical skills—like driving a car or learning to skate. This kind of knowledge is very different from knowing the state capitals; it is more given to individual expression and demonstrated by skills more than verbal explanations. Finally, there is a kind of learning that results in tutored emotions—learning to love intelligently, learning how to celebrate with joy, and learning how to mourn in grief.

Which of these forms of learning are most crucial for Christian believing? The answer to this question begins by exploring the nature of belief.

LEARNING FOR BELIEF

Belief, as the term is used in religious language, frequently reflects two uses, and the distinction between these two uses is important. *The Oxford English Dictionary* identifies one definition of a belief as "The mental action, condition, or habit, of trusting or confiding in a person or thing; trust, dependence, reliance, confidence, faith." The second definition is this: "Mental acceptance of a proposition, statement, or fact, as true, on the ground of authority or evidence; assent of the mind to a statement, or to the truth of a fact beyond observation, on the testimony of another . . ."[12]

Many persons appear to view the task of Christian education as imparting the propositions that can be discerned from the teaching of Scripture. This kind of learning clearly relates to the second definition of belief; however, it is not the kind of learning which the objectives of Christian education, as identified in this chapter, require.

Learning that aids persons in becoming believers, maturing as believers, and functioning as believers cannot be based on one's ability to remember or agree with a catalog of propositions. It must be more. When John says: "He who believes in the Son has eternal life" (John 3:36a, RSV), it does not mean that people who can affirm a variety of facts about Jesus will be saved. That is the kind of believing that even the devils do (see James 2:19)!

The belief of which John speaks is the belief that follows the first definition. It is the individual's putting trust and confidence in Jesus Christ. More than answering "true" to a statement about Jesus, it is a profound confidence in the saving grace of God through Christ; it is a trust in Christ as Savior; it is a commitment—both rational and emotional—to Jesus as Lord of life. Education must be toward the "belief in"—the state of confidence that breeds hope and commitment and the sense of truth that breeds surrender to the lordship of Christ.

Education that cultivates belief is a complex process. Learning what is true or false about a proposition requires nothing more than memorization and recall. However, learning how to place an increasing degree of confidence in Jesus Christ, learning to love God more truly, and learning how to behave in more consistently Christian ways are difficult learning tasks. In fact, this kind of learning is possible only through God's grace.

It is crucial to approach Christian education with the constant awareness that faith is the gift of God. It is not something that can be acquired through the proper kind of education, effort, or religion. Although faith entails careful educational efforts, an individual does not become a believer by education. Belief comes as a gift of God, the kind of gift that must be tutored and nurtured toward maturity.

THE KINDS OF LEARNING FAITH REQUIRES

Learning how to believe requires all of the kinds of learning noted earlier in this section: learning of information, learning to understand, learning to feel, and learning to act.

Learning for faith includes a cognitive dimension—people need to know the content of the Christian faith and to be able to think about the meanings of that content. The Bible provides many guides concerning the content most important for Christians to learn (see, for example, 1 John 4; 1 Cor. 15:1–18). Christians are a part of God's long-term effort to relate to the human family with justice and grace. While belief must be more than assent to propositions, faith is tutored as people learn the story of God's efforts.

Learning must also include the tutoring of emotions—learning how to love and trust. Pascal is right, I think, when he notes, "The mind has its order by premise and proof; the heart has another. We do not prove that we should be loved, by setting forth in order the causes of love; that would be too foolish."[13] He concludes, "The last step that Reason takes is to recognize that there is an infinity of things that lie beyond it. Reason is a poor thing, indeed, if it does not succeed in knowing that."[14] The education that facilitates believing must touch the heart, and also the head.

Belief requires yet another form of learning—learning to act out one's faith consistent with the character of its content. The importance of this characteristic is illustrated in the parable of the Good Samaritan (see Luke 10:29–37). The problem in the story, as Jesus tells it, is that the first two passersby should have stopped to help, but did not. The reason they should have stopped was that helping was a part of their belief system. It is likely that the priest and the Levite knew what they should do to help a wounded person, but they did not act according to the content of their belief. The epistle of James admonishes us not to be hearers only, "But be doers of the word" (James 1:22, RSV).

It is not enough for the Christian to think the precepts of faith; it is not enough just to feel one's faith; and it is not enough for the individual only to do the actions of faith. Belief that is mature reflects the learning of thoughts, feelings, and behavior. This is the kind of learning that the objectives of Christian education require.

TEACHERS, LEADERS, AND STRUCTURES
FOR CHRISTIAN EDUCATION

The kind of learning that cultivates Christian believing leads to several implications for the leaders and teachers of educational programs and also the structures of those programs.

THE PRIORITY OF PEOPLE

People are the key resource for Christian education. The learning of faith requires a person-to-person kind of teaching. It would be all but impossible for persons to learn to be more Christian in contexts apart from close and constant contact with other people. Propositions and facts can be learned from teaching machines or correspondence courses. But learning to love and care or learning to be faithful and obedient are possible only as people share the experience of faith together. John Westerhoff affirms this idea when he recalls Baptist layman Benjamin Jacob's statement that "teaching is leading others by example on the road to spiritual maturity."[15]

People are central in the Christian education task because learning for faith involves not only the accumulation of ideas but also skills and attitudes, feelings and ways of acting on one's faith. People learn these best from other people, as their lives touch under the leadership of God's Spirit. People learn a great deal about Christianity as they encounter others who are confronting the joys, frustrations, anxieties, and burdens of day-to-day life. While "celebrity religion" is very highly valued by some, it is all but impossible to learn about lives that are full of faith when people never come closer to their teachers than the television set. Christian education—at least the kind that facilitates maturing discipleship—is an activity of people with people.

THE REAL TEACHERS

Teachers are critical because faith is learned person to person. The real teachers, however, are not limited to the individuals who fill the formal role of Sunday or church school teacher. They are all the persons who are struggling to live their faith.

John Westerhoff notes that the historical function of the Sunday school "was to give persons an opportunity to share life with other faithful selves, to experience the faith in community, to learn the Christian story, and to engage in Christian actions. Sunday school was not curriculum, teaching-learning strategies, or organization; it was people in community."[16]

Everyone who participates in the life of the congregation becomes a teacher to other persons in that congregation. Church officers are teachers; deacons are teachers; people who speak for or against issues in business meetings are teachers; the people who always come, and those who never come, are teachers. The sinners at church teach people about sin, and faithful believers, usually without knowing it, teach people the most fundamental truths of the Christian faith.

Those who serve as the formal teachers are a part of a larger educational ecology. While they must accept responsibility for certain educational agenda, they must never view themselves as the only teachers in the church.

EDUCATIONAL SETTING AND STRUCTURES

As all of the individuals in a congregation are teachers, the total life of the church becomes the teaching environment. Three kinds of events form the curriculum for the congregation's teaching: (1) those events that are structured and intentional, (2) those that are quite unstructured and unintended, and (3) the teaching a congregation does by avoiding certain subjects or activities. All influence the education of persons, but each differs in the kind of learning it produces.

Much of this book is about the structured, intentional educational experience. Structure, in a program of Christian education, assures comprehensiveness in presenting the content of Christian faith, as well as balance in the sequence with which that content is presented. The structures should be sensitive to the local church environment and should reflect the needs of the people served by the program.

In most administrative structures, basic principles can be followed, but few models should or can be copied. Structures will vary with a congregation's size and its general style of ministry. Congregations are populated with persons of various gifts, and they have needs of various kinds. Christian education structures should be responsive to these gifts and needs.

Learning also emerges from the unstructured events of community life. For example, some have learned from a church leader who failed in his own moral life and hurt the people who had placed their trust in him. Others learned from business meetings where people differed in their opinions and resorted to power plays, deception, and public displays of anger and disgust. Not all the unstructured events are negative, but most negative events in congregational life are never planned for or wanted when they occur. These negative events are profoundly educational, however.

The more positive aspect of the unscheduled curriculum is provided by Christians who are willing to forgive one another and who remain faithful over long periods to their commitments to serve Christ and work with each other. Roger Shinn remembers the teaching value of unplanned events in his own life when he writes about his experience as a soldier in a war. "What I learned was not primarily what the military teachers taught me. Neither they nor I planned that education. But it took hold."[17] A program of Christian education must be sensitive to these unplanned teaching events. It must learn to seize them and incorporate them into the total ministry of education.

Finally, congregations should pay careful attention to the issues they avoid, the parts of the Bible they choose not to teach, the events they choose not to conduct. Maria Harris describes the impact of the combination of things unsaid and undone: things that, by their absence, constitute a "null" curriculum.[18]

In the community of faith, the null curriculum has powerful teaching capacity. If a congregation never helps youth think about social justice issues, or if it never helps adults think through the critical issues of their time, the church has taught that this form of learning is not worth the church's time or energy. The frequent result is that the gospel is truncated—part of it is lopped off, left unexplored, and therefore is unlearned. Congregations need to develop the skills necessary to diagnose their null curriculum and take necessary action to correct it.

QUALIFICATIONS FOR TEACHERS-LEADERS

All people teach, whether their influence is positive or negative. Some people teach in the unstructured emotions and inspirations of life in the community; others teach in the structured environment. While congregations have no control over the broader community of teachers, choices are possible regarding people who teach in the programmed and planned arenas of education. Assuming there are more persons who can teach than there are teaching positions (an assumption that is not always valid), what are the criteria for the selection of the intentional teachers? I would emphasize two qualifications without which individuals should not be entrusted with the faith-lives of others.

First, the teacher must be a person of authentic faith. Because so many unstructured teaching events will be dominated by those who fail to be the Christians they are called to be, the structured teaching events must be careful to use people who take their own lives of faith seriously. If teachers are to lead others toward more mature discipleship, then they must be persons who are seeking to mature themselves.

The qualification is not so much that teachers are fully mature in their faith as it is that they have a measure of maturity and are growing toward more. Arthur Adams, in discussing the qualifications for church leaders, argues for the necessity of faith. "The important requirement is that conviction be powerful enough to give life its main thrust."[19]

The teacher must not, however, teach with the desire to influence everyone to believe exactly as he or she does. Such a position is contrary both to the teaching of Scripture (we are all priests unto God) and to the affirmation that the Holy Spirit may work uniquely among different persons. But the teacher must be a person of convictions and willing to express those convictions and make them available to the students.

Second, those who teach in the intentional program of instruction should be persons who love and are willing to develop skill in sharing that love. Christian education helps individuals understand how they should love the Lord with all their minds, hearts, and souls, and love their neighbor as themselves (see Matt. 22:34–40). People learn to love by experiencing love.

Those who are afraid of love being overemphasized in the teaching ministry of the church would probably be offended by the ministry of Jesus. When Jesus was asked to reduce the law to its most important dimensions, he affirmed the need to love God and human beings. One simply cannot teach the gospel of Jesus Christ apart from some firsthand experience with loving and caring. Long after students have forgotten the point of the Sunday school lesson, they will clearly remember the teachers who cared for them, who rejoiced and cried with them, and who encouraged and chided them.

As persons are taught by individuals characterized by faith and love, the gospel becomes incarnate once again. Christians learn about faith from people of faith—just like people learn a symphony by hearing it, not merely by studying the musical score. Education with a teacher who has neither faith nor love may provide opportunity to explore the content of faith, but it can never provide the experience of it.

These criteria are so important that if there is only one person in the church who possesses these qualities, then the only structured Christian education that church should have is one class with that person as teacher. Education for faith is too important to be left to those persons who are loveless and faithless.

Of course, there are other qualifications that should be pursued in the choice of persons to be the formal faculty. But there is a great gap in importance between these two qualifications and any others. Scripture speaks of those whose gift is teaching, and persons so gifted should be secured for the teaching program of the church.

Teaching is a skill, and skills require training and development. Teachers who are willing to develop skills should be selected. Teaching is hard work—especially if it is done as an expression of one's faith and love. Those who are willing to work should be recruited for the task. Any invitation to teach, however, prefaced by "this job will not take much time" is an invitation to fill a vacancy more than it is an invitation to teach the Christian gospel.

These are only a few of the additional qualifications which could rightly be placed on those who should serve as teachers in the formal educational program. But the theological affirmation is that the qualifications of faith and love must be preeminent. The skills which constitute other qualifications help the message of faith to be delivered with more precision and clarity. They make it more accessible to the persons seeking to learn. However, skills without faith and love are of little value.

EDUCATION FOR FAITH

Education for faith requires qualified teachers, though it recognizes that everyone in the congregation is a teacher. Education for faith requires a special kind of learning—the kind of learning that cultivates behavior and feeling as well as ideas. Education for faith requires a clear sense of purpose and objectives. Education for faith is a function of the church that helps it be the church. It makes a ride on the gospel train rich and full.

CHAPTER 3

The Christian Witness

Bruce P. Powers

What are we trying to do to people? Consider this as a possible answer: The purpose of educational ministry is to develop within persons an understanding of, commitment to, and ability to practice Christian teachings. Another way to answer is to describe Christian education as the ongoing efforts of believers seeking to understand, practice, and propagate God's revelation.

This statement from the first chapter illustrates the foundation for the educational dimension of ministry. Before dealing with the practical issues of leadership and administration in the rest of the book, it is important to clarify the aim for education in the church. Without clarity in biblical, theological, and philosophical foundations for ministry, techniques and methods can become detached from the very vision that birthed them. Just as illustrated in the life cycle (chapter 1), a church can drift away from its reason for existence and become a religious country club. The best way to keep a congregation focused on its educational responsibility is to keep asking the question: What are you trying to do to people? This chapter gives an answer.

A Christian's faith ultimately must be judged by standards generally claimed by those who profess to be disciples of Jesus Christ. These standards at best are accurate interpretations of the message proclaimed by Jesus and incarnated in the beliefs and practices of the church. However, as we have seen, faith takes on many forms, not the least of which are the practices for one's faith tradition. Consequently, it would be difficult to say that there is any one prescribed version of beliefs and practices. Thus, we must rely on biblical and theological foundations to keep us on track from generation to generation.

What we seek to pass on is belief in Jesus Christ, trust of Scripture, and our best interpretation of how we have experienced God. This message— what we know, believe, and do—becomes the dominant force as we seek to influence the young and those whose beliefs and practices are different.

SHARING OUR FAITH

We share faith with others through two primary means: *direct intervention* and *example*. Direct intervention is an action taken by one person trying to influence another. For example, a parent makes a direct intervention when he or she tells a child how to behave or enrolls the child in Bible school. The initiative is with the person who seeks to give or develop in others the knowledge, attitudes, or skills considered important.

Teachers, preachers, and evangelists are prime examples of persons who often seek by direct means to influence the lives of others. Actions are usually direct—such as a lecture, sermon, or testimony—and often in a planned encounter, such as a Bible class, worship service, or visit to someone's home.

How one responds to the direct intervention of another varies. Consider these three situations:

1. A young lady, nicely dressed, knocks at your door. She tells you she is taking a survey of the neighborhood to find persons who would like to be part of a religious group unfamiliar to you. She says, "If it's convenient, I would like to come in and show you some materials and tell you about my beliefs." How would you respond?

2. Jimmy, a lively twelve-year-old, is enjoying himself at the church picnic. He and several cronies are teasing a younger boy who is obviously upset by the barbed comments. Knowing only Jimmy, you walk over and tell him that such behavior might hurt feelings and is not appropriate. How do you think Jimmy would react?

3. In a Bible study class, the teacher places an outline on the chalkboard. Class members have been studying passages in Galatians and now are focusing on the historical setting. The teacher turns and calls attention to a specific chapter and verse, which each person finds and reads. How are these people responding to direct influence?

The response to direct interventions varies depending on one's interest, openness, need, and degree of trust/suspicion. Which of these are present in each of the above situations?

In the first two situations, suspicion and openness might be involved; in the third case, trust and interest would be prominent. This illustrates a basic principle in communication: *a person must be open and willing to be influenced.* Otherwise, one's resolve is strengthened to resist the direct intervention.

Influencing others by example is an *indirect* way to elicit change and growth. Although actions may be intentional, they represent more an expression of the beliefs one holds and are not necessarily directed toward others. The parable of the Pharisee and of the tax collector praying (see Luke 18:9–14) is a good illustration. Both chose to pray, but one did it to impress and the other did it to confess. Which one would impress you?

Indirect influence by example, or by modeling, is possible because the human mind always seeks out discrepancies. That is, whenever there is a difference between what I know and what I would like to know, how I feel, and how I would like to feel or what I can do and what I would like to do, I recognize a need. As I see ways others are meeting these needs, I become very impressionable and open myself to being influenced.

Thus, influence by example is powerful due to the high degree of motivation engendered in the recipient. And as one chooses to be open to another's influence, the potential for growth and learning through direct means increases proportionately.

Influence on others, then, must be approached in a combination of direct and indirect means. We must show in every action the faith we hold and, at appropriate times, use direct testimony and teaching to help others deal with the issues of faith.

This is a crucial issue for teachers, church leaders, parents, and others who have responsibility for helping persons in their spiritual development. Therefore, the authors of this book give primary attention to the biblical foundations and encourage all educational leaders to do likewise.

EVALUATING OUR INFLUENCE

How successful are we in passing on our faith? From a biblical viewpoint, there generally are two dimensions for evaluation: how individuals respond and how the church responds.

INDIVIDUAL RESPONSE

Our efforts to reach and teach people are based on two objectives: (1) that individuals will accept Jesus Christ as Lord and Savior, and (2) that believers will keep Christ's commandments. In John 14:6–7, Jesus describes individual responsibility as the essence of faith and practice. So, one way to evaluate our effectiveness is to look at how those under our influence are responding *individually.*

Two questions must be asked: *Are persons expressing belief in Jesus? Are they living lives that are consistent with Jesus' teachings?* The degree to which you can respond positively to *both* these questions illustrates your or my effectiveness in influencing individuals.

CHURCH RESPONSE

Individuals who have responded to the call of God in Christ must then focus on an added dimension to the Christian life: that those who profess Jesus as Lord unite themselves in a body—the church—to carry out God's will. The New Testament knows nothing of a Lone Ranger approach to Christianity. Where the gospel is preached and the lost come to Jesus, it is always as a part of the life and ministry of the church.

Individuals usually profess Christ as Savior after hearing the gospel message and becoming acquainted with believers. It is in this environment that we relate to others and through which they come to know us. We are saved and come to understand "church" in this relationship with believers, and we become a part of the church so that we might share personally in its life and work.

But what is the life and work of the church? It is the same as God's call to all Christians: to be his people and to continue the earthly ministry of Jesus. The church must be the means through which the eternal purpose of God is declared.

We can evaluate our work in this area by determining the extent to which those under our influence become involved in the life and work of a local congregation.

WHAT ARE THE RESULTS?

Our influence, then, cannot be evaluated apart from tangible results— as individuals respond to God and as they involve themselves in a church. Naturally, we would all want to interpret the specific meaning given to the type and quality of tangible results. But the fact remains that, as we seek to influence the faith of others, there *is* a response. And that response must be judged by criteria such as those described above.

The question now comes back: *How successful are we in passing on our faith?*

REDESIGNING OUR WITNESS

How do you evaluate your influence as a Christian witness? If your response is like mine, there are some ways in which we have been effective; but, also, there are areas of shortcoming or areas that had not previously been considered.

The important thing is to recognize the discrepancies that exist between the faith we *want* to pass on and the faith we *are* passing on. Ideally, these are the same; if they are not, the points of difference represent the areas in which we may need to redesign our witness.

PAUL'S EXPERIENCE

Consider the life of Paul. In his early adult years the focus of his religious experience was on the *form* of worship and belief. There was little room for personal belief and individual commitment apart from following the rules of religion.

Following his Damascus Road experience, however, he began a reorientation that changed his life and furthered the growth of the church in a miraculous way.

In many ways, Paul can be viewed as an ideal example of a witnessing and maturing Christian. He is one who responded fully to Jesus' call to discipleship.

But as Paul considered his own inner being and the lives of other followers, he did not see ideal disciples. He saw persons who were in need of growth, learning, experience, and maturity. And he was convinced that through the power of God they could press onward toward being like their Lord.

Ephesians 4:15–16 and Philippians 3:12–16 give us insight into Paul's view of a maturing, or growing, disciple. One is to speak the truth in love, grow up to be in and like Christ, and work effectively with other believers. The result, according to Paul, is growth of the body and a spirit of love.

The Philippians passage suggests that disciples are not fully developed or perfect just because they have chosen to follow Christ. Believers are to seek continual growth. Even those who are more mature are admonished to keep growing toward the high calling of God in Christ Jesus.

The most impressive idea from these passages is that Christian growth is not optional. For persons who choose to accept Jesus as Savior, there is no question but that they must also make him Lord of their lives. This requires growing toward Christlikeness.

Paul went through a dramatic reorientation in his faith and consequently, in his witness. This change was so dramatic that his former colleagues wanted to kill him (Acts 9:23– 25), and the disciples did not believe he was one of them (v. 26).

A radical change in faith perspective? Yes. But no different from the growth process you and I encounter. Each of us has a frame of reference. When new insight occurs that does not fit easily into this way of knowing, there is a *discrepancy*. We then become unsettled until we decide how to resolve the differences. These discrepancies are the crossing points in life: opportunities to renew ourselves in light of fresh discoveries.

THE ANSWER

What are we trying to do to people? You can probably guess the answer. All of the ways presented are biblical, but the simplest answer is: Our job is to (1) bring people to Jesus Christ, and (2) help them grow in his likeness. As described in Ephesians 4:11–13, it is the task of church leaders to equip, or prepare, God's people for the work of Christian service. Reaching, teaching, and developing are the key words for what we are trying to do. The purpose of Christian education, then, is to make disciples and lead them to live and serve under the lordship of Christ (v. 15).

THE ANSWER

What are we trying to do to people?

Our job is to

(1) bring people to Jesus Christ, and

(2) help them grow in his likeness.

_____

The *purpose* of

Christian education is to

make disciples and lead them

to live and serve under the

lordship of Christ.

SECTION TWO:

Administrative Principles and Procedures

*We, who are many, are one body in Christ,
with many different gifts to serve the Lord!*

Romans 12:5–6

(personal translation)

CHAPTER 4

How to Plan and Evaluate

Bob I. Johnson

Kevin heard the telephone ring, but he decided not to answer it for fear of breaking his train of thought. Trinity Church, where he served as minister of Christian education, was launching an intensive effort to review its past and plan for its future. He was thinking about the first meeting of the steering committee scheduled for that evening. He and the others on the pastoral staff had discussed what approach to take. Kevin knew that one current emphasis in businesses is for individual units to plan and evaluate their work somewhat independently of other units. The overall vision of the enterprise is what ties them together.

He pondered if the various church units could handle this kind of responsibility and still produce workable plans that would be supported by the congregation. He thought of certain advantages. One advantage would be that more aggressive and committed units would not be hindered quite so much by inertia in other units. Another advantage would be that those who oppose change could not have a veto over all new or revised ministries proposed. And, Kevin reasoned, persons in a unit would make more investment in ministry planning and performance if they knew that their ideas counted.

Kevin wanted the Christian Education ministry to be the best. The telephone rang again; it was Molly, his wife, reminding him of the need for an early evening meal because of the planning meeting in the evening.

Planning is both old and new. It is both spiritual and scientific. Planning is as old as God's intention for the universe and as new as the latest theory and principles for effective planning. Planning is spiritual; that is, it is compatible with God's nature. Reliable word has it that God in Christ created all things and from eternity followed careful plans to redeem the fallen. Also, the spiritual nature of planning requires that its every facet be an object of prayer for the Spirit's guidance.

Planning is also scientific (but not an exact science), since theorists and practitioners apply various disciplines to construct approaches to planning. Truth, wherever found, can be incorporated into the search for better ways to serve God. For example, a grasp of the human sciences, such as psychology and sociology, enhances planning skills by providing an understanding of human development and group behavior.

Evaluation may evoke a variety of responses, much of which depend on the respondent, the evaluator, or the one(s) being evaluated. To say that a church does not evaluate equals saying that a church does not teach or preach. In reality the church lives with evaluation. Like preaching and teaching, some evaluation is good, some bad, and some adorned with an abundance of mediocrity.

The term *developmental* will be used concerning both planning and evaluation within this chapter. Such planning and evaluation are intended to focus on developing spiritually the church as a whole *and* the individuals involved. Thus identified, planning and evaluation form a compatible partnership with the potential for freeing the church from spiritual inertia. Such planning and evaluation stand neither in isolation from, nor out of harmony with, an authentic understanding of the nature and function of the church or with healthy personal growth.

It does, however, seem out of character for a church or an individual to set aside these tools and approach the greatest work in the world from a laissez-faire stance. The "if God wants something done, God will get it done" approach sounds noticeably off-key from the melody produced when God's best and the people's best merge intentionally to produce a masterpiece of community and ministry.

The intent of this chapter, then, is to provide both a philosophical foundation and practical help for planning and evaluating a church's Christian education ministry. This foundation is important to the church planner as are the fundamentals of music to the practicing musician. Once one understands the basics, he or she is better equipped with a larger perspective from which to make good decisions and to improvise. The practical help serves as basic how-to guidelines and as stimulants for developing other innovative methods to do the educational ministry of the church.

DEVELOPMENTAL PLANNING

Much church planning can be characterized as troubleshooting. Often energy and time are consumed in simply reacting to a nagging problem or an unexpected crisis. At its best, planning enables the church to act as the servant presence of God in the world, and not merely as a brushfire fighter. Planning helps the church to focus energy on its future rather than on skirmishes (or, God forbid, brawls) over its past.

The term *developmental* is intended to imply spiritual growth and maturity in the church, both collectively and individually. This idea presupposes that the educational ministry as well as the entire church should and can improve in important areas.

As a church educational leader you may profit from considering such planning that seeks the following:

1. *Effective planning develops good decision-making and decision makers.* One crucial question in any church is how are decisions made? Somehow God chose to entrust the church to struggle in prayer and faith to follow the leadership of the Holy Spirit and decide its course. Decision-making is a life constant. Potentially, good decision-making in the church will help individuals to be good decision makers elsewhere. The church should model the mind of Christ in decision-making as a part of its stewardship.

2. *Effective planning consistently develops the best use of nonhuman resources.* Each church has limits on such resources as money, space, and time; therefore, serious attention to their use is a part of Christian stewardship and the planning process.

3. *Effective planning develops the use of human resources.* Each church likely has the persons it needs to staff its educational ministries. Planning helps to relate persons, according to their gifts and calling, to ministry within the church.

4. *Effective planning develops an understanding of the interrelatedness of all areas of the church's life.* The church is made up of parts, the whole of which is greater than the total of all the parts. This synergism demands that the covenantal nature of our existence be respected as basic. We are our brothers' and sisters' keeper.

5. *Effective planning develops a rationale for being and ministering.* The educational ministry is the primary means for the church to reclaim the lost and to mature the believers. This is the reason for its existence and the purpose for its ministry.

6. *Effective planning develops quality individuals.* Educational ministry leaders show astuteness by remembering that they are in the people business. While leaders may have their goals, individuals also have directions for themselves set by what they believe to be God's guidance. The two sets of goals do not have to be opposed. Developmental planning emphasizes individual maturity *and* reaching church organizational goals without either running disrespectfully over the other.

PURPOSE AND DESCRIPTION

As with nearly any enterprise, planning, especially longer-term planning, suffers from some misunderstanding. To clarify thinking about planning, consider some things it is not.

1. *Planning is neither foretelling nor masterminding the future.* The only thing Christians can predict with accuracy is the ultimate victory of God and his people. Could anyone have predicted yesterday's headlines ten years ago?

2. *Planning is not dealing with future decisions.* Instead it relates to the futurity of present decisions. Decisions exist only in the present. The task of the planner is to determine what to do today to be ready for opportunities tomorrow. "How well will today's decisions stand up, for how long, and to what degree of effectiveness?" is a valid question for church educational planners.

3. *Planning is not an attempt to eliminate risk.* Rather, knowing that risks are unavoidable, the planner wants to take the right risks. Actually, good planning provides the capacity to take a greater risk—a fact not out of keeping with the Christian faith. Indeed, long-range planning inherently requires risk-taking decisions.

DEFINITION

Briefly stated, planning is primarily a decision-making process. It is the process of asking and answering questions such as these:

- What is our purpose for being?
- Where are we to go?
- What are our means for getting there?
- Who is responsible for what?

Developmental planning within the educational ministry of the church consists of (1) the search for an understanding of the opportunities available, the obstacles to be overcome, the potential of the persons to be involved, the resources available; and (2) the decisions that bring these factors together with God's will to carry out effectively the purpose of the organization.

THREE IMPLICATIONS OF OUR DEFINITION

This definition possesses certain implications for educational planners.

1. *This planning allows for the expression of faith.* Christianity, while rejecting fatalism, teaches that God's people can have a vital impact on the future. Planning demands the element of hope, and hope thrives best on the nourishment of faith. Jesus criticized those who were so concerned with the future that they filled today with unwar-

ranted worry about tomorrow. He was provoked by those who began projects without counting the cost or planning ahead (see Matt. 25:1–13; Luke 14:28–32.)

2. *Planning identifies with change.* Though certain theological truths remain constant, change is evident in every area of the Christian's existence. The disciple of Christ ought to be changing more and more into Christ's image. Communities and issues change; family structures change; even ministry and training opportunities change. Planning is a means by which we discover together the changes called for by our Lord and by which we have a part in making the church more effective through such anticipated change.

3. *Planning helps the church to maintain an awareness of purpose.* At times individual goals or interests may too easily take precedence over the church's central purpose. Planning which involves many members in clarifying and positioning this central purpose helps avoid self-centeredness and aids the church's maturity.

Planning as discussed here is inclusive—covering operational (ongoing), annual (fiscal year), and long-range (multiple-years) planning. Of course, these various levels of planning are interrelated. Long-range plans are sequenced and assigned to annual plans, which in turn are broken into quarterly, monthly, and weekly details through operational planning. Consistency among the levels of planning should be the goal of each planning group. At times, however, current situations may reveal the need to revise goals developed in long-range planning. The planning process should always maintain the flexibility that would allow for reasonable revision of goals at all levels.

ELEMENTS OF PLANNING

Effective planning in a church also requires these key elements:

Purpose. What overriding vision guides the planning group? Purpose may be seen as the church's timeless intention to act as the people of God.

Assumptions. These are the realities as anticipated by the group making the decisions. What can be counted on to have significant impact on plans made?

Expected Results. These are the things considered likely to result from the implementation of plans.

Alternatives. Because wrong or less-than-best decisions can be made, other avenues of action should be planned and available.

The decision itself. Eventually, the planning process requires a decision. The decision is made, approved, and communicated. Since no decision stands in isolation, each affects and is acted upon by others.

Impact stage. A decision stays in the arena of good intention unless it is carried out. Upon implementation it affects the life of the church to varying degrees.

Outcomes. What has happened because of planning? Are the results good, bad, or yet to be determined? At this point evaluation and then more planning are needed.

PRINCIPLES OF PLANNING

1. *Discern the forces that oppose planning.* Probably one of the most universal is fear of planned change. All ambitious plans are designed to produce new patterns of thought and action. The truth is that people resist planned change, though later they may support it.

     Another force opposing planning is risk-aversion. People immerse themselves in the routine of church to the extent that they see no need for planning. This force works against planning because a new—and perhaps more demanding—commitment to the future will be required.

     The protection of one's own interests is another force that works against planning. Some people feel that planned change would lessen their influence or take away their space or hurt their group. Some might feel that a preferred project would be passed over and others given priority by the planning process.

2. *Encourage as many persons as possible to participate.* Not all the people can participate in every decision to be made. However, if members care about the church's ministry, they like to feel a part of the planning and decision-making process.

     A planning group should attempt to involve and consult with as many people as possible who will be affected by the plan. Involvement decreases inappropriate resistance and increases commitment. People are much more likely to display interest in plans they have helped to formulate. People may even respond beyond expectation when given a chance to participate in planning. See figure 4.1 for a form that may be useful in involving a large number of persons.

3. *Look toward the ultimate destination desired.* Decide where you want your organization or project to be when you get there. Knowing this will aid in determining how to make the trip. This principle applies to all levels of planning, whether designed to formulate a three-year development plan for the Bible teaching ministry or to prepare for next week's classes.

4. *Look for strengths and potential rather than for weaknesses and problems.* Listing your problems can be very depressing. Emphasizing potential can give new life and self-esteem to a planning group

Figure 4.1

CHURCH DREAMER'S PRIORITY LIST

Write the potentials and possibilities our church has. Do not limit your dreaming because of a lack of such resources as adequate finances or leadership.

I believe our church has an opportunity for increased ministry with these groups of persons or needs:

1.

2.

3.

4.

5.

6.

I am interested in our church giving a priority to number(s)_____.

I am interested in active participation in number(s) _____.

and ultimately to the church. A church may struggle to maintain a long-established college Bible study group with few prospects and fail to see the hundreds of other young adults living in the area as a potential ministry target group.

5. *Avoid overkill in planning*. A casual review of the newsstand boggles the mind with the number of periodicals devoted to subjects such as fitness. The person who wants to get a little exercise may be stymied by the abundance of information on the subject. The same thinking might paralyze Christian education planning. An abundance of materials, seminars, and consultations on planning and related subjects is available. In taking advantage of these resources, however, one should not be thwarted by a lack of knowledge. Planning must be intentional, simple, Spirit-led. Starting with what is known, resources can be used advisedly to enhance that starting point.

6. *Look beyond individual agendas*. To say that a planning group is completely objective is naive. The planning effort probably was born because at least one person thought change was needed. The difficulty comes when personal agendas remain hidden. Consequently, planning leaders should give time early in the process to discover how and what the participants are thinking.

   One way to do this is to have persons share with the group information such as who has influenced them most as Christians; what motivated them to take their current position in the church; what is their greatest fear concerning the project(s) under consideration; and what is their greatest hope for the experience.

   Moving beyond these initial feelings will help the group see that their task is not simply to adopt one person's ideas but to search collectively for the best plans possible.

7. *Maintain flexibility*. It is important to remember that you are dealing largely with volunteers who cannot be coerced into decisions. Also, needs may arise which were not anticipated in earlier planning. New information may surface. These and other factors provide evidence that requires planners to maintain flexibility.

8. *Evaluate planning from the perspective of process and outcomes*. The means used and the projections developed have significant influence on the participants, the organizations they represent, and the administrative support systems affected. Consequently, it is imperative to assess the extent and quality of the work done. This information will aid implementation of plans and improve future planning efforts. (Information about evaluation and suggested procedures will be discussed later in this chapter.)

GUIDELINES FOR THE LOCAL CHURCH

THE CHURCH COUNCIL OR CABINET

The church council holds the key planning responsibilities in most churches. Its members include the pastor, who serves as chair, church staff members, directors of program organizations, a deacon representative, and those who chair committees, such as stewardship and missions. Other group representatives may be added temporarily or permanently according to need.

Basically, the church council should serve as a forum for a church's leaders in planning, coordinating, and evaluating the total work of the church. The church depends on the various church organizations to carry out the plans according to their assigned tasks. As chair of the church council, the pastor can lead in the development of a unified program that gives major attention to church priorities. (Additional information concerning the church council is given in chapter 7, "Administering Church Educational Organizations.")

The principle function for the council or cabinet, then, is to help the church to decide its course and to coordinate and evaluate its work. Figure 4.2 illustrates a planning sheet that may be used by the church council and other planning groups.

PROGRAM PLANNING GROUPS

Each educational organization may have a council group responsible for planning its work, depending of course on the size of the church. For example, the director of the Bible teaching ministry serves as the chairperson for that organization's planning group. Great care should be taken to monitor a council's planning activities for consistency with the church's overall objective(s).

CLASS LEADERS' PLANNING

Class leaders should meet as needed to plan for study, outreach, and ministry. Matters to be included are evaluation of the class's effectiveness in fulfilling its purpose, planning for activities growing out of Bible study, and planning to meet outreach and other ministry needs.

DEVELOPMENTAL EVALUATION

"But these persons are volunteering their time and efforts," Kevin pondered. "What are they going to think if we announce some sort of formal evaluation for the Christian education ministry?"

Indeed, the volunteer aspect should weigh heavily when church leaders approach evaluating the church's educational ministry.

Figure 4.2

A PLANNING SHEET

Project Title: _____

Overall church objective(s) to which this project relates:

_____

_____

_____

_____

_____

Project objective or goal: _____

Possible need(s) to be met: _____

Priority listing of needs: (4) _____

(1)_____   (5) _____

(2)_____   (6) _____

(3)_____   (7) _____

Procedures to meet and reach objective

_____   _____

_____   _____

_____   _____

_____   _____

ASSIGNMENT OF RESPONSIBILITIES

Person assigned	Action to be taken	Date assigned	Date to be completed	Resources needed	Cost involved

The hesitation to evaluate formally may grow out of a concern that those who serve are not paid in money and should not be subjected to the kind of accountability of those who are. Such hesitation, however, may be conditioned by past, mostly inadequate ideas of evaluation.

Any of us might recall the shameful feeling of answering incorrectly a question proposed by a teacher. The ease with which another student answered that same question may have been even more devastating. Such experiences are not easily forgotten, and they condition the way we think about evaluation. It is shortsighted to dismiss evaluation on such thinking or to suggest that it be inappropriate in Christian work. Far from being insulting or inappropriate, evaluation properly done may be the greatest favor a church can do for its volunteer workers. (This applies to paid staff persons as well, but that is another subject.)

At best, it is not thoughtful to ask a person to take a place of responsibility in the church without stating what the church expects from that person, providing resources to do the task, and doing some means of evaluation to help answer the sincere worker's question, "How am I doing?" One foundational principle of working with adults holds that they need reactions to their progress. Evaluation is appropriate, then, if for no other reason.

"Evaluate," according to *Webster's New World Dictionary*, means "to find the value or amount of, to appraise." What does this definition mean for the Christian education ministry?

It is presumptuous to suppose that the church can be the judge of a member's work in relation to God's standards or yet unrevealed effects of that activity known only to God. Instead, the appraisal is addressed to the volunteer's performance in specific activities designed to accomplish purposes and goals established by the church, goals to which the member has made a commitment.

Ideally, evaluation makes a person aware of the quality and kind of his or her work and furnishes guidance for improvement. The most important result of evaluation is what happens in and to the persons involved. The church belongs in the people-mending and people-maturing business; therefore, evaluation should contribute to that process.

Consider these benefits of evaluation:

1. Evaluation is a humane process involving an assessment of strengths and weaknesses in the performance of individual human beings.

2. Evaluation is the only way to find out whether the objectives and goals of the education program are being accomplished.

3. Evaluation is a process that has the capacity to promote an attitude of self-improvement.

4. Evaluation requires the involvement of people interested in improving their attitudes and skills for ministry.

5. Evaluation is a process that enables teachers/leaders and learners to figure out how much success each exhibits in the teaching-learning process.

6. Evaluation provides a means by which the need for and use of facilities, materials, and supplies are seen in relation to the total education ministry.

THE PURPOSE OF EVALUATION

People usually care a great deal about an enterprise in which they have invested significant portions of their energy and resources. Because of this care, they display keen interest in what they perceive to be the vital signs of that enterprise. The national government is one example; the church is another. Constituents, as an outgrowth of concern, constantly evaluate such institutions. The evaluation does not always bear the marks of fairness or lead to the proper conclusions and needed change. It does, however, occur.

Because evaluation occurs somewhat constantly, leaders can profit from understanding the following two facets. First, evaluation speaks to the planning process. Evaluation criteria should be established before the final formulation of plans; and if this is done, then planners can proceed knowing the standards by which their work will be assessed. If ineffectiveness results, the persons responsible can seek improvement.

Second, evaluation speaks to learner progress. All the factors already discussed about evaluation exist for the good of the learners involved in the church's educational ministry. The learner should have some indication of what he or she does and does not know, what he or she does and does not do well. Properly done, this kind of evaluation helps the learner discover areas of needed growth and become motivated to do something about it.

To further clarify the purpose of evaluation, consider the following:

1. Evaluation should serve to provide a comprehensive view of the educational ministry.

2. Evaluation should assess the consistency of the program with the educational philosophy of the church.

3. Evaluation should provide a chance for a cooperative effort by everyone involved.

4. Evaluation should serve the church continuously as an ongoing part of the planning and implementing process.

5. Evaluation should highlight quality and growth.

6. Evaluation should provide a serious look at teachers/leaders, learners, and the learning process.

7. Evaluation should identify strengths and feed this information into the general planning process for inclusion when expanded ministries are being considered.

8. Evaluation should identify problems and focus clearly upon them with a view toward proper solution.

9. Evaluation should help clarify good objectives and point out weaknesses in poor ones.

10. Evaluation should provide accurate and relevant information for those charged by the church with the responsibility for improving the educational ministry.

STANDARDS FOR EVALUATION

Standards for evaluation should be determined early in the process before plans are carried out and persons enlisted for places of responsibility. Here are standards that will be helpful in assessing the church's education program:

First, the church's mission (also, objective or purpose) statement should provide an overall guideline to help find out if the educational ministry is contributing to the fulfillment of the church's intention. This standard may be used in a formal process of evaluation or simply in regular, ongoing assessment of various programs and activities.

Next, and growing out of the church's mission, an educational objective provides a standard. A statement might read something like this: To help persons come to know God as revealed in Jesus Christ, make a personal commitment of faith, become a part of the church as maturing Christian disciples, enter the church's worldwide mission, and live in the power of the Holy Spirit.

Additionally, job descriptions or worker covenants (see fig. 4.3) which have been developed, approved, and reviewed with workers provide a base for evaluation. Since all good evaluation seeks the development of the person(s) involved, a job description becomes a vital resource. Performances can be measured, and areas for needed improvement become apparent, when clear guidelines exist.

Furthermore, carefully formulated and tested standards developed by Christian education specialists (usually connected with your denomination or a religious publisher) provide criteria for evaluating the organization and the performance of specified tasks. Of course, such standards can be revised and made more specific for a particular church situation.

Another source for standards may be found in the individual worker's own goals, developed to be consistent with the church's educational objective and goals. For example, a teacher might set a personal goal of making so many contacts with class members each week or of reading several books relating to the worker's responsibility.

The Bible serves as an authoritative standard for all the church does. The standards found there are appropriate, then, for the church's education ministry. One such application is found in Colossians 3:17: "And whatever you do, in word or deed, do everything in the name of the Lord."

Growing out of the biblical teaching is the final standard recommended for use in evaluating the church's educational ministry: teaching of the priesthood of all believers. Five passages in two books of the New Testament refer directly to this basic belief: 1 Peter 2:5, 9; Revelation 1:5b–6, 9b–10, and 20:6. This doctrine, which has long been used to support direct and equal access to God by all believers, also means that every Christian is a minister and has a ministry to perform. First Peter 2:9 states, "you are a chosen race, a royal priesthood, a holy nation, God's own people, *in order that you may proclaim the mighty acts of him* who called you out of darkness into his marvelous light" (emphasis added). Asking questions about how people are living out this teaching is a vital aspect of evaluation.

WHO ARE THE EVALUATORS?

The most effective evaluation occurs when it involves active participation by the persons who are "stockholders" in the enterprise. To be sure, the responsibility for guiding and coordinating the evaluation process belongs to those individuals and groups who have major responsibility for the church's religious education ministry. Somewhere in the total process, however, there should be a place for others who are involved to say what they feel about the ministry. Such persons include teachers, leaders, learners, certain community leaders, and parents of the children and youth.

Caution must be exercised at this point, however. Pushing too hard for formal evaluation may cause more confusion than benefits. Being wise as a serpent and harmless as a dove is good advice in developing an approach to helpful evaluation. An effort should be made to include everyone possible and to get them to practice self-evaluation under the leadership of the Holy Spirit. People can be encouraged to ask, "How am I doing?" type questions, as well as to measure the organization's effectiveness by the previously accepted standards.

Teachers should study and evaluate their role as learning leaders. Guidance and incentives for class or group members will cause them to check their performance and growth. Suggested criteria must be offered by which they can gauge these matters. All can assume responsibility for improvement along with their leader. Above all, planners must be open to evaluation by others and practice it themselves. This provides a good model. Everyone needs evaluation.

Figure 4.3

SUNDAY SCHOOL WORKER'S COVENANT

Believing that the privilege of guiding people
in the Christian way of life is worthy of my best,
I covenant, as a worker in the
Bible Teaching Ministry
of my church, to:

- Order my conduct in keeping with the principles of the New Testament, and seek the help of the Holy Spirit that I may be faithful and efficient in my work. (Eph. 4:1)

- Be regular and punctual in attendance; and, in case of unavoidable absence, give notice as far in advance as possible. (1 Cor. 4:2)

- Make thorough preparation of the lesson and for my other duties each week. (2 Tim. 2:15)

- Use the Bible with my group and help them to understand and love it. (Psalm 119:16)

- Contribute, proportionately and cheerfully, to my church's budget. (1 Cor. 16:2; 2 Cor. 9:7)

- Attend the regular planning meetings. (Luke 14:28–30)

- Visit prospects frequently and make a special effort to contact absentees each week. (Acts 2:46)

- Study one or more training books each year. (Prov. 15:28a)

- Cooperate wholeheartedly in the plans and activities of the church and school. (1 Cor. 3:9)

- Be loyal to the program of the church, striving to attend all worship services. (Heb. 10:25)

- Make witnessing a major endeavor. (Prov. 11:30)

- Seek to discover and meet the needs of those with whom I come into contact, especially fellow church members and prospects for my church. (Gal. 6:2)

- Pray regularly for the church, the Bible teaching ministry, the workers, and for the pupils and the homes from which they come. (1 Thess. 5:17)

- Apply the teachings of Christ in moral and social issues of my everyday life. (James 1:22)

With the help of God, I will do my utmost to keep this covenant.

Additionally, the people should become more objective in their evaluation through regular practice and by including themselves in the process. They should learn to judge by standards other than their own prejudices toward people and programs. Remember, Jesus did not forbid us to judge; he simply said that we should evaluate by using the standards with which we wish to be judged by others. Getting broad participation means broader ownership by the people involved, a genuine benefit for the church.

AREAS TO BE EVALUATED

Several major areas should be included in a balanced effort to assess the church's educational ministry. It must be recognized that these areas cannot be neatly compartmentalized, standing in isolation from one another. They are all inseparably bound as a part of an active, living organism that we call the church. Consider the following areas for evaluation:

The curriculum materials. Speaking inclusively of the term "curriculum," one means everything that goes on in the church that relates to learning. That is an important idea to consider. However, when the word "curriculum" is mentioned, most people think of the printed, recorded, computerized, or projected materials used. This latter way of thinking is what is being considered here. Although curriculum plans and materials are available from a variety of publishers, the church still needs to make choices based on its own situation. In the selection process, the characteristics of good curriculum become a very basic consideration.

Characteristics to look for in curriculum resources are these:

1. Biblically and theologically sound.

2. Relevant to the learner's situation.

3. Contain comprehensive, essential material for well-rounded growth.

4. Balanced in emphases.

5. Sequenced to assure the best order of learning.

6. Flexible to fit a variety of situations and needs.

7. Relate well to other parts of the total teaching plan of the church.

Teachers/leaders. What happens to the individuals involved is a prime factor in evaluation. Assessing teachers and other workers, therefore, must be done with tact and with their cooperation.

It is essential for the evaluator to follow the principle of helping the individual in the most profitable and expeditious use of his or her gifts, skills, and attitudes. It is not the responsibility of the evaluator to judge or recommend dismissal; rather, it is to encourage, to guide, and to help every member of the church in a God-given ministry. The responsibility includes studying personalities with their related gifts and then seeking to place them where they can function most effectively for God. A person may be moved from one responsibility to another; however, according to biblical principles, no one in the program of God is restricted to the role of passive listener.

It is common knowledge that not everyone should be a teacher or leader (leaders are teachers also by how they lead). Paul faced this problem when he wrote in 1 Timothy 1:7 about those "desiring to be teachers of the law, without understanding either what they are saying or the things about which they make assertions" (NRSV).

One important function of the educational leader or minister is to help persons who should not be leaders or teachers avoid the painful experience of being placed in an inappropriate job. Before enlisting, certain questions should be asked about prospective workers:

- Do they manifest Christlike characteristics?
- Do they understand the goals of Christian education, and, if not, are they willing to learn and apply them?
- Can they learn to use proper methods of teaching and leading?
- Will they participate in outreach?
- Are they lazy?
- Do they know the Bible adequately?
- Can they work with others?
- Are they willing to use the curriculum materials properly?

Once the person takes a place of service as a teacher or leader, self-evaluation is probably the most effective means of detecting strengths and weaknesses, and planning for improvement. For evaluation to occur, workers need a guide or standard. The guide might be a Worker's Covenant (such as illustrated earlier in fig. 4.3) that the church has approved and to which the persons involved have agreed.

Another approach would be for the person closest to a supervisory relationship to visit with the volunteer (preferably in the worker's home) and ask some "How are you doing or feeling?" kinds of questions as they discuss the job description or covenant. Out of this exchange should come ways of improvement or even the decision that a person could profit from a change in responsibility.

For a teacher in the Bible teaching ministry of the church, a checklist such as suggested in figure 4.4 can be used regularly. As persons become more aware of the type questions that are appropriate in evaluation, they are likely to become more conscious of the factors regularly.

Observation is another method of evaluation, although it can become a sensitive issue. The person being observed should be aware of such a procedure and should have agreed to it. The results should be shared and carefully assessed with the worker.

Here are four principles to follow when using observation: (1) the worker should be able to respect the observer as competent and caring; (2) the worker should enter the process voluntarily; (3) the observation should be planned and carried out with the least disturbance possible; and (4) a conference after the observation should be carried out as mutual evaluation.

Some leaders have supervisory responsibilities. If you are one, you can use these questions for self-evaluation:

- Do I have concern for those who serve under my leadership?
- Do I delegate responsibility to my workers?
- Do I ask for and respect the opinion of those I lead?
- Do I promote loyalty to the entire church?
- Do I give deserved and specific praise?
- Do I keep the workers informed?
- Do I include all workers in the planning and evaluation?
- Do I deal with problems rather than personalities?
- Do I have a checkup system to ensure that assignments are completed successfully?
- Do I consult those who will be affected by an action before it is taken?
- Do I see that a new worker gets proper orientation?
- Do I seek to measure up to the standards for my position?

The learner's experience. Learners must benefit in increased knowledge and understanding of the Bible, fellowship and acceptance, and opportunities for participation in ministry activities. Leaders need to listen so they can know what the learners are learning and how they are making application. The quality of instruction can be measured also.

There are some observable signs available to those seeking to understand the learner's experience: attendance, attention and comments in class, growth in Christian understanding and character, and enthusiasm for reaching new persons.

Tests may be used to help find out learner knowledge and understanding. Such tests may be essay (which usually begin with a word such as discuss, explain, or compare); objective (short answer, based on simple recall and completion); interest and attitude (reaction to a series of statements). Some tests are included in the curriculum material, and others are available from religious publishers.

Another effective way to determine learning is to interview individual members of the class or group outside the regular sessions. The questions should be more open and informal than questions on a written test. This type of evaluation shows a measure of Bible knowledge and suggests the degree to which learners are serious about the learning experience.

Figure 4.4

CHECKING YOUR BIBLE TEACHING

Grade yourself as a teacher by circling beside each question the number which you feel is most accurate. Add up the total of the circled numbers. A score of 85 or above would be an excellent score and 40 or below would be a poor score. In between would range from fair (41–60) to good (61–84).

PREPARATION

I look through the lesson topics
in advance.   Always 5 4 3 2 1 Never

I begin lesson preparation more
than one week in advance.   Always 5 4 3 2 1 Never

The Bible is the center of my
lesson preparation.   Always 5 4 3 2 1 Never

I have a systematic plan of lesson study.   Always 5 4 3 2 1 Never

I keep in mind the specific needs of all
my pupils as I prepare.   Always 5 4 3 2 1 Never

I write down or have in mind a specific
objective for each lesson.   Always 5 4 3 2 1 Never

I seek constantly to improve my teaching
by general reading, by attending workers'
meetings, and taking training courses.   Always 5 4 3 2 1 Never

I pray regularly about my task.   Always 5 4 3 2 1 Never

PRESENTATION

I am able to stimulate interest from
the beginning.   Always 5 4 3 2 1 Never

I seek to have the Bible passages
read meaningfully.   Always 5 4 3 2 1 Never

All of my learners participate in the
lesson discussion.   Always 5 4 3 2 1 Never

I use a balanced variety of
teaching methods.   Always 5 4 3 2 1 Never

I am able to follow the main subject to a
desirable conclusion without getting
unduly diverted.   Always 5 4 3 2 1 Never

I pace the presentation schedule to give
proper emphasis to the central truth.   Always 5 4 3 2 1 Never

My pupils and I reach helpful conclusions
by the end of each lesson period.   Always 5 4 3 2 1 Never

EVALUATION

My pupils are stimulated to more
Bible study.   Always 5 4 3 2 1 Never

My teaching helps change learners' moral
and social standards.   Always 5 4 3 2 1 Never

My teaching helps to reach the unsaved.   Always 5 4 3 2 1 Never

My teaching helps make pupils more
faithful in their church relationships.   Always 5 4 3 2 1 Never

My teaching helps make me a better
Christian.   Always 5 4 3 2 1 Never

Facilities and equipment. Place is important in Christian education. The physical characteristics of that place contribute significantly to the learning experience. Although many buildings in which Christian education programs are housed do not provide ideal arrangement for classes or groups, evaluation should begin with time-tested standards. Usually, denominational offices or publishers can provide such help.

Church workers need to be aware of how much the physical surroundings affect learning. Each time workers enter the room where they teach or lead they should observe the physical characteristics with the eye of a stranger. Things such as littered and unattractive areas, surplus materials out of place, and inappropriate room arrangement can be corrected with little or no money. Problems with lighting, heating, seating, and audiovisual equipment will require varying costs to correct.

Organization. Organization is the structuring of persons and other resources for accomplishing a given task. Because organization contributes to the effectiveness of a program or ministry, it also should be evaluated, at least annually. This usually is done by each organization's program council, using questions such as these:

- Are there adequate classes, departments, and other units?
- Do we have the right number of leaders and support staff?
- Is coordination appropriate for each level of work?
- Where can we start new units?

- Are we making good use of all resources (participants time, volunteer leaders, facilities, ministerial staff, and administrative support services)?

For more information on organization, see chapter 5, "How to Organize and Coordinate."

USING EVALUATION INFORMATION

Effective developmental evaluation always maintains the role of a servant, never a tyrant. For something to serve, it must be used. Failure to use the results of evaluation is a disservice to the people with whom you work and, if done intentionally, dishonest. The same people who helped in planning and conducting evaluation should be included in drawing conclusions and helping choose what steps to take. In that way, evaluation serves the people most affected by it.

The process of using evaluation should include these elements: (1) careful examination of the information to determine its validity; (2) determination of the reasons for past success and failure; and (3) the feeding of information back into the process for future ministry planning.

As Kevin and Molly shared the meal, they discussed their thoughts. The more they talked, the more they realized the awesome task of planning and evaluating the church's ministry. This chapter is for all those, like these two, who want to do the best job possible.

CHAPTER 5

How to Organize and Coordinate

Bob I. Johnson

Brother Mike was feeling fine, more refreshed than recent memory told him. His week away for meditation, study, and rest furnished a welcome rejuvenation for weary mind and body. This was an exciting time for the church as it celebrated one hundred years of ministry and the tenth year of the pastor's leadership. So on this Sunday Brother Mike sermonized about building on tradition for the church's next century and the new millennium. The message centered on the positive ministry of the church and the need to dream for the future. He cautioned the congregation about the danger of clinging to the past and fearing the future.

Anna had recently graduated from a seminary and had joined the church staff as the associate minister for Christian education. As she sat before the congregation that day listening to the sermon, her thoughts were captured by a desire to lead a ministry of education effectively and with clear purpose. She remembered that a seminary class on leadership had emphasized the power of a clear vision of what God wanted the church to be and to do. So all that the pastor was saying sounded good. But Anna knew that vision needed to be translated into a tangible and workable structure for ministry.

Among other things, such a structure means good organization and coordination. She felt that doing business as usual would not enable the church to face effectively a new century and the new millennium. So she began to compose a mental image of a possible future state of the church and what the structure might resemble, especially as it related to her responsibilities. For one thing, change would be inevitable—not with God's timeless intention for the church, but with the expression of that intention and how it relates to the times.

The vision of such a future state, however, must be widely owned and not just confined to the staff. It has to become a magnificent obsession possessing at least a significant core of church members. Yes, Anna, this inevitably involves good structure. It means, among other things, good organizing and coordinating, the subjects of this chapter.

ORGANIZING PRINCIPLES AND PROCEDURES

Why do we organize? The answer is simple. Organizing provides the structure through which a group of persons committed to and involved in a common enterprise do their work. The simplest form involves two persons communicating and working toward a common purpose.

We know that organizing developed soon after the early church was established and is a constant and essential factor in successful ministry. It is the means through which the church expresses itself as a living, dynamic, and servant extension of the Lord Jesus Christ.

Churches sometimes establish organizations without adequately deciding what work is to be done. This virtually assures that the organization will become the end instead of the means. Starting with organization instead of purpose may involve church members in ways that are less valuable than those dealing with a church's essential work.

One of the challenges for the staff person who wants to gear organization to the church's essential work is the fondness of many members for the status quo. For example, as Anna pondered the future she could not help thinking about several of the Bible study classes (such as Dorcas, Friendship, and Baraca), with long histories and designated rooms which class members had decorated. These had been taught for many years by the same highly respected teachers. But what about the classes that require staffing by persons who can serve only for a matter of weeks or months at a time?

Her thoughts also encompassed the almost mind-boggling changes in society and church ministries she had read about as she studied at the seminary. She had learned that a church as old as this one is not likely to grow unless it develops ministry structures that will reach new persons, especially younger generations. Also, the facts show that churches with high expectations of their members generally grow while others decline.

But how do you reorganize a church to encourage high commitment to Christian discipleship when low commitment has been the basic church culture? How is this done without usurping the place of the Holy Spirit? In other words, what can be done in the future so the church will be the church God intends?

THE NATURE OF THE CHURCH

At the heart of the church's existence is the need to know the purpose for which God intended it. This demands the question, "What is the nature of God's presence in the world?" When the answer emerges, the believing church finds ways to join God at work. Organization then forms itself around that purpose and responds to the leadership of God.

Serious Bible students know that God's activities focus on creation and redemption. So, to begin, one must start thinking about getting organized for creative and redemptive expressions of ministry. Also, one must think about ways to lead the church to discover its high calling in Christ as partners in creating and redeeming.

Increasingly there is an attempt by churches to approach organizational structuring from the viewpoint suggested above. What are the tasks of the church? What does the church plan to do about its God-given assignment? Needed organization then grows from the soil produced by answers to such questions. This makes organizing a means to an end, not an end in itself. It should also reduce competition and enhance cooperation and coordination.

Terminology used to describe important features of organizations has varied both in the professional literature and in practice. To gain initial perspective for this study of organization, it is helpful to understand several related terms.

Organizing is the process by which the structure of an organization is created and maintained. This process includes the determination of the specific activities necessary to accomplish the objectives of the organization, the grouping of those activities according to some acceptable pattern, and assignment of these grouped activities to a responsible person. Organizing (with other activities such as planning, motivating, communicating, and evaluating) is considered a part of the responsibilities of church staff members and elected lay leaders.

Organization refers to the structure determined to be the best framework for a church to carry out its ministry. Of course, the emphasis of this book is on the church's educational ministry. As a vital part of the whole, many people think immediately about the educational ministry when they think about church organization. Academic inquiry about organizations often is described as the study of organizational theory, or the theory of organizations.

CHURCH ORGANIZATIONAL MODELS

Three main types of organizational structure have prevailed in recent history. These three are found in churches as well as business, government, and other institutions.

Executive model. The executive, or mechanistic, structure usually is depicted in charts by titles of job roles contained in several boxes. Some are joined by continuous lines to show an executive relationship between the roles and some by dotted lines to indicate communications relationships only. The former are "lines of authority"; the latter, "lines of communication."

This organizational model may be viewed as a system of people in a structure of *work* roles—in which people may change, but the roles remain the same. The people thus must be fitted to the roles rather than the roles to the people.

Such organizations are structured into a hierarchical system of specialist roles or functions. Each individual role carries carefully defined rights, duties, and technical requirements. There is little or no overlap among the various positions or components. Consequently, information must be directed upward in the hierarchy, where executive officers have most knowledge of the enterprise's needs and send down instructions accordingly to lower levels.

Communications therefore are mostly vertical; that is, between supervisor and the supervised. Work is done according to instructions devised by the head of the hierarchy.

Some churches practice this style with a strong directive pastor serving like a chief executive officer. Most often, where this seems effective, such a pastor has served in the church since it began or for an extended time and has gained the confidence of the members. Pastors and other staff members who attempt this system on their own nearly always fail at being effective leaders and rarely have long tenure.

Probably no more than one in ten ministers can be effective with this approach. Those who succeed have a system for listening to key people before they move ahead with plans and pronouncements. Also, they are benevolent enough not to run over too many people who might appear to stand in the way of progress.

Human relations model. The second organizational structure may be designated by the term *human relations.* Human relations theorists claim that a key task of leadership and management is to create groups strongly committed to the achievement of organizational objectives. Individual incentives should be replaced by group incentives to help workers gain a sense of togetherness. Team work and participation in decision-making are expected at all levels.

The advocates of the human relations structure claim that organizations should not be depicted as sets of relationships among *work* roles but as relationships between interlocking and interdependent *groups.* This strengthens the work force and, therefore, provides more energy for the achievement of organizational objectives. A potential weakness, however, is that leaders can become so focused on building up good human relationships among the various interlocking groups that major tasks are neglected.

When used in a church, the human relations structure is benevolent, permissive, and friendly; everyone is encouraged to be involved. As such, the church may be perceived by its members as a social group, just like other groups in society. Its main concern is with itself, and its objective is to enlarge its social nexus. An example might be the Bible study group whose main purpose is to "fellowship," to have an abundance of activities with little or no reference to the heart of the gospel and its call to servanthood.

Organic model. The third approach to organization is the organic structure, also known as the systems approach. This group of managers and scholars has viewed the executive and the human relations structures as unable to achieve both organizational objectives and the personal fulfillment that each person seeks. They contend that organizational purpose and meaningful personal involvement can be found only in an organic structure.

In the organic structure, knowledge is no longer confined to the top of the hierarchy; it is shared with each member of the organization who needs it for the achievement of his or her task. Work, to be effective, must be coordinated with that of other group members. This requires that communication become less a matter of passing down instructions from above and more a matter of sharing information and mutual consultation among the organization's members. Communication is both vertical and lateral.

Advocates of the organic approach say that people do not function in little boxes, as in the executive structure, but must constantly relate what they are doing to what is being done by others in the organization. The organization is not static, but it is in a state of continuous interaction with the environment in which it exists.

To understand something of its intent and approach, contrast the organic (or systems) approach with that of the human relations and executive (or mechanistic) theories. The executive approach focuses on achieving the organization's goals, while the human relations organization focuses on achieving the goals of its people. The organic approach, however, holds that organizational growth and goal achievement, as well as the growth of persons and the achievement of their own goals within the organization, are equally important.

CHURCH LEADERS AND ORGANIZATION

These three descriptions briefly characterize the major approaches to organization. But more must be said for organization as current and future needs present themselves. A church's pattern of organization and its forms of ministry will become less effective or even obsolete at some future point. Only faith, hope, and love will survive. The ways in which we do things will change. Therefore, built into the fabric of any organization should be the element of flexibility and the acceptance of the fact that change is not the exception but the rule.

Some have talked about necessary *disorganization.* Unsettling suggestions like, "if it ain't broke, break it," are offered here and there. Such radical thought arises from the need to address a rapidly changing environment with all of its new challenges. Churches confront challenges similar to those of businesses and other institutions.

For churches the primary challenge is what to change and what to keep the same as, or similar to, what we have been doing. Who would dare think that the Sunday morning Bible study and worship times should or could be changed? Such changes are happening in places where the organization is flexible and the need exists for additional opportunities of study and worship. A church may expand its program to include a Saturday night Bible study and worship. Or a church may have a Thursday night "Sunday school" for singles because many of them leave the large metropolitan area on the weekend.

The point is this: organization(s) should be flexible, responsive, and always subservient to the God-given ministry of the church. Of course, we must continue to question how much change a local church can tolerate. Additionally, we must ask what to change and when to make the changes.

VOLUNTEER WORKERS AND ORGANIZATION

Furthermore, consideration must be given to the volunteer leaders/ workers in a church. What are their characteristics and how do they relate to these organizational studies?

Volunteers, of course, are not paid monetarily, but they do get their rewards in other ways. They usually serve for a short duration. In churches that do not require high commitment, volunteers may view the church as one among other volunteer organizations.

Their leaders are confined to using persuasive power rather than position or other kinds of power. Usually volunteers are generalists and not highly trained in their work in the church organization. On the positive side, they are interested in achieving the organization's goals as they understand them. Their motivation comes from a personal desire to serve rather than to earn money.

Evidence exists today that people will respond positively to organizations requiring greater commitment by volunteers. One has only to consider the music ministry that has certain standards for those who wish to sing in the choir for the worship service(s). Members understand and expect to abide by those standards. This is true even in churches where other organizations do not have high expectations of their participants.

REASONS FOR ORGANIZATION

When negative feelings arise about organization, they probably come from confusing bad or ineffective organization with good organization. When organization is right, one is hardly aware of its existence. The benefits, however, are enjoyed by all.

In an effective Bible teaching ministry, the persons blessed by it are not going to sing praises of "the organization." They will speak in terms of teachers or other persons who have extended themselves in Christ's name to meet their need. Or they will comment on what a great Sunday school the church has.

But the people who have put the organization in place, humanized it, and led it to be sensitive to the moving of the Holy Spirit, know that such development requires substantial effort. They are, however, quite happy for that effort to be invisible to the observer and not to call attention to itself.

Some benefits of good organization to consider, then, are these:

1. Good organization establishes responsibility and clarifies roles.

2. Good organization channels need authority for the work to be done.

3. Good organization allows for proper distribution of work.

4. Good organization establishes how the parts of the whole relate to one another.

5. Good organization fosters a team concept based on shared responsibility.

6. Good organization lives and breathes flexibility in order to accomplish its ministry.

PRINCIPLES OF ORGANIZING

How to organize is a subject of highest importance for a leader in designing an educational ministry. Here are seven principles of organization for educational ministry.

Principle #1: Let the work to be done provide overall structure. The purpose for organizing, plus the time and resources available to accomplish it, are the basic factors that indicate how to organize.

Determining these factors may be done by using a council meeting in a retreat setting. One plan for such a retreat is to bring staff and lay leaders together for a listening session, during which the staff listens to the volunteer leaders.

Over the next several weeks staff members project plans based on what they have heard. Having selected, for example, the need for teacher training, the next step is to find the most effective organizational vehicle to accomplish the task.

Principle #2: Put together work functions that share important common concerns. Work that is similar should be combined. Again, the need for teacher training is an example. Another concern might be leadership training. Instead of each organization conducting its own training program, one central unit in the church could be responsible.

Another example is from a ministry in which many churches have become involved—disaster relief. Such a ministry can best be provided organizationally through one unit rather than by separate classes or programs.

Principle #3: Push decisions as low in the organization as adequate information is available for making them. This is done to provide for maximum growth and participation of each leader and worker. Also, this leaves ministers as free as possible for their primary responsibility: to focus on articulating the vision God has given the church. Then, at different levels, others have their duties and the authority to do them.

As you encourage workers to make decisions appropriate for their level of responsibility, you should remember that leaders will always need to be available for consultation. One must be careful, however, that people do not use "upward delegation" of some of their tasks to avoid tough decision-making and difficult responsibilities at their level. This is their church, too.

Principle #4: Avoid overorganization. If you have analyzed needed work and the other factors involved, you have a reasonable idea of the numbers and kinds of persons required to do the job. But organization should be kept to a minimum.

Every additional component and layer of organization add to the difficulty of communication and increase working time devoted to coordination, relationships, and information exchange. All these factors impede accomplishment, decrease efficiency, and lessen the likelihood that all will feel a partnership in the work and accomplishment of the task.

Since the purpose of organization is to establish an easy flow of work and to help its accomplishment, formal structure should be kept at a minimum.

Principle #5: Make good communication a priority. An organization consists of a system of interrelated parts. When these parts work well together, the organization functions most effectively. Communication is essential for peak efficiency to occur.

Good communication in a volunteer organization begins and ends with a leader who listens. Such a leader puts himself or herself in the place of the volunteers and tries to anticipate how they feel and think. Such a leader finds the best method for communication, such as staff meetings and newsletters (see also the section in this chapter on coordination). Good communication is aimed at creating a sense of community and belonging.

Principle #6: Seek to understand the informal groups that are not included in the church's organizational chart. Every organization has informal groups. These groups evolve slowly—almost unnoticed—until they become an influential, though still informal, part of the structure. Sometimes these are called "kitchen cabinets" because of the decisions which they make on an informal basis. Being close-knit and usually friends, these groups often discuss issues and answers that ultimately may carry a great deal of weight. The term "clique" is often applied to such unofficial groups.

Since informal groups may devise plans of action on their own and catch others off-guard, it is good practice to identify, understand, and seek to maintain working relationships with those involved.

Informal groups cannot be prevented, but should they be discouraged? Not always. Cliques and informal groups are not always detrimental to a church's welfare and often can enhance the fellowship.

Consider a church that is located in a community with a high turnover in population and a comparable turnover in church membership. Cliques and informal groups in this situation may form a core of leadership and thereby provide a source of stability and strength for a church in the midst of its changing constituency. Without such groups, churches in changing communities or with a high turnover in staff members might find themselves deprived of capable leadership.

This principle also relates to the amount of informal influence exerted on the formal organization. Informal influence may be physical presence, economic control, knowledge, performance, personality, and ideological strength. A leader exhibits critical awareness when recognizing the informal power structures which affect the organization.

Principle #7: View the persons within the organization as those for whom Christ died and as capable of doing God's will in their lives. They have received the gift of God in Christ Jesus and are now trying to express their commitment to him through their gifts from the Spirit. Decide how you will treat these persons who have volunteered to work within the organization. The leader's attitude toward and understanding of people will directly affect the organizational approach taken.

AN ORGANIZATION IS PEOPLE

Decades ago Douglas McGregor popularized the "Theory X" and "Theory Y" approaches to relating to people in an organization. A Theory X approach means that the leader views persons as basically disliking work, being lazy and irresponsible. They need to be strictly controlled because they are not trustworthy.

In contrast, Theory Y assumes that people naturally enjoy work, that they will demonstrate great loyalty to an organization in which they believe, and that every person possesses to some degree the gifts of creativity and imagination. If people seem passive to the needs of the organization, it is because the organization has failed them rather than the other way around.

If both X and Y theories seem extreme, perhaps there is another way of viewing the situation. Consider a secular work situation as it relates to job enrichment. We recognize that some employees do not want their jobs enriched. Some prefer easier work. Some are troubled by too much challenge. Others prefer a friendly situation and are not as much concerned about job content.

Consider a church example. Some people have served for many years as record-keepers for the Sunday school or a class within the school and are perfectly contented. They do not wish to move to any other position or "get a promotion."

For leaders of Christian organizations, valid theological questions are involved. For example, how do we view humanity and their response to Christian commitment? How does the warfare of the old nature and the new nature play a role in a person's volunteer ministry through the organization? Since there is not much reward for volunteers except the pride of accomplishment, how are they to be motivated? (See chapter 6 on "How to Staff and Motivate.") The leader of volunteers will need to choose a way of leading which allows for the greatest involvement in and satisfaction for these volunteers.

Volunteers may be involved in helping to plan, choose curriculum materials, and evaluate. This involvement will help them with the larger view of the organization and its purpose. Also, it allows them to provide ideas as to the strengths and weaknesses of the organization. Participation in these ways should enlarge their vision for and commitment to the ministry of the organization. Enhanced commitment will make them more open to needed change and should forestall their saying, "We never did it that way before." (Might these be called the "seven last words of the church"?)

GUIDELINES FOR ORGANIZATION

The following actions will be helpful for designing a new organization or in redesigning existing organizations:

Guideline #1: Preview the existing situation. What is the present plan of organization? What has the church stated in its official documents such as its constitution and bylaws? What, if any, long-range plans does the church have involving the educational ministry? What are the real needs for ministry?

Churches differ in size and therefore have different organizational needs. The smaller membership church, for example, is not merely a scaled-down version of the larger membership church. The truly small church is a unit, or single cell, in which everyone identifies with and relates to everyone else.

In the larger church this interrelatedness is impossible. However, the larger church must be organized so that there are enough small units that everyone may find a place to belong, love and be loved, and express ministry.

Guideline #2: Assess the future in relation to the present and past. What are the opportunities for the church and what structure is needed to be ready to meet those challenges? What problems existed in the past that can and need to be corrected?

Using the appropriate persons will help determine answers to such questions. Lists of responses can be made for future evaluation.

Guideline #3: Formulate a plan for the organizational needs to be met. This begins by putting together the structure that seems best. One must leave plenty of room in the mind and on the paper for change. Should changes in procedures be made? What do the church's constitution and by-laws say? Do they need to be revised?

When can the plan be put into effect? What are the snags along the way? What can be done to overcome inertia? How much money is involved?

Guideline #4: Prepare a report for information and action. Depending on where responsibility for development of the plans lies, the key coordinating group or council should review and approve such plans for organizational change and then take them to the church for approval (or in whatever way the church stipulates the process to take place).

Guideline #5: Implement approved plans on an effective schedule. Timing is an important factor. Moving too quickly or too slowly can prove to be detrimental. This issue should be discussed with church staff members and with the educational ministry leaders.

KEEPING THE ORGANIZATION UP-TO-DATE

Setting up the organization is one activity. Keeping it up-to-date is quite another—and just as important. Ongoing effort to maintain it is essential. Here are some ways to monitor the situation and keep the organization alive:

1. *See that people, both members and visitors, are properly cared for by the existing organization.* Are meeting rooms attractive and inviting? Will total strangers and first-time visitors be able to tell when meetings occur and where they should go to enter the flow of activities? Are greeters well-placed, or is there a welcome center, for the arriving visitor?

2. *Study the organization through the year.* What needs have arisen since the beginning of the church year? What is the ratio of teachers to students in classes, groups, and departments? The addition of

workers and the creation of new units as necessary will maintain a good ratio for growth and effective teaching-learning.

3. *Check enrollment and prospect lists.* Are classes and other units appropriate in size to function effectively for outreach as well as study? Are additional units needed?

4. *Identify untapped resources in the organization.* These resources are the people through whom God is, or could be, working. You probably will find a tremendous gap between what some people are doing and what their potential is for ministry.

   Matching this potential with performance is the source of true joy in your leadership. With computers or other filing systems, you can develop a data bank to help the matching of people's gifts and skills with needs of the organization. No organization ever becomes great until it is focused, dedicated, and disciplined. A central storehouse of information is a starting place for the effective stewardship of gifts.

5. *Regularly assess and redream the vision of the organization.* This starts with the leader(s) but involves all participants. Regular evaluation times should be scheduled to assess how well the organization is helping the church fulfill its mission. Ways to improve should be considered but changes are not to be made merely for the sake of change.

6. *Assess your role as the leader.* Ask questions: Am I a person of spiritual authenticity at the deepest level? Do I get along with people? Am I aware of cultural and other background differences in people? Am I openminded and willing to listen both to God and the people? Am I flexible where flexibility is in order? Do I adjust to new conditions? Do I deal with facts and not stereotypes?

7. *Learn to anticipate.* Anticipation allows for making internal changes in the organization in response to a changing society. A successful leader consciously practices the skill of anticipation. This skill requires having the big picture and possessing good response timing.

RELATING TO TRADITION

A church, like other organizations, develops within a tradition that is an evolving system of assumptions, habits, behavior, and attitudes. This tradition has been shaped by leaders in the past as they dealt with situations inside and outside the organization.

As situations change, new leadership may reinforce, reinterpret, or seek to change traditions. New leaders can never afford to forget the effect the group's history has on members.

Before much time passes, a body of people develops momentum. Sudden changes court disaster. Stopping and then starting in a new direction take more time and energy than building on parts of tradition which are allies of biblical imperatives or of responses to new needs.

Thus, a church organization that has become a self-centered, mutual-help society may awaken to its evangelistic obligations when the people vividly recall the missionary zeal of its founders and first members. An organization that has been building itself but neglecting its community may begin to show more of the compassion of its Lord when reminded of the priorities he had and how they were carried forth by earlier faithful workers.

An important first step for a new staff member is the study of the church documents, history, and both oral and written traditions.

COORDINATING PRINCIPLES AND PROCEDURES

You wonder how it can happen. But somehow it really does. Two groups in the church have planned activities requiring the fellowship hall for the same date. Neither checked the calendar, and each learned of the conflict only after significant amounts of time and energy had been invested in preparations. Both groups had good intentions, but a lack of coordination caused the problem.

This simple example points out that the church's educational ministry has unique needs for coordinated, integrated plans and procedures. Since the church is largely dependent on volunteers who see each other for relatively brief times each week, coordination becomes absolutely necessary and also more difficult than in situations where people are together for a regular workweek.

When someone exclaims out of a sense of frustration, "We need to get better organized around here!" coordination may be what is meant. When people know what is expected of them and how they relate to others, then coordination can begin. The prerequisite for good coordination, however, is good organization.

Organizing, as described at the beginning of the chapter, is a process going on all the time in any social system, including the church. It involves, among other things, developing a vision in the members' minds of how they are to live, serve, and worship together. It also includes maintaining an atmosphere for continued commitment to the vision.

Coordination, then, complements the organizing process and may be defined as the means of bringing together all the parts of an enterprise into a relationship that harmoniously achieves the organizational goals.

Good church leadership requires comprehensive, coordinated planning. The church functions best as an organization when all the parts join together under this leadership to make a larger whole with a unified mission. In addition, the church as the body of Christ functions best as a unified, coordinated, and directed whole—allowing for diversity of gifts and people as well as the leadership of the Holy Spirit.

PRINCIPLES OF GOOD COORDINATION

Principle #1: Basic agreement on the purpose of the organization is necessary for good coordination. Understanding of purpose must be reached early in the process of organizational relationships so all members of the team can work together. Such understanding must begin with the church's own determination of an overall purpose and then come to maturity as the church's purpose filters into and influences the purpose of each organization.

Principle #2: Planning is essential for good coordination. Agreement on purpose is followed by careful planning. By matching agreed purpose with thorough planning, a leader can place a general strategy before everyone. Detailed plans can be made with a minimum of overlapping. Remember, a lack of coordination often is not detected until a crisis has arisen.

Principle #3: Good coordination should include all groups involved. At times individual groups exalt their own importance in relation to the whole. Groups may become self-centered and feel that everything must revolve around them. A group or a leader may feel that a room or equipment is exclusive property when in reality it belongs to the larger body, the church, and is to be shared with others.

Coordination involving all groups or units helps to maintain a perspective and to remind people of the common task the church has undertaken.

Principle #4: Specific efforts to communicate with the constituency are a part of good coordination. Communication is essential to effective coordination of activities because the achievement of group purposes is dependent upon dividing the required tasks among the members. Good communication makes options clear and opens the way for wise choices by individuals and groups. It clarifies the relation of actions to the desired results and increases motivation. It makes coordination easier through developing awareness of the actions of others.

GUIDELINES FOR COMMUNICATING

Guideline #1: Use a variety of means. The church council (or other group assigned the responsibility) is the administrative body for planning and coordinating a church's work. The pastor, who chairs the council, leads this group of key leaders representing church programs in maintaining order and relevancy in all phases of church life.

This group should meet monthly or often enough to function properly and carry out its task. Members should be encouraged to prepare properly for the sessions so that effective coordination can be accomplished.

Program councils and staff plan the direction of the program(s), coordinate efforts, and relate to the church council for general coordination. Directors of major units in the program become members of the program council and serve for as long as they are in their particular responsibility. See figure 5.1 for a suggested agenda for such a group.

Sunday School Council Plan Sheet

Getting Ready for the Meeting	Person Responsible	Date to Be Completed
I. Prepare an agenda.	Sunday school director	
II. Mail copy of agenda to all council members one week before the meeting.		
Suggestions for the Sunday School Council Agenda		
I. Encouragement Perhaps the pastor could be used to speak briefly.	Pastor or other respected leader	
II. Information Discuss "how" to get the work done.	Division/ department directors	
III. Evaluation Discuss events and activities that have been conducted. Consider how they could be improved or whether they should be held again.		
IV. Communication This period can be used for a progress report on current activities.		
V. Preparation This period is time to schedule, plan, and assign responsibilities for upcoming projects.		
VI. After the Meeting Prepare a summary of the meeting and mail a summary to absent council members.		

Figure 5.1

Age-division coordination is accomplished through either self-coordination, age-division conferences, or age-division coordinators (or directors). The complexity of the organization should determine the approach used.

In self-coordination, the organization leaders of an age division voluntarily coordinate their work and the use of space, equipment, and supplies.

Age-division coordination conferences serve as counseling, advisory, and coordinating groups. Members are leaders of units of a particular age division (choirs, mission groups, Bible teaching units, and discipleship units).

Age-division coordinators counsel teachers/leaders and coordinate the work of units within the age division.

The church calendar lists the regularly scheduled activities of the church for the year. It is distributed to all officers, workers, staff personnel, and church members. The distribution should be well worth the cost involved and should help promote greater effectiveness of the program.

A long-range view will provide the businesslike planning inherent in an annual church calendar; it will also motivate leaders and others to plan their personal programs, with the church coming first rather than last in their thinking. A definite process for creating and amending the calendar should be established, preferably through the church council.

Planning guides and coordination materials for program organizations are available from your denominational bookstore or church literature distributor.

Written reports will update the church calendar. There will undoubtedly be activities planned which have not been included in the annual church calendar. Reports describing projected activities and submitted to the organizational leaders and/or the church council, will give sufficient opportunity to coordinate these with the activities already listed in the church calendar. If there is any conflict, the activities previously scheduled in the annual church calendar usually take priority.

The organizational chart shows the relationships among persons in leadership positions. A chart of this nature should be distributed to all officers and workers to help them visualize the organization.

If the church distributes a manual to new members, an organizational chart should be included, thereby providing an excellent means for their orientation to the administration of the church. This chart becomes a coordinating device in that each person knows to whom to go for assistance, rather than moving from one office to another seeking the person with the knowledge and authority concerning the matter at hand. See figure 5.2 for a checklist that helps in detecting strengths and weaknesses in such an arrangement.

The administrative handbook is a manual prepared by many churches for communication and coordination. It should be available to all who function in a leadership capacity. Responsibilities should be defined

Figure 5.2
Checklist for Coordination Review

1. In your organization have you found:		
(1) Unassigned areas of responsibility? (Describe)	Yes	No
(2) Inadvertent overlapping areas of responsibility? (Describe)	Yes	No
(3) Procedure difficulties between tasks? (Describe)	Yes	No
(4) Fuzzy lines of communication? (Describe)	Yes	No
(5) Other (Describe)	Yes	No
2. In your personal contacts with other organizations, have you found:		
(1) Unassigned areas of responsibility? (Describe)	Yes	No
(2) Inadvertent overlapping areas of responsibility? (Describe)	Yes	No
(3) Procedure difficulties between tasks? (Describe)	Yes	No
(4) Fuzzy lines of communication? (Describe)	Yes	No
(5) Other (Describe)	Yes	No
3. With respect to your relationship with other persons:		
(1) Is the relationship between your task and overall organization goals clear?		
(2) Are any of your responsibilities unclear?		
(3) If you reach all the results planned, will your organization make its full contribution to the overall purpose of the church?		
(4) If the person to whom you look for leadership carries out the planned work, will you receive adequate help from him or her?		
(5) Is the communication channel adequate?		

clearly, procedures for contingency situations explained, and other items of an essential nature included. Handbooks—which some churches or groups issue annually—often include the names, addresses, and telephone numbers of officers and leaders, important activities and their dates, constitution and bylaws, and scheduled programs and projects for the year. Some handbooks are comprehensive, while others are designed for a specific program or ministry group.

Worker's meetings, both weekly and monthly, are absolutely necessary if activities are to be kept coordinated. Examples include Sunday school workers' meeting and music leaders council.

The dominant idea or motto is a coordinating device that may have value for achieving a sense of unity. The idea should be directly related to the supreme mission of the church and be emphasized regularly through printed materials, brochures, and other communication media.

Ex-officio memberships are usually extended to persons at the upper levels of organizations so that they can gain information for coordinating the general program. The pastor, associate pastor, minister of education, or others may be given ex-officio privileges. This allows them to be members of selected committees with voting rights, as determined by the group or by the constitution and its bylaws, but without responsibility for leadership.

The church bulletin is perhaps the most commonly used device for coordinating church activities. It is distributed to all worshipers on Sundays and lists the activities for the coming week. The disadvantage of this method as a coordinating device is that most people plan many of their business, educational, social, and recreational activities a month to three months in advance.

Those church bulletins which announce important events for a month ahead are doing the church members a genuine service, but even this monthly notification cannot begin to replace the more efficient method of distributing annual church calendars to the entire membership.

The church paper is published by some churches in addition to the bulletin. This too may be employed for publicizing and coordinating activities. The problem that most churches find in producing a paper, apart from the financial aspect, is that of recruiting the necessary journalistic talent with sufficient time and dedication to produce it regularly. If a paper is to be started, there should be reasonable assurance that there are persons who can make it a meaningful tool.

Delegating responsibilities to one person is one of the most important methods of coordination available to the administrator. It permits such a person to clarify and expect performance of duties assigned to others. Both the person delegating and the one receiving delegation should agree that each understands the other's perceptions of what is involved.

Informal conferences are another way leaders consider matters of coordination. In this technique the persons responsible meet on a very informal basis (over cups of coffee, for example). Through such conferences many hindrances to coordination can be reduced to a minimum or eliminated before they pose any serious problem.

Budget allotments as a coordinating technique are sometimes overlooked. However, this technique can be of value if the activities of a group are funded by the church's budget.

A church may emphasize ministry-oriented budgeting; that is, it may determine the ministries the church should be doing and give priority budgeting to those ministries. Coordination becomes crucial in such a process. What if, seemingly, there is not enough money? What should be trimmed? consolidated? reconsidered? prioritized?

The church mailbox is an in-house mail system that can be effective and much less expensive than regular mail service. For this method to be most effective, members must be made aware of its use and importance. Also, the quality and timeliness of the information communicated in this way are extremely vital.

Guideline #2: Deal proactively and wisely with change. The need for coordination becomes more acute when dealing with change. Whether dealing with a matter as small as reassigning meeting places for two groups or as large as planning for the changing demographics of society and finding ways to reach people over the next decades, change cannot be ignored.

All change involves taking risk. Indeed, planning for change is a risk-taking decision. Natural barriers to risk abound. For the church, tradition holds great power to resist change. Logically, the church wants to remain unwaveringly true to its two thousand years of tradition. Also, people rally to take care of what they have rather than to risk taking a new way. People need stability, and they favor it rather than innovation.

To make changes in an organization a leader must (1) have the kind of power to make decisions and announce them as official policy (Few will ever have that power!), or (2) enlist a group of supporters who are committed to the changes sought. The second approach requires strategy and innovation that stretch beyond regular routine. It involves a disruption of usual activities and a redirection of the organization's resources that may result in new approaches for ministry.

To initiate and carry out innovative change, people need power to move the organization off automatic pilot. Change also requires enough power to mobilize people and resources to get something new done.

Plenty of time must be allowed for people to think about and reflect on the anticipated changes. If possible, some of the old can be kept with the new to make the new more acceptable. Patience with people who react negatively is vital while a leader keeps up the positive pressure for the change.

The environment after change is very important also. A leader should seek to keep the change effective and to detect any loss of support and understanding from those involved. He should strive to evaluate and encourage, admit mistakes, solicit and listen to suggestions, and help answer people's questions—while maintaining a positive, prayerful attitude.

Guideline #3: Introduce new ideas effectively. Ideas are the stuff from which changes are born. How do new or untried ideas come and how shall they become a part of the coordinating process? See figure 5.3 for a diagram of a suggested process.

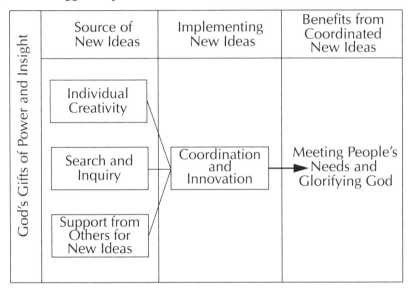

Figure 5.3

In any Christian enterprise, God gives many gifts—such as gifts of power, understanding, insight, and knowledge. Although some people are more creative, all have some ability to create. Christian education leaders can become more creative in an atmosphere that provides them uninhibited opportunity to dream and brainstorm. Free speculation and disciplined reaction to it are important, for there is a persistent force that works against creativity. We humans often want something new and simultaneously try to protect ourselves even from our own new ideas.

Search and inquiry is another source of new ideas. Thus, reading from others is important as well as doing research related to the educational ministry.

New ideas should be tried on some trustworthy person(s) capable of giving an objective viewpoint. Such a person may point out a pitfall not previously considered or make a simple suggestion which not only provides affirmation but perhaps improves the original idea. A reflection group whose members are committed to being shock-proof may be willing to give you their honest opinions.

Guideline #4: Harness conflict for good. Conflict is not all bad. It is bad if it evolves because of spiritual or psychological sickness of the participants. Conflict is evil if it hurts persons without opening possibilities for their redemption or prevents the church, which is the body of Christ, from carrying forward its mission.

While the Bible assures us that God can make the wrath of humankind to praise him, the family concept of the universe that dominates the Christian revelation places great stress on the blessedness of peacemaking. It is the responsibility of the Christian leader to join in the prayer that all may be one (see John 17:21) and to do what can be done toward this purpose. Paul, writing to the Corinthians, mourned over the harm done to individuals and to the body of Christ by divisions and quarrels (see 1 Cor. 1:10–17).

Conflict is inevitable when coordination of the church's programs and ministries is attempted. This conflict is not all bad, as has been said. Actually, most conflict is good. Disagreement that results in open confrontation can be creative and even consistent with Christian commitment. Such conflict may cause both parties to reexamine ideas and procedures. It may result in new ministries which bring glory to God and benefit to people.

Conflict that arises when coordination is sought should be handled seriously and objectively. One cannot avoid personality clashes in the church, but as a rule one can deal with the problem and not with the personality. At least, that approach should be taken first.

When handling innovation, change, new ideas, and/or conflict, it is best to bring to the occasion resources which were gained before they were needed. That is why we go to school, attend seminars, and experience other kinds of learning for our tasks. If a leader wants innovation and change to happen more easily in an organization, he or she should train people to deal with them beforehand. If conflict is to be energizing and serve the organization's purpose, then people need to be taught how to handle conflict before the conflict comes.

ONE MORE WORD

You need allies! It is more fulfilling as well as more effective to enlist others in sharpening and empowering the organization. Strength is found in diversity.

But Anna knew that. She listened to the sermon and thought of her next step.

She thought of Steve and Nancy, who had shown special sensitivity and commitment to the church's future. Perhaps they could serve as possible early allies in discussing ways to improve the organization and coordination of the church's educational ministry. They were fairly new to the church but were already serving in the Bible teaching program and seemed to be progressive persons. They could be mixed with other volunteer leaders who were long-term members as a think tank about the future.

After mulling over the idea of a think tank and discussing it with other staff members, she and husband Dean invited such a group to their home to consider everyone's ideas about effective ministry. The group understood their unofficial nature. But they delighted in anticipating what the church might be like in its new century.

CHAPTER 6

How to Staff and Motivate

Jerry M. Stubblefield

Staffing and *motivating* are two tasks ministers deal with almost daily. Often new opportunities for ministry and mission present themselves. As they do, questions arise: Is this a task already assigned to an organization or committee? Do we need to recruit someone to do this? Will people feel fulfilled and excited about doing this? Staffing and motivating are critical needs consistently found in every church.

Leadership is approached differently with volunteers than with paid workers. Volunteers are recruited differently and their motivational factors are unlike paid persons. This is true whether trying to staff or to motivate. The approach taken in this chapter is that of working with *volunteers*.

Successful ministry in a church depends upon the recruitment and development of many leaders who give freely of their services. Many volunteer organizations, including churches, complain that people will not volunteer or there are not enough workers willing to engage in a particular activity. My experience, however, is that people will volunteer if approached and recruited in the proper way and if the needed work is challenging, fulfilling, and meets genuine needs.

This chapter gives practical ideas and guidelines ministers can use in staffing the educational organizations and in motivating volunteer workers. Every minister is involved in staffing and motivating, whether serving as a bivocational pastor or as one of several ministers in a large church.

Good staff leadership comes from an awareness of what people are doing to help the church fulfill its purpose. All activities should contribute to and enhance the church's objectives and goals. The lack of established, clearly defined plans invites distrust that ultimately leads to poor morale among volunteer workers. The result is that the church loses some or all of its potential effectiveness in its ability to reach and develop people in its mission and ministry. This is what the educational ministry is about.

The success and effectiveness of a local church are largely decided by its ability to develop and motivate its staff, whether it is paid or volunteer or a combination of the two. Even the small church has a staff—a pastor and a corps of volunteers. Every minister must have a thorough knowledge of the church's educational organizations and the educational processes used by each age group within the organizations. This is true whether a person is the only minister in a church or the senior minister of a multiple staff church. The pastor is the supervisor of the educational organizations whether working with volunteer leaders or with other professionally-trained ministers.

Pastors who fail to do this soon discover that either morale among lay leaders is decaying or educational ministers feel that the senior minister does not understand or appreciate what they are doing. Wise ministers learn while in school all they can about educational programs and continue to be students of Christian education throughout their ministry. Then they can supervise either volunteers or other staff members more knowledgeably and more efficiently.

If a church is to have an effective educational program, it will, of necessity, be heavily dependent upon volunteer workers. This is also true of its programs of mission and ministry. For example, volunteers can serve in these areas: Bible teaching activities, discipleship training, missions education organizations, choirs, committees, deacons, councils, groups of church visitors, shut-in ministries, youth activities, and mission projects. The list is endless. A church cannot have paid staff members doing all the ministries necessary to carry out the mission of the church.

Some churches have used paid teachers in their Christian education programs. However, these programs were limited primarily to classes for children and youth. Many were professional educators or students training for educational careers. Churches using this approach usually focused on the quality of classroom instruction, with teachers having little or no contact outside the classroom.

Effective Christian education requires its leaders to share not only what they have experienced but also their relationship with Jesus Christ. Quality instruction must occur in the classroom, but also involves teachers interacting with learners outside class time.

Could your church function without the dedicated corps of volunteers working in every facet of its educational program? What would happen without volunteers in Bible teaching, discipleship training, missions education, youth ministries, single and senior adult groups, family life education, choirs, and recreational activities?

This discussion does not depreciate or minimize the role played by paid church staff members. It acknowledges the impracticality and impossibility of a church employing enough people to minister effectively to persons with whom it has contact and for whom it has responsibility.

For five years I served as minister of education in a church that had two thousand people enrolled in its Bible teaching program. Even with two other educational ministers, it was impossible for the three of us to minister effectively to that many people. We worked to equip, train, and enable more than two hundred church-elected volunteers to work directly with those enrolled in the Bible teaching program. In addition, many classes and departments had other volunteers helping those elected by the church. The three staff members had personal contact with many people, but not to the extent and intensity of that of the two hundred volunteers.

Volunteers are crucial in the daily ministry and functioning of the local church. If the church is to have volunteers, they must be recruited to staff the church's educational organizations. Those recruited must be inner-directed by the Holy Spirit to fulfill tasks to the maximum of their ability.

HOW TO STAFF

Staffing the church's educational organizations is the responsibility of the church nominating or Christian education committee in consultation with staff ministers. Responsibility for deciding the necessary units and organizational patterns, however, rests within each educational organization or unit, not with this committee. Before beginning the staffing process, each organization should submit in writing the organizational pattern and volunteers needed. The committee's task is to discover and enlist potential leaders as requested by the various educational units, not to decide organizational patterns or needs.

STAFFING PRINCIPLES

Six principles enhance the staffing process.

Principle #1: Develop a master file of potential church leaders. Several months before beginning work, the committee should see that the church has a service record of resident members. These records should show areas of interest and positions currently or previously held by each member.

Many churches use computers to compile this information into a membership profile. The master membership profile shows those who are or would be interested in specific tasks and positions in which a person has served previously. Information is retrieved from the church's information bank.

For churches without computers, cards have been designed that follow the same procedures as the computer but are maintained by hand. The cost is reasonable. No matter whether one uses a computer or a card system, setting up the information bank takes time but is an important investment. This can be done by secretarial staff or volunteers. Once the data is entered, it is easy to update the files so they are current.

No system can be more effective than the membership information it contains, so records must be kept current. New service commitments need to be recorded and cards filled out on each new member who joins the church. Often a church can meet many of its staffing needs by those who have previously served in these or similar roles. You may find that there are already people trained for the leadership areas in which you are searching. With minimal training, they may be ready to function quickly.

Principle #2: Encourage church leaders to suggest potential leaders. Ministers and the committee have limited knowledge of people's spiritual gifts and leadership potential. They cannot know the church's membership in a personal, intimate way. An excellent reservoir of potential church leaders can be made up of persons known to the present church leadership. Church leaders should be asked to submit the names of persons they feel are ready to assume a place of leadership or are potential church leaders. Potential church leaders can be encouraged to participate in the church's training activities.

It is important for leaders to keep the opportunity of service before their groups. They should not only speak about these possibilities, but also affirm those who go forth in service. The highest compliment paid to a church teacher is not the size of one's class, but the number of persons from that class involved in places of leadership within the church.

Principle #3: Describe Christian service opportunities. Asking for volunteer workers during a worship service is usually futile. These appeals often attempt to place guilt upon the people. Public appeals for volunteers are invitations for someone to solve a crisis or emergency. Such needs are seldom presented as a challenge but as a stopgap measure.

Talking about the opportunities for Christian service and the potential rewards or blessings that are inherent in the task should be a common feature of church life. The chance to grow spiritually while ministering to others through Christian service should be emphasized. Service opportunities should be promoted and described long before they are to begin.

Recently, I visited three churches. Each minister made an "annual" appeal for volunteers to staff the church's organizations. Each stressed the idea of doing "one's spiritual duty" (whatever that means), thus making the work of the nominating committee easier. No mention was made of Christian growth, of the opportunities to influence and enrich lives, or that you should pray about what God wants you to do in the church.

Once a need is identified, it should be conveyed to the church. Members should be asked to pray that God will call one out to meet the need. While serving a church, I discovered that we were not reaching the newlyweds, primarily because there was not a Bible study class for them. I shared this concern with the deacons. No'one responded immediately. Two months later a couple came to me and said, "We have been praying for a place to serve and would like to teach the newlyweds." He was a deacon, and they possessed the skills vital to working with this group. Several years later, they continue to teach the class. God has used them effectively to teach and reach young adults.

Principle 4: Develop written job (position) descriptions. To help in recruitment and training, job descriptions must be developed for all major positions. Many churches distribute denominationally prepared documents to elected leaders. These documents are written in broad, general terms. It takes time, energy, and some creativity, but every church should adapt these or develop their own written job descriptions for all elected positions.

Job descriptions should contain the following information:

1. position title;

2. brief description of the task to be done;

3. specialized or specific skills essential to effective achievement;

4. resources available (curriculum items, age group books, additional helps, etc.);

5. time commitments (regular meeting time, training opportunities, in-service training, etc.);

6. length of service;

7. objectives and goals of the educational organization (what you are seeking to achieve and how you plan to do it).

See figure 6.1 for a sample job description for a Sunday school teacher, and figure 6.2 for a sample work sheet.

Principle #5: Emphasize the service to be rendered, not the position or its title. People fill many positions in the church. Different skills are necessary for people to carry out their assignments. As persons competently complete individual responsibilities, they help the church fulfill its mission and ministry challenges. Every task is important. Therefore, magnify the service rendered by each person, not the position or its title.

Principle #6: Discover the individual's gifts or abilities. It is a tragic waste of spiritual and human gifts when more than 80 percent of the church's leadership positions are filled by 20 percent of the resident membership.

Figure 6.1

SAMPLE JOB DESCRIPTION

ADULT SUNDAY SCHOOL TEACHER

Tasks to be accomplished:

1. Understand and use the principles of effective teaching and learning.
2. Prepare for each week's Bible study session with your class.
3. Accept personal responsibility in enlistment and witnessing actions.
4. Share in and encourage your class to participate in ministry actions.
5. Be knowledgeable about the role of the class in the work of the church.
6. Lead the total work of the class.
7. Help care leaders to minister to members and prospects.
8. Plan regularly with class outreach and care leaders.

Essential skills:

1. Ability to converse effectively.
2. Skill in planning and execution of plans.
3. Leadership—ability to challenge others to follow your example.
4. Desire to be a sincere, dedicated student.
5. Desire to be a learner—from the Bible, the Holy Spirit, and class members.
6. Ability to be a personal visitor.

Available Resources:

1. *The Adult Teacher*
2. *Sunday School Adults*
3. *Biblical Illustrator*
4. *Sunday School Leadership*
5. *Teaching Adults the Bible*

Time Commitments:

1. Be in your classroom fifteen minutes before Sunday school begins.
2. Attend the planning meetings for teachers.

3. Participate in the church's outreach program.

4. Attend Sunday school training sessions.

Length of service:

September 1 to August 31.

Organizational objectives:

1. Reach persons for Bible study.

2. Teach the Bible.

3. Witness to persons about Christ and lead persons into church membership.

4. Minister to Sunday school members and nonmembers.

5. Lead members to worship.

6. Interpret and undergird the work of the church and the denomination.

Organizational goals:

Each church and class must set its own. These are suggestions:

1. Each class visitor contacted within six days.

2. Increase class enrollment by 10 percent.

3. Increase average class attendance by 10 percent.

4. Achieve 50 percent of class members bringing Bibles and studying the lesson.

5. Each teacher lead at least one person to Christ this year.

6. Minister to members and nonmembers as needs occur.

Figure 6.2

JOB DESCRIPTION WORKSHEET

Position or title:

Tasks to be accomplished:

Essential skills:

Available resources:

Time commitments:

Length of service (elected for how long):

Organizational objectives:

Organizational goals:

This situation creates two major problems: (1) those who are elected carry more than one major responsibility; thus, they are not able to do any task well due to the limitations of time and energy, and (2) many capable, trainable people within the congregation are never asked to do anything. Skills can be developed through adequate training and opportunities for service.

God has given each Christian a gift or ability that can be used in Christian service; however, not everyone is conscious of such capabilities. Sermons and Bible studies can be used to help members become aware of their gifts. Another way is to conduct a spiritual gifts survey or simulation exercise. (These resources are available through your religious bookstore.) Christian educators strive to equip and enable *all* the people of God to use their gifts in ministry, not just a few.

ESSENTIAL CHARACTERISTICS OF CHURCH LEADERS

Many churches have elaborate criteria for church leaders. So many items are listed that it is impossible for anyone to meet all these qualifications. I recently worked with a church that had so many requirements for church leaders that even Jesus was not qualified. Rather than describe a long list of characteristics, let me suggest six essential requirements. A church should take these, modify and expanded them as needed, and adopt them for guidelines:

Characteristic #1: A church leader should be a Christian. It seems trite to say that a church leader should be a Christian. All church leaders must have a personal experience with Jesus Christ. Many people in our churches have equated knowing *about Jesus* with knowing *Jesus*. Anyone who does not personally know Jesus as Savior and Lord will find it difficult, if not impossible, to lead others to follow Christ in their daily lives.

Characteristic #2: A church leader should be a member of that local church. All persons filling leadership positions in a church should be members of that church. Any person who is unwilling to join should not be elected to a position of leadership. Nonmembers usually are less sensitive to the total needs of the church than people who invest themselves fully. A nonmember may do things in a way that would destroy morale or be in direct violation of the church's objectives and goals. Nonmembers are more difficult to supervise than members.

A church should elect only those persons who have shown their commitment to Christ and his church. New church members should become active in various activities before being considered for leadership positions. One cannot set an arbitrary time limit, but there should be enough time to observe Christian character, commitment, and leadership potential before a new member begins serving.

Characteristic #3: A church leader should love people. The work of the church involves working with people. Ideally, a Christian should love people. Practically, however, there are many persons who are not people-oriented. They are directed toward the achievement of goals or building a successful organization.

Successful church work involves teamwork. One must know how to interact effectively with others. A leader must have a keen appreciation for the worth and dignity of others.

Characteristic #4: A church leader should be a person of aptitude or ability. Church leaders should possess the skills for the work they are asked to lead. Ability, interest, and a desire to make a contribution to the church and to people's lives are desirable traits.

Present leaders can provide information about the potential worker's skills and interests. To enlist a person for a job if success is not likely threatens the future growth and Christian usefulness of that person. Also, it may hinder others in continuing in that activity and consequently affect the growth of the church.

Characteristic #5: A church leader should be a person who has shown dependability and responsibility. Church leaders are selected from those members who have shown that they are faithful, dependable, and responsible to the life and work of the church. A church should expect that its leaders are actively involved in the worship experiences, the Bible teaching program, and discipleship training, and that they contribute to the church financially. A pastor once said that "The weight of the church should be placed on the shoulders of those who support it."

Characteristic #6: A church leader should be willing to learn. Church leaders should not feel that they presently know all that is necessary to do the task. Leaders must be willing to participate in the church's training opportunities that equip and enable them to do the job effectively and successfully.

In summary, a church leader should have the following characteristics:

1. be a Christian;
2. be a member of that local church;
3. be a person who loves people;
4. be a person of aptitude or ability;
5. be a person who has shown dependability and responsibility;
6. be a person who is willing to learn.

THE ENLISTMENT PROCESS

Assume that the committee decides a specific person is the right one to do the assigned task. This decision comes after much prayer. The committee feels led by the Holy Spirit to contact this person. What do they do?

First, a decision is made concerning who should make the enlistment visit. Usually the person who will work with or supervise the worker is asked to do this. For example, a Sunday school teacher should be contacted by the department director in whose department he or she will teach. However, if the committee thinks there is someone else who is more likely to get an affirmative response, then this person makes the enlistment visit. The person who will be the supervisor or under whom the person will work may accompany this person.

Before describing the steps to follow in enlistment, one additional idea needs to be discussed. Election to serve on the church's nominating or Christian education committee does not automatically qualify a person to make enlistment visits. The church should provide training for those who will visit. Included should be members of the committee, the ministers, department directors, committee chairpersons, and others who will seek to enlist persons to staff the church's organizations and committees.

Recruitment of workers is a serious task. Though she describes it in relationship to teaching, Carolyn C. Brown's comments are pertinent for recruiters for all church positions:

> So our first task as recruiters is to remind ourselves what it is we are doing. Recruiters are asking people to share their faith with other Christians. Teaching is a calling ranked high among the spiritual callings by Saint Paul. To be asked to teach is an honor, and also a challenge. These teachers are going to be given carefully prepared and selected materials to work with and will have the support of the entire church. All of this is being done because the church places a very high value on Christian growth. So, set aside the cloud of doom, and approach the task of recruiting teachers for the church's educational ministry with the prayerful energy it deserves.[1]

One training technique could be a simulated enlistment visit. Persons skilled in interaction processes should conduct the simulated experience. Guidelines to use in the enlistment effort need to be written, duplicated, and distributed to each trainee. A training model would be to use the approach described below. No one should go out to contact prospective church leaders who has not participated in the training process. This training is scheduled each year before the committee begins the enlistment effort.

After the committee chooses the contact person, what steps should this person follow in the enlistment process?

Step #1: Set a time to talk with the person when you have privacy and adequate time. Persons should never be enlisted in the hallways of the church or when pressed for time. Someone could see the person at home, go to lunch together, or talk over coffee. The meeting should be in a friendly, relaxed environment, recognizing the pressures of time.

Step #2: Pray for the leadership of the Holy Spirit as you prepare for the interview. The challenge should be presented as well as the opportunity for Christian service in this task. The person should ask God to prepare the person to be receptive and responsive to his leadership.

Step #3: Present the challenge of the position. The position is described and the job description reviewed. The prospective worker should be told what the duties are and how the position relates to the total ministry of the church. No one wants to be asked to do a job that is insignificant or that can be achieved with little or no effort. Enlistment must be honest.

The person should hear that this job will call forth the very best that one can give, that it will require time, energy, and prayer. The person should be made aware of the opportunities for personal Christian growth and of how the prospective leader can influence the lives of others by doing it.

The person should see that this task is important to the lives of Christians and benefits the work of Christ and his church. The prospect should hear of your confidence and that of the nominating committee that he or she can do this job effectively and can expect to have a sense of personal achievement.

Step #4: Prepare and present prospective workers with a packet of curriculum materials and other available resources. Not every church leader will be in a teaching/training role, but job descriptions, organizational charts, and other materials should be prepared and given to the potential worker. These materials should be briefly reviewed and described, particularly in terms of how each item will help in doing this task. The person should have time to study the materials and know that you are available to respond to any questions.

Some churches have a Christian education worker's covenant. As you present the above materials to the prospect, it is appropriate to share the church's expectations of workers and what workers can expect from the church.

What should the church expect? Here is a suggested list for Bible study teachers:

We expect teachers to . . .

- pray for class members and prospects
- prepare for weekly sessions (two to four hours)
- be present fifteen minutes before starting time and to begin on time
- use church-approved curriculum

- attend worship
- visit class members and prospects
- attend weekly workers meeting and other training opportunities
- notify the director early when a substitute is needed.

  The church will . . .

- pray for you and your work
- provide curriculum and basic resources required in curriculum
- provide substitutes through your director
- provide basic audiovisual equipment
- pay fees and travel costs for training activities
- support you and your work.[2]

Step #5: Be realistic about the job. The challenges and problems a person might expect to encounter if this assignment is accepted should be presented. The Chinese have a way of looking at a crisis that can help us see this more clearly. "When the Chinese write the word 'crisis,' they do so in two characters, one meaning danger, the other opportunity."[3]

Opportunities for Christian service usually are not crises, but every responsibility has its positive and negative aspects. In presenting the situation, it is best to be realistic rather than idealistic. There are two practical reasons for this approach: (1) the person should accept the assignment with as much knowledge about it as possible; (2) you must continue to work with and have a relationship with this person. Supervision, morale, and motivation are more difficult if you have not told this person as much as you should have.

Step #6: Describe scheduled activities for preservice and inservice training opportunities. The person should be given the dates for training events. Some church positions require attendance at monthly or weekly planning meetings where additional training is offered. The prospective leader should see that these training activities are planned by the church to provide skills and information so that its volunteers may do an effective job. The prospect should realize that accepting this assignment will provide opportunities for Christian growth and improve relationships with fellow Christians.

Step #7: Ask the prospect to pray and study for a week or two before giving you a decision. A person needs time to review the materials you have left and to pray about this responsibility. You say you will call in a few days to clarify further the role and to answer any questions.

Step #8: Set the date when you will call or return to receive an answer. The prospective leader should know that you and other church leaders will be praying as he or she makes this decision. It is good to pray, asking God to guide and lead during this time.

Step #9: Check with the person in a few days to clarify the role and answer any questions.

Step #10: Call or visit to receive the answer. If it is affirmative, the training schedule in step number 6 should be reviewed. The person should be assured of your continued prayers as he or she prepares for and begins this new work.

What do you do if the prospect declines? First, you must thank the person for considering the job and express gratitude for the privilege to become better acquainted. You can assure him or her of your continued prayer support in finding God's direction for service. You might also ask about future interests and if you might share this information with the committee in case of other possibilities or future needs. However, no commitments should be made about other positions without committee approval.

Step #11: Follow up. Your task of enlistment is not complete until the person is functioning effectively in the new role. Periodic conferences will be scheduled to see how the new worker feels about the job, to consider any problems encountered, and to provide encouragement and support.

CONSIDER ENLISTMENT FOR MORE THAN ONE YEAR

Churches usually enlist persons to serve on committees and boards for terms of three to five years. Yet persons serving in educational positions—Bible study and discipleship training, for example—are usually enlisted for one-year terms. Initial enlistment should be for one year; it should then be reviewed and extended in two or three-year terms, when mutually agreed on by the committee and the worker.

The person's desire to continue in the position should be reaffirmed annually, but the enlistment process described above would not be followed. Thus, the staffing task of the church would be simpler and would not require the large amounts of time usually spent by the committee.

HOW TO MOTIVATE

Some time ago I went to my doctor on a Monday. In talking about his church and his Sunday worship experience he stated, "I really felt sorry for my pastor yesterday." I sat in stunned amazement. His pastor was recognized as an outstanding preacher. Having heard the sermon myself, I felt that the minister had eloquently proclaimed his concern for people in the inner city. His invitation had been a plea for volunteers to go into the inner city and minister there.

Finally, I asked the doctor, "Why did you feel sorry for your pastor?" His reply was that no one had responded to the invitation to go into the inner city. The doctor believed that the reason no one responded was the minister's inability to motivate the congregation.

Many ministers and congregations believe that motivation is just like administration. Administration requires the ability to understand certain ideas and procedures—including human nature. However, to say that one person can motivate another person is a myth. Motivation is a product of an individual's will. Leaders can motivate by their actions and the quality of their lives— their character and core values. A minister can help establish the climate or environment under which good motivation can happen, but he or she cannot cause another person to be motivated.

It has been assumed that a person's behavior can be decided from without; however, the opposite is true. One's behavior is decided from within. Motivation is internal, not external.

There is no magic formula church leaders can follow to motivate others. What causes one person to respond positively may generate a negative response from another. Therefore, ministers must know as much as possible about each member. They must know at what need level the person is presently responding.

TRUST: A KEY MOTIVATIONAL INGREDIENT

Stephen R. Covey points out, "Trust is the highest form of human motivation. It brings out the very best in people."[4] Trust comes from relationships that come over time. He calls this "an Emotional Bank Account." The trust account is built up through acts of courtesy, kindness, honesty, and keeping commitments to others. He notes, "When the trust account is high, communication is easy, instant, and effective."[5] A key to building up the emotional bank account is seeking to truly understand another person.

A demotivating factor comes when there are conflicting or ambiguous expectations around roles and goals. Expectations and goals must be clear from the beginning.

Covey, emphasizing the role of personal integrity, says, "Personal integrity generates trust and is the basis of many different kinds of deposits. . . . Honesty is telling the truth—in other words, conforming our words to reality. Integrity is conforming reality to our words—in other words, keeping promises and fulfilling expectations. . . . Integrity also means avoiding any communication that is deceptive, full of guile, or beneath the dignity of people."[6]

Leaders do make mistakes but people will forgive mistakes of the mind and of judgment. They will not easily forgive mistakes of the heart, ill intention, and bad motives.

The greatest deposit is that of unconditional love. Covey continues:

> When we truly love others without condition, without strings, we help
> them feel secure and safe and validated and affirmed in their essential worth,

identity, and integrity. Their natural growth process is encouraged. We make it easier for them to live the laws of life—cooperation, contribution, self-discipline, integrity—and to discover and live true to the highest and best within them. We give them the freedom to act on their own inner imperatives rather than react to our conditions and limitations.[7]

Trust is critical for motivation to take place; it personifies what happens in relationships. We build relationships through courtesy, respect, and appreciation for others and for their point of view. As a result, "You stay longer in the communication process. You listen more, you listen in greater depth. You express yourself with greater courage. You aren't reactive."[8]

Without trust or a common vision, the leader tends to hover over, check on, and direct workers. There is a tendency to try to control people.

MOTIVATIONAL PRINCIPLES

Here are guidelines that will benefit church leaders as they seek to lead others:

Principle #1: Realize that you cannot motivate another person. Motivation comes from within. People can be led by the Holy Spirit working through their needs, but they, and they alone, can respond to the guidance of the Holy Spirit.

You are not the motivator, except for yourself. Your role is to be the instrument, the facilitator who helps the other person become motivated. You must recognize who you are—that you are a servant of God responsible only for yourself. Many leaders ask, "Why didn't I get them to do this or that?" The real question is this: "Why didn't they want to do it?" Motivation is internal, not external. Your opportunity to help motivate others comes from the quality of your work, your example, and your character.

Principle #2: Believe the volunteer worker can do the job. Church leaders must have confidence both in the ability of the membership and the equipping, enabling power of the Holy Spirit. You must trust the person to do a good job. People accepting new jobs may not begin with expertise, but you must believe that with proper training, inner motivation, and the help of the Holy Spirit they can do a good job.

Principle #3: Permit people to work in their own way. You are asking persons to accept an assignment, so you should allow them to do it their own way. Training sessions tend to teach methods designed to cause each trainee to become a reproduction of the trainer. God has endowed each person differently, so individuals will approach the task from their own perspective. They might discover a better way to do it, particularly if they are self-actualized persons.

Principle #4: Emphasize results, not methods. This is not to say that the end justifies the means. Means should always be consistent with the principles of Jesus Christ. A church elects a person to be a teacher, a committee chairperson, and so forth. The important factor is performance: that the person is an effective teacher, and that the committee does its assigned work. The methods are secondary. Be sure that the assignment is clear, and then stand back and let the people work.

James K. Van Fleet, a generation ago, began urging: "You can motivate people to do their best for you when you emphasize skill, not rules; results, not methods. To do this, use mission-type orders. (A mission-type order tells a person what you want done and when you want it, but it does not tell him how to do it. The 'how to' is left up to him.) A mission-type order opens the door wide so people can use their imagination, initiative, and ingenuity to do the job for you."[9] Thus, you keep your attention focused on the result, not the techniques used to get there.

Principle #5: Rule people by work: do not work people by rules. This keeps all eyes focused on the job to be done—the mission and ministry to be accomplished. People have something worthwhile and meaningful to do, which keeps them physically and mentally occupied. They will be happy and contented with their work.[10]

CREATING A CLIMATE FOR SELF-MOTIVATION

To encourage volunteer leaders, the minister seeks to develop an atmosphere in which motivation is under the guidance of the Holy Spirit. Reginald M. McDonough explains, "A leader's role in motivation is to be sensitive to the needs and gifts of persons, to help persons understand their needs and gifts, and to help them live out their Christian calling in satisfying and fulfilling ways."[11]

If ministers are to become self-actualizers, they must develop some specific skills. They must *be* self-actualized and practice a leadership style characterized by the following:

1. *Leaders are genuinely interested in other people.* People yearn for attention from others. They want to feel their ideas and opinions are heard. The desire for attention is present in all of us. People need to be important to someone else. If you wish to be a self-actualizer, you must become truly interested in others and their problems. You must place more emphasis on others' problems than on your own. What is needed is an attitude of complete unselfishness.

2. *Leaders must learn to listen.* You must put aside your own interests, your own pleasures, and your own preoccupations. You must learn to listen with your eyes and your ears. Changes of facial expression are significant communicators. You must learn to be a good listener.

3. *Leaders must practice patience.* In working with others, you do not criticize or offer snap judgments. Instead, you learn to make allowances for inexperience; you do not expect perfection.

4. *Leaders must never take another person for granted.* No matter how faithful the worker is, you must express gratitude and appreciation for the work being done. A word of praise serves as a significant self-motivator. People will work harder when they feel appreciated—knowing that what they do really makes a difference. The parable of the talents contains a well-known affirmation: "Well done, thou good and faithful servant" (Matt. 25:21, KJV).

5. *Leaders must be concerned about others.* A minister's heart must be filled with compassion toward others. Feelings of concern or genuine interest in others cannot be faked. Attention to others must be accompanied by honest concern for them. A person cannot do this unless he is really willing to share another's pain and help solve personal problems.[12]

6. *Leaders must treat each person as an individual.* What stimulates one person to action may not be appropriate in another situation; in fact, it might have the opposite effect. There can be no bag of motivational tricks. Self-actualizers are motivated from within.

7. *Leaders must create team efforts.* The work of the church depends upon effective teamwork. Every task is important to the church's achievement of its mission and ministry. McDonough notes that teamwork relates to the needs each person has to belong and to be loved and that an effective "team relationship enables persons to receive and give affection."[13]

    Three keys to creating team efforts, are these: (1) a team must have a reason for being to which all members are committed, (2) a team cannot function without good communication, since teamwork requires interdependence, and (3) a team must have openness and trust.[14]

8. *Leaders must generate excitement about the mission.* Excitement and enthusiasm are contagious. For people to be self-actualized motivationally, they must believe that what they are doing has meaning and purpose. They must feel that they really do make a difference. Excitement must be genuine. A minister who has no excitement about what is happening in and through the church has ceased to be a self-actualized person. The achievement of objectives and goals brings a sense of exhilaration and expectancy to church leaders. Being involved with God through the church should generate excitement.

9. *Leaders should be willing to share responsibility and authority.* Volunteer leaders should be given authority commensurate to their responsibilities. Asking a person to lead without appropriate authority creates potential for poor morale and failure of the project. No one wants to do only the mechanics. McDonough concludes, "A person's

motivation will soar when he realizes he has been entrusted with decision-making responsibility."[15]

10. *Leaders must get the right person in the right job.* Many people accept volunteer leadership positions in a church out of a sense of duty or loyalty to the person who asks them. They must also feel that they have the skills necessary to do effective work. In doing the task there should be a sense of accomplishment, and the job should be pleasurable.

11. *Leaders must keep working toward goals.* A goal-oriented environment encourages workers to do their best. The organizational objectives and goals should be clear. This is why volunteer leaders are enlisted. Each person should be led to establish individual goals that will contribute to the organization's goals; this provides opportunity for gaining a sense of personal achievement and satisfaction. Periodic review of objectives and goals will enhance the motivational environment. Goals should be realistic and attainable, yet challenging, calling forth the best from the person.

12. *Leaders must challenge persons to become involved in a mission.* When volunteer leaders see their task as a mission, they become self-actualized. There is a reason for what they do and it becomes an energizing force for them. They are in pursuit of a goal. They will not be satisfied until that goal is reached. It must call forth the very best in them. What joy comes to a person who is engaged in a mission! Once this challenge has been successfully met, they are ready for new, more challenging experiences.[16]

QUALITIES OF A MOTIVATOR

For ministers to become facilitators and equippers of volunteer workers, they must develop certain qualities and skills. McDonough, in summary, provides a description of effective leaders and the ways in which they seek to influence others.[17]

1. *They are committed to a specific, meaningful task.* Effective ministers focus attention on the achievement of a goal: the equipping and enabling of the people of God for ministry. Their sense of mission causes others to capture a vision of what the church is all about. They help others to high levels of commitment to achieve assigned tasks.

2. *They concentrate on concerns outside themselves.* Self-actualized ministers seek the realization of goals not for themselves but for others—the church, Christ, and the kingdom of God. They help others see beyond themselves—to be unselfish in service, time, and energy.

3. *They are capable of meaningful relationships.* They are capable and willing to share much of themselves with others. Their relationships with others are characterized by self-confidence and trust of others. They help others to concentrate on the mission before them. Through this relationship they call forth the best effort from others.

4. *They perceive issues clearly.* They are astute in solving problems. Their healthy self-image protects them from being easily threatened. Their keen perception aids their ability to see and challenge the potential in others. They see what people can become in Christ, not what they are now.

5. *They are spontaneous and direct.* There is a sense of authenticity about them. They have freedom both in expression and in their own personhood. They are not trying to impress others. Their spontaneity makes others feel comfortable around them. They share opinions about issues, not final decisions. Their leadership style encourages others to respond naturally and honestly.

6. *They are courageous in the face of opposition.* Because of their sense of security and self-esteem, opposition does not paralyze them. They are open to new ideas. Followers feel open and free to exchange viewpoints. Leaders perceive conflict as healthy and normal, not something to be shunned or avoided at all costs. Their sense of security aids the development of healthy self-esteem in their followers.

7. *They have self-confidence.* Others see their strength of character. They feel good about themselves. Little energy is spent in defense mechanisms or in second-guessing. Their dedication and commitment to the task before them move them forward with great objectivity. It is easy for others to capture their spirit of self-confidence, thus stimulating others to do more effective work.

8. *They have a positive attitude toward life.* They focus on the positive. They are happy and transmit this happy, joyous attitude to others. They encourage others to be optimistic about life. Others are captivated by this positive attitude.

9. *They are capable of deep spiritual experience.* Self-actualized ministers not only have had a deep spiritual experience but also continue to maintain a close, personal relationship with God. They help those with whom they work to have similar experiences with God and with each other.

CHAPTER 7

Administering Church Educational Organizations

Bruce P. Powers

As described earlier, education in a church is a support function that enables a congregation to make disciples, help members grow, and develop spiritual power in their lives. Education, along with the other church functions of worship, proclamation, ministry, and fellowship is one of the distinguishing characteristics of the New Testament church. Whereas the other functions have value in and of themselves, education must always exist to *serve*, functioning as a midwife to enable persons to learn.

So it is with educational organizations. They are *means,* or *ways,* for achieving the mission or purpose of a church; they are not *ends* in themselves. Each organization exists to achieve a specific purpose or portion of a church's educational ministry. And each, theoretically, should be the most effective structure to achieve the purpose for which it exists.

ORGANIZATIONAL DISTINCTIVES

Because of common objectives among evangelical churches— making disciples, enabling members to grow and mature, and developing spiritual awareness and power in the lives of believers—similar structures have evolved among denominations to enable churches to do their work. For example, most churches have organizations to facilitate Bible study, discipleship development, mission activities, and worship experiences. Although names of these may vary, such as Sunday school, Bible school, and church school, the functions and general organizational principles are remarkably similar from denomination to denomination.

BASIC CHURCH PROGRAMS

These structures or organizations are the primary channels for the ongoing, functional education provided by a congregation. Educational experiences are usually graded according to the ability and/or need level of participants. Basic church programs are designed to help a church achieve its objectives and, also, to meet the general needs of people in the congregation.[1]

Five basic programs that are essentially educational and exist in some form in most evangelical and protestant churches will be covered in this chapter. Each program has a cluster of tasks that are essential, continuing, and important to the work of a church. (See fig. 7.1 on p. 115.) The sixth program, pastoral ministries, focuses primarily on general church leadership; it is included only for reference.

Other organizations are necessary to provide effective Christian education in a church, but they are not considered basic programs for all the congregation. These are primarily service-oriented (like media or recreation ministries) or specialized programs for subgroups in the congregation (like a club for senior adults). Chapter 8, "Administering Specialized Educational Activities," will deal with the many ways in which service and special group ministries can be developed.

DETERMINING ORGANIZATIONAL STRUCTURE

The essential elements in deciding how to organize an educational program include the following.

1. *Identify the specific purpose of the organization.* Why does (should) it exist? What is its unique contribution to the church? What would happen if we did not have this organization?

2. *Find the best way to achieve the stated purpose.* What resources (leaders, facilities, denominational assistance, financial support, and such) are available? What are the priorities within and among the educational organizations? What structures will provide efficient and effective team work among leaders and also help the achievement of educational objectives?

3. *Define clear areas of responsibility and decision-making in the total educational ministry, and in each component.* What is the distinct responsibility for each position? What decisions should the person in each position be able to make without consultation? What are the positions that link each level (or unit) with the larger body for purposes

of planning, evaluation, communication, and such? Do all leaders have someone to whom they are responsible?

GENERAL COORDINATION

An effective organizational structure includes a church council or education committee, which would be charged with planning, coordinating, and evaluating the church's educational activities. (Information about a church council is given in fig. 7.2 on p. 116.)

In most churches, this group would be chaired by the pastor and would include these persons:

- church staff members,

- leaders of all church programs and service organizations,

- leader of the deacons (or church board), and

- chairpersons of key committees (those closely related to the work of church program organizations, such as missions, stewardship, and nominating committees).

In larger churches with a full-time educational leader, activities might need to be planned, coordinated, and evaluated through a separate, specialized group, usually an education council or committee. Members would include leaders representing the various educational components, church staff personnel who have educational duties, and age-group coordinators (if used) as illustrated in figure 7.3 on p. 117.

Similarly, each program organization would have an administrative council or staff to guide the work for which it is responsible, as shown in fig. 7.4 on p. 117. (Information about a program council/staff is given in fig. 7.5 on p. 118.)

AGE-DIVISION COORDINATION

Whereas most administration is handled *within* programs, those who work with similar age groups in different organizations often need to link up to coordinate work and support each other. This can be achieved through age-level coordination.

The simplest approach is for leaders of a particular age division to meet periodically to coordinate their work and the use of space, equipment, and supplies. This is most effective for small churches and age divisions with few workers.

Another approach is to schedule periodic conferences for age-division coordination, the purpose being to deal with issues of common concern among leaders within each age group. Persons in each group could elect a convener to facilitate meetings and channel messages.

In large churches, age-group coordinators often will be necessary (some churches use directors or ministers in this role). Their principal function is to facilitate the work of all programs within the age division for the total educational ministry. Coordinators should serve on the education committee, or church council. (Descriptive information concerning age-division coordination is given in fig. 7.6 on p. 118.)

GROUPING OR GRADING OF PEOPLE

There are three general approaches to dividing congregations for educational purposes: *age, compatibility,* and *interest.* To a lesser extent, some churches choose to create additional subgroupings by using distinctives such as gender and marital status.

AGE

Age grouping, or grading, is used most often when trying to match developmental needs of individuals with the educational experiences provided. This is the approach usually recommended by denominational program leaders to facilitate an ongoing, systematic study of curriculum materials by all ages.

Under this plan, educational groupings follow a general pattern, but these often are adjusted when subgrouping to allow for compatibility and/or interest groups. For example, the Organization Planning Chart, figure 7.7, lists the major divisions, suggested maximum enrollment per unit and worker-pupil ratio for preschool and children's departments. By completing the chart, you can figure out the number of classes/groups/departments needed and the approximate number of workers.

In a small church, you may need a nursery plus at least two departments for preschoolers (up through age two and ages three through five) and two for children (grades one through three and four through six). Only if space is not available should all preschoolers or grades one through six be together.

If space and leaders are available, three groups can be set up for preschoolers (up through age one; ages two and three; and ages four and five). Also, three groups for children can be provided (grades one and two; grades three and four; and grades five and six).

At least two classes for youth are best if space and leadership are available and there are sufficient participants for each group (six or more enrolled). Older and younger youth could be divided, possibly using the same grading system as the local public school—junior high/middle school and high school.

If possible, there should be a class for each group of twenty-five adults enrolled. This can begin by dividing younger and older (using some midpoint age) or by having a class for women and a class for men. Additional classes might be graded as shown in the organization planning chart (see fig. 7.7 on p. 120) or formed according to compatibility or interest.

Larger churches would add more classes/groups/departments for each of the age groups according to enrollment and the availability of leaders and space.

COMPATIBILITY

Grouping according to compatibility is used in many churches—particularly among adults—to allow persons who have the most in common to be together. People congregate due to factors such as preferred learning style or fellowship needs, and these preferences are established as a regular part of the organizational structure.

This grouping approach typically is used in combination with age grading and may be seen, for example, in a fellowship Bible class. Sometimes the compatibility groupings develop informally, such as in a class of persons who have chosen to remain together despite suggestions that they "promote" to another age-group class.

INTEREST

Interest grouping is used when persons are free to select the most appealing study or activity. These groups exist as long as the particular study or activity is provided; consequently, this approach is used primarily with *short-term* educational activities and special emphases.

In some churches, all three approaches will be used; however, age-group divisions remain the foundation. Additional groups can be organized as necessary or appropriate to meet the needs of participants and to fulfill the purpose of the organization.

CHOOSING A PATTERN

Ultimately, every church has to make its own decisions concerning the best way to organize and administer its work. The guidelines and options which have been described will help you assess possibilities; but, in consultation with other church leaders, you must choose the most appropriate arrangement.

As an additional resource, a list of possible patterns for church organization is given in figure 7.8 on pages 122–123. By studying these options you could probably clarify how best to proceed with any adjustments needed in your church.

GUIDELINES FOR THE ADMINISTRATOR

Here are guidelines that will enable you to give effective and strong leadership to church educational organizations:

1. Determine the purpose and organizational structure for each educational program. A chart should list every position and unit and the

name of every officer and teacher. This information should be at the front of a reference notebook/folder devoted to educational administration.

2. Use, or establish, a church council or committee of key leaders to plan, coordinate, and evaluate the church's total educational ministry. Meetings should be held at least monthly. (Suggestions for forming such a group are included in chap. 4, "How to Plan and Evaluate.")

3. Prepare job descriptions for all positions. This should include duties, decision-making authority, and the person to whom the worker is responsible.

4. Make annual plans for each organization. Following the enlistment of officers for a new church year, a planning workshop should be scheduled to develop goals and make plans for the next twelve months. Before the meeting, each leader should receive the appropriate purpose and organizational statements, along with suggested areas for evaluation and goal setting. Each organizational leader can then consult with his or her coordinating group for orientation, evaluation, and to develop proposed goals and plans to be considered at the planning workshop. (See fig. 7.9 & 7.10 on p. 127.)

5. Budget for regular expenses such as curriculum materials, and for all special items in the annual plan. This can be delegated to organizational leaders as appropriate.

6. Maintain a master calendar listing all plans, person(s) responsible, and budget provisions, if any. This is used as a monitor of educational activities and a record of progress toward goals, as well as a diary of your reactions concerning educational activities and a guide in planning with the church staff.

7. Maintain a complete record system for each organization listing persons involved, contact information, officers, and attendance records. This information is needed for communication purposes and for planning.

8. Use information to keep work focused. Information gathered and the materials developed will be especially helpful when enlisting and orienting new leaders, planning for enlargement, determining organizational problems, and other similar administrative duties.

9. Evaluate the educational ministry periodically and annually. Spend time before each church council or educational committee meeting assessing the effectiveness of the church's educational ministry. Look at records, review your master calendar, and check any information you have received or gained from your contact with classes,

departments, or committees. Discuss current needs with other leaders and adjust the annual plan as necessary. Prepare annually an extensive evaluation to present to the congregation and to the planning workshop; use these in developing future goals and plans.

10. Follow the basic principles of working with, for, and through people in administering church educational organizations. The three I's will guide you:

Inform. Everyone should know specifically what is happening and why. This means a clear understanding of all plans and procedures, providing opportunities for open discussion of pertinent issues. The leader keeps in touch with key leaders in the educational organizations.

Inspire. There is ministry to and support of the persons with whom you work. Whatever you are as a leader will be the most powerful influence on those through whom you must work. Administration is not doing the work yourself, but eliciting, combining, and guiding the resources of the congregation. Your leadership will be multiplied through others.

Involve. Leadership duties should be shared widely among responsible people. This requires giving major attention to

• equipping leaders to do their tasks,

• delegating to them responsibility,

• supporting and encouraging them as they do their jobs, and

• involving workers in making decisions that will affect them or the duties for which they are responsible.

HOW TO RELATE TO ORGANIZATIONAL LEADERS

Administration, as described throughout this book, focuses on working with and through people. It does not mean that you make all the decisions, attend all the meetings, or do all the work yourself. Your job is to coordinate and guide many areas of work rather than to immerse yourself in the details of one or two organizations. This requires serving as a primary leader in one group and as an advisor to several others.

The person responsible for educational ministry (minister of education, pastor, educational director, or other designated person) is the chair of or staff to the general body that plans, directs, and evaluates all educational activities sponsored by the congregation. This person then serves in an advisory capacity (or as a general officer) to the leader and administrative council for each educational organization. In this way, thorough coordination can be maintained while spreading the load of responsibility and decision-making.

Thus, the educational leader has direct, administrative responsibility for one group and serves as advisor to the members of that body as they, in turn, lead their respective organizations. This organizational arrangement is illustrated in figure 7.11 on p. 128.

STARTING NEW EDUCATIONAL UNITS

The following steps can be used to begin a new unit in any educational organization or, if necessary, to begin a new program.

1. *Determine the need.* This means examining prospect files and membership rolls for the educational program or church to learn possibilities. Attendance patterns are reviewed and growth potential figured out. The appropriate leadership council must also be consulted.

2. *Choose the organization needed and provide facilities.* Using the guidelines given earlier for the appropriate number of members and leader-member ratio, selection is made of the best organization for your situation or the arrangements you would like to provide. Appropriate facilities are provided.

3. *Enlist and train leaders.* You will need persons who are enthusiastic and willing to start new work. There must be careful orientation to the job expectations and the necessary training, materials or supplies, and personal support provided. People must feel involved in making subsequent plans for starting the new unit(s).

4. *Secure materials and supplies.* When a beginning date is set, plan for sufficient study materials and supplies for the number of people expected.

5. *Promote the new unit(s) and enlist members.* General promotion through posters, announcements, and bulletin articles will be helpful. These will not, however, replace enlistment activities—visits, phone calls, notes, and other personal contacts—to secure new members.[2] Extra attention and support should be given the new unit(s) and leader(s) until it has been fully integrated into the larger organization.

CURRICULUM MATERIALS

Curriculum materials are vital to the life and growth of Christians who participate in the programs of a church's educational ministry.[3] The study guides and teaching aids which are used in classes and groups provide stimulation for the spiritual growth and intellectual development of members. Consequently, it is imperative that church leaders understand the needs in each situation and choose appropriate learning resources.

SELECTING CURRICULUM MATERIALS

There should be an approved procedure in your church for selecting and ordering curriculum materials for all educational programs. A church might delegate the responsibility for selecting materials to the education committee or church council. This body, in consultation with the minister of education and pastor, recommends the curriculum line or lines for the church to approve.

Leaders of classes or departments who want resources not available from the approved lines present requests to their program leader. If the program leader and the minister of education agree, the request is forwarded to the education committee or church council. For minor changes, such as choosing an undated unit of study, the church may develop guidelines that will authorize the minister of education or program leader to approve the request.

Use the Curriculum Selection Checklist in figure 7.12 on p. 129, to help in the selection of the curriculum line most suited to the needs of your church or for a particular program.

Curriculum materials should be provided by the church and paid for through the church budget. In anticipating costs, allowance should be made for current enrollment, new members, special outreach and ministry projects, and new items that might be produced during the year.

ORDERING, SECURING, AND DISTRIBUTING CURRICULUM MATERIALS

Curriculum publishers usually provide order forms and information bulletins for their materials. The order forms provide a complete listing of all items available. New materials and special emphases are highlighted for ease in ordering. News bulletins, available from most publishers, usually include announcements of new items, feature articles, special order blanks, and instructions for ordering. If you need information, your denominational office can provide the phone number and address for publishers with appropriate materials for your church.

To get best results in ordering materials, follow these guidelines:

1. Study information bulletins, catalogs, and order forms before ordering.

2. Order early. For regular curriculum materials, order twelve weeks in advance. For special studies and undated items, order six to seven weeks before you need the materials.

3. Appoint one person to handle all your orders.

4. Establish a permanent mailing address to which all materials will come.

5. If a regular order form is provided, use it to speed processing.

6. Be accurate and complete in filling out the order form.

7. Order adequately but not excessively. For example, you should order one pupil's book for each pupil enrolled, each teacher, and some for new members. You will need a teacher's book for each regular and substitute teacher and one resource kit or teacher's packet per class. (A sample requisition form is in fig. 7.13 on p. 131.)

8. Open and check materials upon arrival. There should be time for any "stray" packages to arrive. Report discrepancies immediately to the publisher or bookstore.

9. Develop and follow a literature handling schedule, such as the one in figure 7.14 on p. 132.

Media center/library personnel or other volunteers can be helpful in the distribution of curriculum materials. They can plan together to make sure the materials are sorted and distributed to the locations where they will be used. This is especially true of materials which serve across organizational lines, such as materials for the family.

RECORDS AND REPORTS

Each group, class, department, division, and program should keep records of its activities, and report regularly to the next larger unit.[4] All basic programs and organizations, such as Sunday school, discipleship training, music ministry, and missions, should report regularly to the church. An update of activities in monthly or quarterly business meetings, and a summary report at the end of the church year, are also needed.

RECORDS

Program and ministry leaders should determine what information they and others need to keep informed and to give adequate guidance to the work of each organization. A record system usually is in place that can be adjusted as needs for information change. Religious book stores and publishers have a variety of record-keeping and report forms that can be used as-is or adapted for your situation.

Some have found it feasible to use computer systems to serve the records needs in a church. Individuals and companies are in business to help congregations with their use of computers not only with educational records, but also with financial and church membership records. Instead of taking several hours to prepare and type a report for the monthly business meeting, it can be processed in a few minutes using a computer.

Once leaders select an appropriate record system and secure the essential supplies for its operation, there should be training to assure proper use of the system. An annual training session for those who "do" the records can be a great help in getting accurate and complete information. For example, training would be useful for Sunday school group leaders, class secretaries, department secretaries, division secretaries, the general secretary, and hosts who work at welcome desks (including those who receive guests, get information from them, and help them find the appropriate group according to the church's grouping and grading plan).

Good records enable leaders to discover needs and opportunities so that appropriate and timely responses can be made. A secondary benefit concerns their historical value. Not only are records necessary when studying church heritage or dealing with legal issues, but data over the years can be studied for trends and needs which can be of significant use in determining leadership actions and planning strategy.

REPORTS

Each unit in an organization should report essential information to the leaders of the next larger unit of which it is a part. General leaders of a church organization need accurate and complete information about the effectiveness of the major units within the organization. Report forms which summarize the key items of information should be prepared by designated persons within each unit and sent to the general secretary.

It is important that organizations of the church periodically report on their work. This can be done in a monthly or quarterly business meeting, through a church newsletter, or by using promotional displays in major traffic areas. A summary report should also be presented at the end of the church year.

Church publications can feature educational programs and ministries. Highlights of special events, as well as regular items such as a weekly or monthly report, schedule of activities, and other pertinent information, will keep the congregation informed. Bulletin or information boards can report key items of information, such as attendance, number of visitors, and offerings. And, of course, the announcement period in regular services can be used as well.

RESOURCES FOR GENERAL ADMINISTRATION

On the following pages you will find basic information concerning programs. This is not intended to be exhaustive nor to substitute for guidebooks published specifically for directors of church programs. Rather, you will find reference and administrative helps useful in providing general guidance for your church's educational ministry.[5]

In each case, a brief overview of the organization is given, including definition and a statement of its purpose and scope of work. An organizational chart follows showing a typical arrangement. For the Bible Teaching program, job descriptions are given for many of the volunteer positions used in churches. Additional items helpful for instructional purposes or in preparation for meetings are included for your convenience.

Note that many aids located in the Bible Teaching program section are useful in other organizations; you will want to adapt from them as appropriate.

BIBLE TEACHING PROGRAM

Definition:

The planned educational activities provided by a local church for the primary purpose of involving people in Bible study.

Purpose and scope of work:

The purpose of the Bible Teaching program is to facilitate Bible study at an appropriate level for all persons who will respond to a church's invitation. This usually includes a weekly study period following a prescribed curriculum and periodic extra studies devoted to specialized topics. Additional Bible classes and informal study groups often are provided in members' homes or in other settings to involve more people.

The Bible Teaching program is considered the primary means for facilitating outreach and witnessing for a congregation.

DISCIPLESHIP TRAINING PROGRAM

Definition:

The planned educational activities provided by a local church to (1) orient new Christians/new members to the faith and practice of the local congregation; (2) equip church members for discipleship and personal witness/ministry; and (3) equip church members for positions of leadership in and beyond the congregation.

Purpose and scope of work:

The purpose of the Discipleship Training program is twofold: to enable church members to live distinctively Christian lives and to prepare persons to assume leadership and ministry responsibilities in the church and community. The former involves (1) short-term studies for integrating new members into the life and faith of the congregation, and (2) ongoing, curriculum-guided study of topics such as doctrine, ethics, history, and church polity. Additional studies may be provided on a short-term basis on just about any topic that would help a person apply biblical teachings to life.

General training for discipleship, personal ministry, and interpersonal effectiveness is part of the ongoing training curriculum and the foundation for leadership development. In addition, specialized training is provided at appropriate times during the year for committee members, teachers, group leaders, church visitors, and other similar positions.

MUSIC MINISTRY PROGRAM

Definition:

The planned educational, worship, and witness activities provided by a local church to develop musical skills, attitudes, and understandings that can contribute to worship, witness, and Christian living.

Purpose and scope of work:

The purpose of the Music Ministry program is to develop appreciation for and ability to use musical experiences to enhance worship and witness in all dimensions of Christian life.

Musical experiences extend from congregational singing and choral anthems to participation in graded choirs for all ages. A structured curriculum often is provided for younger choirs, focusing on music skills and appreciation. Youth and adult choirs, on the other hand, spend most of their time learning and performing music. Although sometimes considered more of an aid for worship and witness rather than an educational function, music ministry nevertheless influences the lives of those who are not performing and teaches those who are.

BROTHERHOOD/MEN'S MISSION PROGRAM

Definition:

A church organization for men and boys devoted to equipping for and involving members in Christian service.

Purpose and scope of work:

The purpose of this organization is to inform, motivate, and involve men and boys in praying, studying, giving, ministering, and bearing witness to Christ at home and throughout the world. Great emphasis is placed on developing a style of Christian living and personal ministry that is a natural part of one's life.

Age-graded leadership and study materials often are used to provide guidance for groups of members ranging from first graders through adults.

This organization should not be confused with the fellowship-oriented meetings held in some churches. A Brotherhood program is a serious, ongoing educational organization that is highly committed to mission support and service.

WOMAN'S MISSIONARY UNION/ WOMEN'S MISSION PROGRAM

Definition:

A church organization for women, girls, and preschool children devoted to teaching, promoting, and supporting missions.

Purpose and scope of work:

The major purpose of this organization is to lead persons to explore the nature, implications, and evidences of God's missionary purpose, and to respond in personal commitment and active participation.

Personal witnessing, participation in mission projects, and support of missionary efforts through prayer, study, and contributions are activities usually associated with this group. Age-graded leadership and study materials often are used to provide guidance for groups of members ranging from older preschoolers through adults.

Figure 7.1

BASIC CHURCH PROGRAMS

There are six established church programs, each with a cluster of tasks that are basic, continuing, and of primary importance to the life of a church. Each program develops organization and seeks to involve the congregation in its work. These organizations form the foundation of church structure, and thus are called basic church programs. Listed below are the tasks which each program assumes in the life of the church.

Bible Teaching

1. Reach persons for Bible study.
2. Teach the Bible.
3. Witness to persons about Christ and lead them into church membership.
4. Minister to persons in need.
5. Lead members to worship.

Discipleship Training

1. Reach persons for discipleship training.
2. Orient new church members for discipleship and personal ministry.
3. Equip church members for discipleship and personal ministry.
4. Teach theology, doctrine, ethics, history, and church polity.
5. Train church leaders for their tasks.

Music Ministry

1. Provide musical experiences in congregational services.
2. Provide church music education.
3. Lead the church to witness and minister through music.
4. Assist the church programs in use of and training related to music.

Brotherhood/Men's Mission Program

1. Engage in missions activities.
2. Teach missions.
3. Pray for and give to missions.
4. Develop personal ministry.

Woman's Missionary Union/Women's Mission Program

1. Teach missions.
2. Engage in mission action and personal witnessing.

3. Support missions.

Pastoral Ministries

1. Lead the church in accomplishing its mission.

2. Proclaim the gospel to believers and nonbelievers.

3. Care for the church's members and other persons in the community.

All programs interpret and undergird the work of the local church and the denominational groups with which the congregation cooperates in mission and ministry efforts.

Figure 7.2

CHURCH COUNCIL

The church council serves as a forum for a church's leaders to guide planning, coordination, conducting, and evaluation of the total work of the church. The council depends on the various church organizations to implement the church's program according to their assigned tasks. As chair of the church council, the pastor is able to lead in the development of a unified program that gives major attention to priority needs.

PRINCIPLE FUNCTION: to assist the church to determine its course, and to coordinate and evaluate its work.

METHOD OF ELECTION: church leaders become members of the church council as a result of election to designated church leadership positions.

TERM OF OFFICE: corresponds to term of office in church-elected position.

MEMBERS: pastor (chair), church staff members, program directors, deacon chair, stewardship committee chair, missions committee chair, and other committee chairs as needed.

DUTIES:

• Help the church understand its mission and define its priorities.

• Coordinate studies of church and community needs.

• Recommend to the church coordinated plans for evangelism, missions, Christian development, worship, stewardship, and ministry.

• Coordinate the church's schedule of activities, special events, and use of facilities.

• Evaluate progress and the priority use of church resources.

Figure 7.3

Organization for Educational Administration

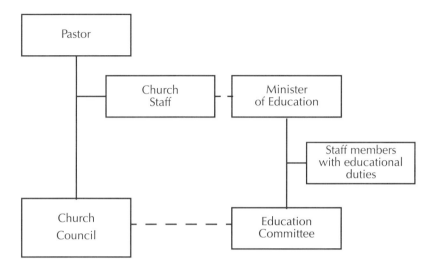

Figure 7.4

Organization for Church Program Administration

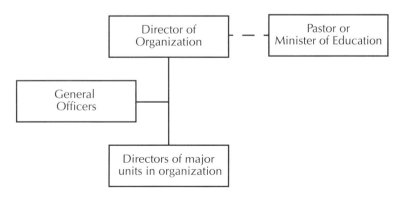

Figure 7.5

PROGRAM COUNCIL AND/OR STAFF

PRINCIPAL FUNCTIONS: to assist the program to determine its course, to coordinate program efforts, and to relate to the church council for overall coordination.

MEMBERSHIP AND METHOD OF ELECTION: Directors of major units/age divisions in the program become members of the program council as a result of election by the church to program leadership positions. If there are no age division directors, the leader of each department represents his or her group.

TERM OF OFFICE: Corresponds to term of office in church-elected position.

REPORT: As a program, to the church; director serves on church council, or other general coordinating body.

DUTIES:

• Help the program understand its mission and define its priorities in the light of church priorities.

• Conduct studies of church and community needs related to program tasks.

• Coordinate the program's activities and schedules.

• Evaluate progress, effectiveness, and the priority use of church resources.

Figure 7.6

AGE-DIVISION COORDINATION

Age-division coordination may be accomplished in three ways: self-coordination, age-division conferences, or age-division coordinators/directors. The approach used by a church is determined by the complexity of the organization within the age division.

SELF-COORDINATION

Self-coordination exists when organization leaders of an age division voluntarily coordinate their work and the use of space, equipment, and supplies. It is the simplest and most effective. It is particularly suited for small churches and age divisions with few workers.

AGE-DIVISION COORDINATION CONFERENCES

Principal function: to serve as a counseling, advisory, and coordinating group when self-coordination is not adequate.

Members: leaders of departments, choirs, and other organizational units of a particular age division.

Convener: one of the members of the group elected by the group.

AGE-DIVISION COORDINATORS/DIRECTORS

Principal function: to counsel age-division leaders and coordinate the work of units within the age division as assigned.

Age-division coordinators are elected by the church and responsible to the pastor or minister of education as designated by the church. The pastor leads in developing procedures for providing consultative and advisory services to the minister of music and other staff members as needed.

DUTIES:

- Consult with department leaders to resolve philosophical, procedural, and scheduling problems.
- Give assistance in classifying and enrolling new members.
- Consult with department leaders to coordinate the use of program materials, supplies, equipment, and space.
- Give individual guidance to department directors and workers.
- Work with church program leaders to provide training opportunities for department leaders and workers.
- Work with director of recreation to provide appropriate services.
- Give assistance as needed to department directors in discovering and enlisting department workers.
- Coordinate age-division visitation.
- Encourage and provide assistance to leaders in planning and evaluating their work.
- Serve as ex officio members of program council.

Figure 7.7

ORGANIZATION PLANNING CHART

	Enrollment		Prospects		Total Possibilities		Suggested Maximum Enrollment	Departments Needed	Suggested Maximum Enrollment	Classes Needed	Suggested Worker/ Member Ratio[a]	Approximate No. of Workers Needed
Member Classification Age (Grade)	M	F	M	F	M	F						
	1	2	3	4			5	6	7	8	9	10
DIVISION / PRESCHOOL — Birth–1 — Cradle Roll							35		×	×	1/6	
Babies							9		×	×	1/3	
Ones							9		×	×	1/3	
2							12		×	×	1/4	
3							16		×	×	1/4	
4							16		×	×	1/4	
5							16		×	×	1/4	
CHILDREN — Special Education							20		×	×	1/4	
6 (Grade 1)							30		×	×	1/6	
7 (Grade 2)							30		×	×	1/6	
8 (Grade 3)							30		×	×	1/6	
9 (Grade 4)							30		×	×	1/6	
10 (Grade 5)							30		×	×	1/6	
11 (Grade 6)							30		×	×	1/6	

ORGANIZATION PLANNING CHART (Continued)

		1	2	3	4	5	6	7	8	9
YOUTH	12 (Grade 7)					60		12		1/8
	13 (Grade 8)					60		12		1/8
	14 (Grade 9)					60		12		1/8
	15 (Grade 10)					60		12		1/8
	16 (Grade 11)					60		12		1/8
	17 (Grade 12)					60		12		1/8
ADULT	18–24 (College)					125		25		1/5
	18–24 (Single)					125		25		1/5
	25–34 (Married)					125		25		1/5
	25–34 (Single)					125		25		1/5
	35–44 (Married)					125		25		1/5
	35–44 (Single)					125		25		1/5
	45–64 (Married)					125		25		1/5
	45–64 (Single)					125		25		1/5
	65–up					125		25		1/5
	Weekday S. S. Classes					X		25		1/5
	Adults Away					75		5	X	1/5
	Homebound				X	75		5	X	1/5
	Outreach Bible Study Group	X				X	X			X
	New Sunday Schools		X			X	X	X	X	X
	Pastor/Staff/Gen. Officers	X		X		X	X	X	X	X
	Total	X				X		X		X

a. Adult ratio in column 9 includes care group leaders in the classes

Figure 7.8a

CHURCH ORGANIZATION

Organization is grouping persons in a way that enables individuals and groups to accomplish their goals. In organization:

- Activities and responsibilities are assigned to individuals and groups.
- Working relationships are established.
- Responsibility and authority are delegated to enable individuals and groups to use initiative in their work.

Organizational Patterns

Possible Organization Components. There are many organizational components a church can design to perform its work. Components commonly found include staff, deacons, church officers, church committees, coordinating units (councils), Sunday school, discipleship training, music ministry, mission organizations, media center/library, and recreation.

Effective Organization. Effective organization grows out of an understanding of the church's mission, resources, and traditions. No pattern is best, even for churches of a similar size. Each must develop its own organization. Objectives, priorities, tradition, availability of leaders, needs and numbers of people, space and equipment, and time considerations will influence decisions about organizational patterns in a church.

Evaluating Options

The following chart gives suggestions and describes alternatives for organization. By studying these options you could determine how best to proceed with any adjustments needed in your situation.

Figure 7.8b

Possibilities for Church Organization

Type of Unit Position	Churches with Fewer than 150 Members*	Churches with 150 to 399 Members	Churches with 400 to 699 Members	Churches with 700 to 1499 Members	Churches with 1500 or more Members
Staff	Pastor Music Director[a]	Pastor Music Director[a] Secretary[b] Custodian[b] Pianist/Organist[a]	Pastor Minister of Music and Education Secretary Custodian Organist[a] Pianist[a]	Pastor Minister of Music Minister of Education Secretaries[c] Custodians[a] Organist[a] Pianist[a] Age-Division Ministers[c]	Pastor Associate Pastor Minister of Education Minister of Music Business Administrator Minister of Recreation Evangelism/Outreach Minister Age-Division Ministers Organist-Music Assistant Family Life Minister Secretaries[c] Custodians[c] Hostess Food service personnel[c]
Deacons	Deacons (1 deacon per 15 family units; minimum of 2 deacons)	Deacons (1 deacon per 15 family units)	Deacons (1 deacon per 15 family units)	Deacons (1 deacon per 15 family units)	Deacons (1 deacon per 15 family units)

Possibilities for Church Organization (Continued)

Type of Unit Position	Churches with Fewer than 150 Members*	Churches with 150 to 399 Members	Churches with 400 to 699 Members	Churches with 700 to 1499 Members	Churches with 1500 or more Members
Church Officers	Moderator (Pastor) Trustees Clerk Treasurer	Moderator Trustees Clerk Treasurer	Moderator Trustees Clerk Treasurer	Moderator Trustees Clerk Treasurer	Moderator Trustees Clerk Treasurer
Church Committees	Nominating Stewardship Missions Evangelism	Nominating Property and Space Stewardship Ushers Missions Preschool[d] Evangelism	Nominating Property and Space Stewardship Personnel Missions Preschool History Ushers Weekday Education[d] Public Relations Evangelism	Nominating Property and Space Stewardship Personnel Missions Preschool Food Service History Ushers Weekday Education[d] Public Relations Evangelism	Nominating Property and Space Stewardship Personnel Missions Preschool Food Service History Ushers Weekday Education[d] Public Relations Evangelism Other committees as needed
Service Programs	Media Services Director	Media Services Director (up to 3 workers) Recreation Director	Media Staff Recreation Staff	Media Staff Recreation Staff	Media Staff Recreation Staff
Special Ministries		Senior Adult Ministry	Senior Adult Ministry Singles Ministry	Senior Adult Ministry Singles Ministry	Senior Adult Ministry Singles Ministry Intergenerational Activities

Possibilities for Church Organization (Continued)

Type of Unit Position	Churches with Fewer than 150 Members*	Churches with 150 to 399 Members	Churches with 400 to 699 Members	Churches with 700 to 1499 Members	Churches with 1500 or more Members
Coordination	Church Council	Church Council WMU Council S. S. Council Brotherhood Council	Church Council S. S. Council C. T. Council Music Council WMU Council Brotherhood Council Division Coordination Conferences	Church Council S. S. Council C. T. Council Music Council WMU Council Brotherhood Council Division Coordination Conferences	Church Council S. S. Council C. T. Council Music Council WMU Council Brotherhood Council Media Services Council Division Coordination Conferences
Bible Teaching	General officers and organization for each age division	Departments of each age division	Multiple departments as needed	Multiple departments as needed	Multiple departments as needed
Discipleship Training	Discipleship Training Director Age-group leaders[4]	Member training groups and departments for each age division Equipping Centers New Church Member training	Member training groups and departments for each age division Equipping Centers New Church Member training	Member training groups and departments for each age division Equipping Centers New Church Member training	Member training groups and departments for each age division Equipping Centers New Church Member training
WMU	WMU Director Age level organizations as needed	Age level organizations as needed	Age level organizations as needed	Age level organizations as needed	Age level organizations as needed

Possibilities for Church Organization (Continued)

Type of Unit Position	Churches with Fewer than 150 Members*	Churches with 150 to 399 Members	Churches with 400 to 699 Members	Churches with 700 to 1499 Members	Churches with 1500 or more Members
Brotherhood	Brotherhood Director	Age level organizations as needed	Age level organizations as needed	Age level organizations as needed	Age level organizations as needed
Music Ministry	Music Director[e] Pianist Choir	Music Director[e] Organist Church Choir or Ensemble Age-division choirs when possible	Age-division choirs Instrumental groups as needed	Fully developed music ministry	Fully developed music ministry

a Volunteer or part-time
b Part-time
c As needed
d If needed
e Person serves as program leader

*NOTE: It is important to encourage, in any way possible, churches of 150 members or less to have choir, recreation, and other needed ministries even though directors or other leaders for those activities might not be listed in column one of this chart.

Figure 7.9

GOAL PLANNING WORK SHEET

Use the following when exploring and planning goals for your committee/workgroup/church.

1. Proposed goal:
2. What we hope to accomplish by this goal is to . . .
3. This goal is related to the following objective(s):
4. What is already being done related to this goal?
5. Specific age or interest group(s) to which goal is related.
6. We will feel we have made progress toward this goal when:
7. Major obstacles we see in implementing this goal:
8. Major resources needed to begin:
9. Decision regarding proposed goal:

    *   Approved.
    *   No decision at this time.
    *   Hold for further discussion/development.
    *   Develop action plan(s).
    *   Secure input from . . .
    *   Other.

Figure 7.10

SAMPLE FORMAT FOR PLANNING REPORT

Page ___ of ___
Program, Organization, or Officer _____ Date Prepared:_____
Objective:
Goal:
Action Plan #____:

Action	Person Responsible	Completion Date	Estimated Budget

Figure 7.11

LINE AND STAFF RELATIONSHIPS

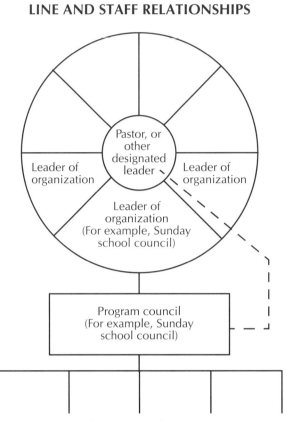

Organizational Units
(For example, age divisions, departments, and classes)

Figure 7.12

CURRICULUM SELECTION CHECKLIST

Use this checklist to compare lines of curriculum you might consider for use with a given age group. Secure samples of each line you wish to consider. Examine the materials carefully. Check each item on the list below. Indicate by ✓ which line is best on each factor. Compare the basic pieces of each line; the pupil's material; the teacher's material. Choose and use the curriculum that best meets your needs.

FACTOR TO CONSIDER	CURRICULUM LINES		
	A	B	C
1. There is ample, appropriate use of the Bible.	__	__	__
2. The teachings are doctrinally sound.	__	__	__
3. Doctrinal emphases are balanced.	__	__	__
4. Coverage of the Bible is comprehensive.	__	__	__
5. The educational philosophy is valid.	__	__	__
6. Concepts presented are suited to the age group.	__	__	__
7. Content addresses life needs appropriately.	__	__	__
8. Teachings encourage appropriate responses.	__	__	__
9. Methodology is properly related to content.	__	__	__
10. Methods are suited to our workers' skills.	__	__	__
11. Training materials are available to develop workers' skills.	__	__	__
12. Learning activities are right for the age group.	__	__	__
13. The materials support the church program.	__	__	__
14. Materials advance purposes of this organization.	__	__	__
15. Quality teaching/learning aids are readily available.	__	__	__
16. Supplementary commentaries are available.	__	__	__
17. Art use is in good taste.	__	__	__
18. The layout is attractive to the user.	__	__	__
19. The binding is sufficiently durable.	__	__	__
20. The paper quality is adequate.	__	__	__
21. The print size is right.	__	__	__

22. The print is clear and easy to read.   __ __ __

23. Use of color in materials is attractive.   __ __ __

24. Service for ordering, receiving, paying is good.   __ __ __

25. Consultation in use of materials is available.   __ __ __

26. Volume (number of pages) in each piece
    is adequate.   __ __ __

27. The cost in relation to the benefits is suitable.   __ __ __

28. The cost per comparable items is least.   __ __ __

29. (Other factor we consider important.)   __ __ __

30. (Other factor we consider important.)   __ __ __

Based upon this comparison, curriculum line ____ seems best for us. It is available at the following address:

_____

_____

_____

_____

Figure 7.13

Literature Requisition Form (Sample)

(This form will also be used to guide in distribution.)

Name:		Organization:		by: (date)
Grade:		Age Group:		Room No.: (class, dept., or office)
Quarter: (circle one)	Oct.–Dec.	Jan.–Mar.	April–June	July–Sept.
Item Number	Title	Current Quarter	This Quarter Last Year	Quanitity Needed

Special Instructions (distribution of leadership materials, etc.)

_____

_____

_____

_____

_____

Signed (Organizational Leader) Date

Figure 7.14

LITERATURE HANDLING SCHEDULE

1. *Plan with church leaders.* Study Church Materials Catalog and other materials pertaining to changes in literature and circulate to church leaders. Review with church and/or organization leaders the literature to be ordered.

2. *Collect information from teachers and leaders.* Fill out all items on literature requisition form except "Quantity" and "Special Instructions." Distribute literature requisition forms. Give to organization directors or directly to each leader in Sunday School, discipleship training, music ministry, media center, recreation, and mission organizations, as well as the pastor and other church staff members. Call or see all leaders who have not returned the forms. All forms should be collected before beginning to tabulate the main order.

3. *Prepare order.*
   (1) Transfer the requests onto the literature order form. Remember that a monthly or weekly publication is ordered only one time per quarter.
   (2) Multiply the number of each title ordered by the price, and enter the amount in the space provided.
   (3) Total the amount, using an adding machine if available. Check several times or have someone else check your multiplication and addition.
   (4) Subtract any allowable discount, if remittance is enclosed, and enter total. Add sales tax if applicable.
   (5) File church's copy of order form.
   (6) Check address label attached to literature order form.
   (7) Enter customer account number on every order.

4. *Mail the order.* Request check from church treasurer. Enclose check and order in return envelope. Check return address. Mail order. To assure having your material on time, have your order completed and in the mail by the date suggested on the order form. For rush orders, indicate the required date. The materials services department will determine the method of shipment and bill the buyer for shipping charges.

5. *Verify the shipment.* Open packages immediately upon arrival and check against your copy of the order. Keep notes on discrepancies or damage and notify the publisher. Allow time for

"stray" packages to arrive. Store literature until time to begin distribution.

6. *Distribute the literature.*

EACH QUARTER

Write names of teachers and leaders on their materials to expedite distribution and the return of lost items. Insert mediagraphy (list) of supporting media center materials. Distribute leadership materials to teachers and leaders either directly or through organizational directors. Distribute member materials to classes and/or departments. Suggest to teachers and leaders that members write their names on their materials.

EACH MONTH

Distribute the monthly reading pieces on the first Sunday of each month, and the monthly leadership pieces for the coming month on the third Sunday.

EACH SUNDAY

Distribute the weekly reading pieces.

OTHER TIMES

Distribute materials for groups which do not meet on Sunday such as deacons, missionary organizations, and persons engaged in outreach projects.

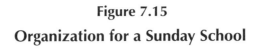

Figure 7.15

Organization for a Sunday School

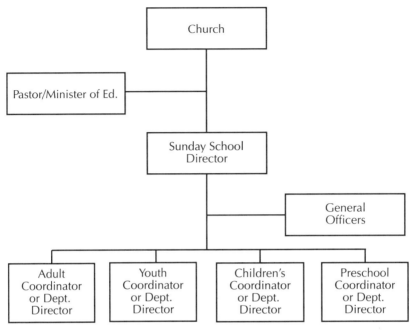

Figure 7.16

Organization for a Sunday School of up to 100 Members

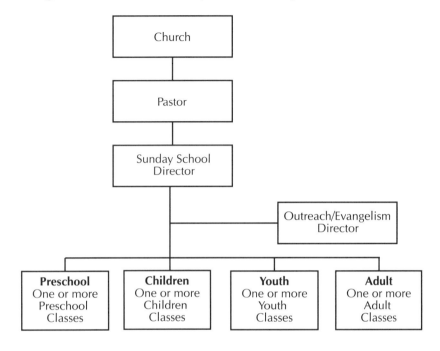

Figure 7.17

Organization for a Sunday School of 200 Members

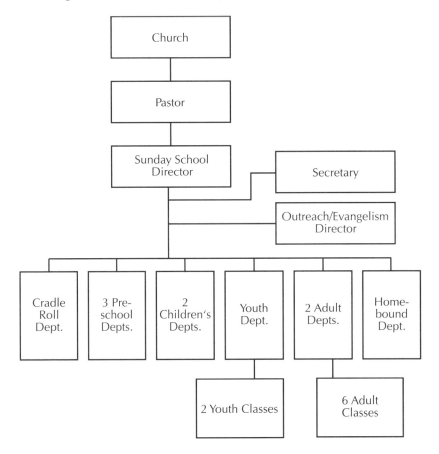

Figure 7.18

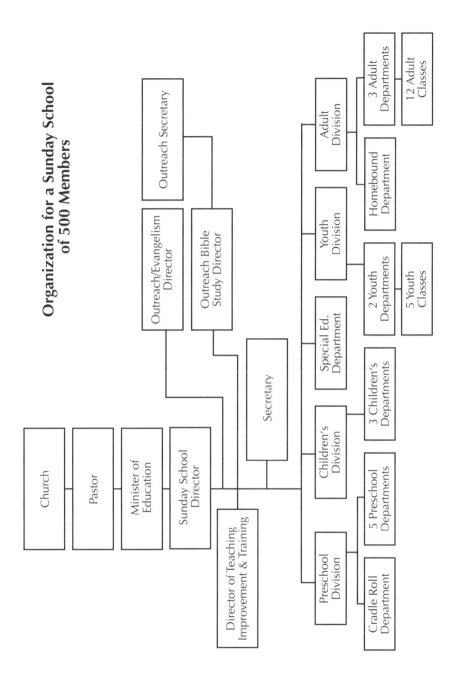

Organization for a Sunday School of 500 Members

Figure 7.19
Organization of a Sunday School
of 1000 or More Members

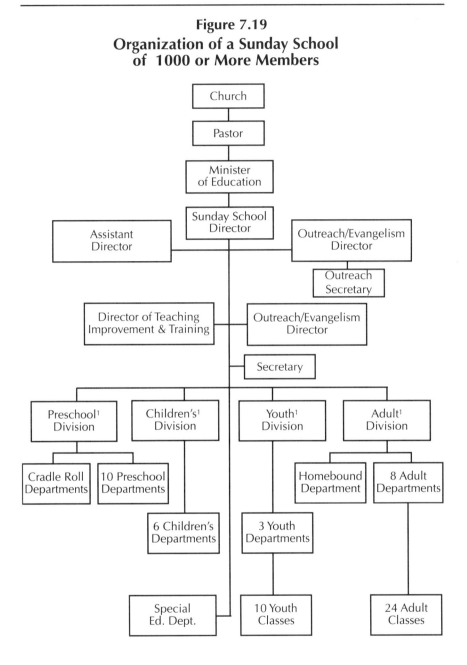

1. Churches with this many departments of each age group would probably want to have divisions for each focus within the age group.

Figure 7.20

JOB DESCRIPTIONS FOR SUNDAY SCHOOL WORKERS

I. General Officers of the Sunday School (Volunteer Leaders)

A. *Sunday School Director:* The Sunday school director is responsible to the church for all phases of Sunday school work. He/she will look to the pastor (and/or minister of education if a church has one) for counsel and leadership. The director leads the Sunday school council in planning and evaluating the work of the Sunday school and represents the Sunday school on the Church Council.

The Sunday school director's full responsibilities include the areas of outreach, Sunday school Bible-teaching improvement and worker training, witnessing, ministering, and Bible teaching projects (such as Vacation Bible School). The Sunday school director also should plan ways to lead the Sunday school to support the work of the church and the denomination. He/she may delegate some of these responsibilities to one or more of the officers listed under Expanded Organization.

B. *Sunday School Secretary:* The general Sunday school secretary is responsible to the Sunday school director for compiling and maintaining weekly, quarterly, and annual records and reports for the Sunday school.

C. *Outreach-Evangelism Director:* The outreach-evangelism director is responsible to the Sunday school director for planning, conducting, and evaluating efforts of the Sunday school in reaching, witnessing, and ministering. The director of outreach-evangelism is responsible for looking at training needs in outreach and working with appropriate persons to see that needed training is provided. This leader would coordinate plans for prospect discovery and enlistment activities, witness training, and evangelistic outreach with the Sunday school director. If the church uses the Sunday School Outreach Communication Plan, this officer would be the project director or enlist someone to do this work in cooperation with the Sunday school director.

II. Expanded Organization

Many churches will need one or more of these officers:

A. *Assistant Sunday School Director:* The assistant Sunday school director may be the only general associate, aside from the secretary, in smaller Sunday schools and is responsible to the Sunday school director for performing assigned duties. The duties usually will include one or more functions of outreach, evangelism, leader training, and teaching improvement.

B. *Vacation Bible School Director:* The Vacation Bible School director is responsible to the Sunday school director or an educational member or pastor for planning, promoting, and conducting the church's Vacation Bible School. The pastor or minister of education may serve as the Vacation Bible School director.

C. *Bible Study Groups Director:* The Bible study groups director is a member of the Sunday school council and is responsible to the Sunday school director for planning, conducting, and evaluating the work of various short-term and ongoing Bible study groups. One or more directors may be needed.

D. *Leader and Member Development Director:* The leader and member development director is responsible for: (1) planning, conducting, and evaluating activities to improve Bible teaching-learning in Sunday school; (2) recommending to the church's Discipleship Training director activities/ studies to improve discipleship development among Sunday school members and then assisting with curriculum selection and scheduling or with activity planning; (3) discovering training needs of present and potential Sunday school workers and then planning, conducting, and evaluating training activities to meet those needs; (4) working closely with the church's Discipleship Training director to schedule Sunday school training events; and (5) making Sunday school leaders and members aware of discipling studies that will meet the expressed needs of Sunday school members.

E. *Mission Vacation Bible School Director:* The mission Vacation Bible School director is responsible to the Sunday school director for leading the church to conduct mission Vacation Bible Schools and/or Backyard Bible Clubs. This person will find and recommend locations, select projects, request church approval, set dates and meeting places, obtain materials, enlist workers, and provide training for these workers; conduct and evaluate the projects; and work with the Sunday school leaders to take appropriate follow-up actions.

F. *Bus/Van Ministry Director:* When a church has a bus/van ministry, the bus/van ministry director is responsible to the Sunday school outreach-evangelism director for planning, promoting, conducting, and evaluating efforts to reach persons for Bible study through a bus/van ministry. The bus/van ministry director also works closely with appropriate department directors in assigning bus/van ministry members to age-groups for ministry.

G. *Mission Sunday School Director:* The mission Sunday school director is responsible to the church Sunday school director or the church missions committee for planning, conducting, and evaluating the mission Sunday school. The director may need one or more of the associates described above.

III. Officers Common to All Age Groups

A. *Age-Group Department Director:* The department director is responsible to the Sunday school director (or division director if the church has this structure) for planning. The director's work will include organizing the department for effective reaching, teaching, witnessing, and caring; enlisting and training leaders; administering the department's work; leading department meetings; leading in planning for Bible study, and working with teachers to identify and recommend to the leader and member development director training needs for discipleship development. In preschool and children's departments, the department director also serves as the lead teacher.

B. *Age-Group Department Secretary:* The secretary is responsible to the department director for handling all matters related to department records. In the preschool and children's division, the department director maintains the records or assigns the responsibility to a teacher. In youth and children's departments, the role of department secretary may be combined with the role of department outreach leader.

C. *Age-Group Division Director:* When there are multiple departments within an age division, a church may choose to elect a division director to coordinate that age division's work. The division director then might be asked to represent the departments within the division on the Sunday school council. The division director is responsible to the

Sunday school director for coordinating the age division's work in accomplishing the tasks of the Bible Teaching Ministry.

IV. Leaders Unique to Adult Departments

  A. Department Leadership Team

   1. *Department Outreach–Evangelism Leader:* The department outreach evangelism leader is responsible to the department director for leading the department to discover, witness to, enroll, and minister to the lost and unchurched prospects. This officer's work is to develop and maintain a department prospect file and make prospect assignments to class outreach evangelism leaders. The department outreach–evangelism leader is responsible for training department and class leaders and members in outreach and evangelism. This officer is also to welcome and introduce visitors and prospects to the department and assign them to an appropriate class.

   2. *Department Fellowship Leader:* The department fellowship leader is responsible to the department director for planning and conducting department fellowship and assimilation actions. This officer is also to assist adult class fellowship leaders in their responsibilities.

  B. Adult Class

   1. *Teacher:* The Adult teacher is responsible to the department director (or Sunday school if there is no department organization) as the administrator of the class. This person is the Bible teacher of the class. This officer is to lead the class leadership team in its work, enlist and train the class leadership team, and work with the department director to identify training needs for discipleship development.

   2. *Class Outreach–Evangelism Leader:* The outreach-evangelism leader is responsible to the teacher and is to lead the class to discover, witness to, enroll, and minister to lost and unchurched prospects. This officer is to develop and maintain the class prospect file, make prospect visitation assignments to members, and assign prospects to members for cultivation, evangelism, and discipleship.

3. *Care Leaders:* The care leaders are responsible to the teacher for contacting, ministering to, cultivating, and discipling as many as six assigned class members. Care leaders are to encourage class members to cultivate, visit, witness to, and enroll lost or unchurched prospects as assigned. Each leader is to report ministry and fellowship needs to the teacher and department fellowship leader. It is recommended that a male care leader be enlisted to work with men and a female care leader be enlisted to work with women. In some cases it may be appropriate in married co-ed classes to have as many as six married couples or up to twelve individuals in a care group led by a husband and wife. In this case, the husband would be primarily responsible for working with the men in the care group and the wife would be primarily responsible for working with the women.

4. *Fellowship Leader:* The fellowship leader is responsible to the teacher for planning, coordinating, and conducting all class social and assimilation actions. This leader is to work with the department fellowship leader to plan and conduct department social events.

5. *Secretary:* The secretary is responsible to the teacher for compiling and reporting class membership records. These membership records are to be reported to the teacher, department and/or general Sunday school secretary.

6. *Prayer Leader:* The prayer leader is responsible to the teacher for leading the class to pray during the week for needs, praises, etc., of class members and prospects. This person can serve as prayer leader in addition to another class or department leadership position. The prayer leader will organize a class network of prayer support through the class care leaders. This person will inform other leaders and members of prayer concern, encourage members to have a daily devotional time, and enlist persons to pray regularly for Sunday school and church needs.

V. Officers Unique to Youth Sunday School

A. *Teacher:* The youth teacher is responsible to the department director (or Sunday school director if there is no department organization) as the administrator of the class.

This person is the Bible teacher of the class. This officer also is to lead the class leadership team, enlist and train the class leader and care leaders, and work with the department director to identify training needs for discipleship development.

B. *Class Leader (Youth):* The class leader is a youth class member who has been selected for a period of time determined by the teacher—usually three to six months. By rotating class leaders periodically, more youth have an opportunity to serve in this leadership role. Each class leader relates directly to the teacher of the class. Each class should have one class leader.

C. *Care Leader (Youth):* Care leaders are youth class members who have been selected by the teacher or elected by class members to serve for a period of time determined by the teacher, usually three to six months. By rotating care leaders periodically, more youth have an opportunity to serve in the leadership role. Each care leader relates directly to the class leader, and indirectly to the teacher of the class. There should be one care leader for every one to four youth enrolled in the class.

D. *Minister of Youth:* If the church has a minister of youth, he or she relates to the highest level of the youth Sunday school organization as an equipper in the areas of administering, planning, organizing, evaluating, conducting, training, and motivating. Some churches choose to elect this staff person to one of the youth Sunday school jobs listed above. In this case, the minister of youth would also assume the job responsibilities described under the position. However, to have a balanced youth educational ministry, the minister of youth should help the church develop enough lay leaders so that all youth Sunday school jobs may be filled by lay persons. Such a plan will allow the minister of youth more time for involvement with all youth program organizations through the youth ministry council.

E. *Other Leadership Positions:* At least two reasons exist for having other youth Sunday school positions: Larger youth Sunday school organizations may require additional positions at the division level in order to (1) assist the division director with the administrative details of the division (2) increase the effectiveness of special Bible studies that are needed to complement the Sunday morning Bible studies.

1. Optional Division Positions

    a. *Division Outreach–Evangelism Leader:* The division outreach–evangelism leader relates directly to the youth division director. The responsibilities of the job should be determined by the need that exists for such a position. These responsibilities should be a blending of some of the responsibilities described under the department outreach–evangelism leader's job and assistance responsibilities to the division director as they relate to reaching, witnessing, and caring.

    b. *Division Secretary:* The division secretary relates directly to the division director. This position may be needed in larger youth Sunday schools in order to coordinate the multiple reports of the department secretaries. The responsibilities relate to the work of the division director.

2. *Special Bible Studies Positions:* Job descriptions for youth workers in special Bible study opportunities may be found in the base design papers for those special Bible studies.

VI. Officers Unique to Children's Sunday School

    A. *Teacher:* The teacher is responsible for teaching a group of children and for cultivating the friendships and interests of pupils and their families; and is responsible for home visitation and ministry to those pupils and their families. The teacher also works with the department director to identify training needs of children and parents of children for discipleship development.

    B. *Outreach–Evangelism Leader:* The outreach–evangelism leader is responsible for leading in the planning, conducting, and evaluating of the inreach, home-reach, and outreach activities of the class/department. The outreach-evangelism leader may also serve as a teacher, a substitute teacher, or as the department/class director.

VII. Officers Unique to Preschool Sunday School

    A. *Teacher:* The teachers participate with the department director in the tasks of reaching, teaching, caring, witnessing, fellowshipping, and worshiping. The teacher also works with the department director to identify training needs of parents of preschoolers for discipleship development.

B.   *Outreach–Evangelism Leader:* The outreach–evangelism leader is responsible for leading in the planning, conducting, and evaluating of the inreach, home-reach and outreach activities of the class/department. The outreach-evangelism leader may also serve as a teacher, a substitute teacher, or as the department/class director.

Figure 7.21

THE SUNDAY SCHOOL STANDARD

A Guide to Basic Sunday School Work

I. Outreach and Growth

___ 1. The Sunday school has an outreach director and someone has been designated to direct outreach in each class and department.

___ 2. The Sunday school maintains and uses up-to-date prospect information.

___ 3. There is a planned program of Sunday school visitation, and each class and department participates.

___ 4. The school sets and works toward an annual enrollment goal.

___ 5. The school works to enroll all resident church members and all prospects in Sunday school.

II. Bible Study

___ 1. The Bible is used as the textbook of the school.

___ 2. Age-graded Bible study materials are provided for the members and teachers.

___ 3. The school provides weekly a minimum of one hour of Bible study for each age group.

___ 4. The school provides annually at least one special Bible study opportunity for members and prospects at times other than Sunday morning (such as January Bible study, VBS, weektime Bible study).

III. Evangelism

___ 1. The school discovers and enrolls unsaved persons in Bible study.

_____ 2. Specific action is taken to involve workers and members in sharing Christ with unsaved Sunday school members and prospects.

_____ 3. The school has participated in at least one witness-training project.

_____ 4. The school actively participates in other evangelistic efforts of the church.

IV. Member Involvement

_____ 1. Each class or department carries out a systematic plan for ministering to members and prospects.

_____ 2. An average of 70 percent of the members present attended a morning worship experience or extended session during the month preceding application.

_____ 3. Members have been made aware of the church's stewardship and mission program.

_____ 4. Each class and department provides its members a plan for daily personal and/or family Bible study and prayer.

_____ 5. Each class/department has conducted at least one fellowship project.

V. Organization

_____ 1. The school is organized by age or school grade and the organization is maintained by annual promotion.

_____ 2. The school seeks to provide departments and classes based on annual enrollment and prospect possibilities.

_____ 3. The church elects all teachers and officers and receives regular reports from the school.

_____ 4. The school maintains and uses a record system that records enrollment, attendance, and other pupil information.

VI. Learning Environment

_____ 1. The Sunday school director led the Sunday school council in studying available space and making adjustments where needed.

_____ 2. The Sunday school director and leaders of departments and classes studied furnishings and equipment and made recommendations to the church.

_____ 3. Department and class workers examined and evaluated meeting areas and storage areas and disposed of unusable materials.

___ 4. The church budget includes funds for Sunday school materials and supplies.

VII. Planning

___ 1. The church provides a weekly or monthly general and age-group planning meeting for all the Sunday school workers.

___ 2. General officers and age-group workers are organized and functioning as the Sunday school council.

___ 3. The Sunday school council conducted an annual meeting to plan and evaluate the work of the Sunday school, using the *Sunday School Plan Book* or *The Standard* as a guide.

VIII. Leadership Development

___ 1. Workers are personally enlisted and are elected by the church.

___ 2. Each worker has received a written statement of duties.

___ 3. At least one-half of the Sunday school workers have received credit for one Sunday school study course book related to their area of work.

___ 4. At least one Sunday school training course of five hours or more has been promoted by the church.

___ 5. Each general officer, including the pastor, holds one or more training awards in general Sunday school.

Figure 7.22

Directory of Leaders

Sunday School Council

Position	Name	Address	Phone
Director			
Assistant Director			
Outreach-Evangelism Director			
Director of Teaching Improvement and Training			
Bus Ministry Director			
VBS Director			
Secretary			
Pastor			
Minister of Education			
Age-Group Representatives:			

Division/Department/Class Leadership Team

Position	Name	Address	Phone

Figure 7.23

_____ Council Roster

	Position	Name	Address	Phone
General Officers	Director			
	Assistant Director			
	Secretary			
Staff	Pastor			
	Minister of Education			
Departments and Department/Division Directors				

Figure 7.24

SUNDAY SCHOOL COUNCIL MEETING
(OR DEPARTMENT PLANNING MEETING)

Date of Meeting:_____   Focus of Meeting:_____

PREPARING FOR THE MEETING   ### PERSON RESPONSIBLE

1. Plan, prepare, and mail a copy   Sunday school director/
   of the agenda to all council   Minister of education
   members one week prior
   to the meeting.

2. Contact every council member.   General secretary

SUGGESTED AGENDA

1. *A Time for Inspiration*   _____

   Devotional

   Pray for _____

   _____

2. *A Time for Information*   _____

   Review pertinent articles in
   Sunday school leadership materials.

3. *A Time for Evaluation*   _____

   Discuss events and activities
   that have been conducted.
   Consider how they could be
   improved or whether they
   should be repeated.

   _____

   _____

   _____

4. *A Time for Communication*   _____

   Secure progress reports
   on current activities.

   • Church calendar

   • Age-group concerns

   • Worker training

SUNDAY SCHOOL COUNCIL MEETING (Continued)
(OR DEPARTMENT PLANNING MEETING)

PREPARING FOR THE MEETING   **PERSON RESPONSIBLE**

SUGGESTED AGENDA (Continued)

- Other _____

  _____

  _____

5. *A Time for Preparation*   _____

   Schedule, plan and assign
   responsibilities for upcoming
   projects and/or emphases.
   - Outreach activity
   - Quarterly training event

     _____

     _____

AFTER THE MEETING

1. Prepare a summary of the   General secretary
   meeting and mail to absentees.

2. Follow up on all assignments.   Sunday school director/
                                          all council members

Figure 7.25

DIVISION ORGANIZATION GUIDELINES

Preschool Division Organization		
Preschool Possibilities	**Enrollment Guidelines**	**Ideal Provisions**
Cradle Roll—Babies (birth through 1 year).*	1 department for each 50 members.	1 visitor-teacher for each 6 homes.
Birth through 5 years—where projected enrollment is less than 8.	One department *only* if the church cannot provide leadership and space for more.	At least two departments (birth through 2 years; 3 through 5 years) if the ages are distributed widely across the age range.
Babies (birth through 1 year).*	1 department for each 12 members.	Infants, creepers, and toddlers separate if enrollment justifies.
2- or 3-year olds.	1 department for each 20 members.	Separate departments for 2- and 3-year-olds if enrollment justifies.
4- and 5-year-olds.	1 department for each 25 members.	Separate departments for 4- and 5-year-olds if enrollment justifies.
*New babies born into the homes of members or prospects are considered prospects for Cradle Roll and Preschool Departments.		
Children's Possibilities	**Enrollment Guidelines**	**Ideal Provisions**
Children (6–11 years or grades 1–6)—where projected enrollment is less than 10.	One department *only* if church cannot provide leadership and space for two.	Two departments (ages 6–8 and 9–11) if the ages are distributed widely across the age range.
Children (6–11 years or grades 1–6) where projected enrollment is more than 10.	One department for each 30 enrolled (including workers).	Two departments (ages 6–8 and 9–11) if enrollment justifies or three departments ages 6–7, 8–9, and 10–11) if enrollment justifies. Provide a separate department for each year (or grade) if enrollment justifies. Larger churches will need more than one department for each year or grade.

DIVISION ORGANIZATION GUIDELINES (CONTINUED)

Youth Division Organization		
Youth Possibilities	**Enrollment Guidelines**	**Ideal Provisions**
Youth 12–17 years (or grades 7–12) where the projected enrollment is less than 15.	One class *only* if leadership and space are available for only one class.	A class for boys and class for girls or class for boys and girls 12–14 and class for boys and girls 15–17.
Youth 12–17 years (or grades 7–12) where projected enrollment is 15 and above.	A department for each 2 to 6 (and not more than 8) classes; maximum enrollment of department not to exceed 50 for younger youth and 60 for older youth.	At least two departments in the division if at all feasible in light of projected enrollment.
	Maximum enrollment for classes: 10 for younger youth and 15 for older youth.	
Adult Division Organization		
Adult Possibilities	**Enrollment Guidelines**	**Ideal Provisions**
Young Adults (18–29).	40 to 125 in departments; 15 to 25 in classes.	Separate provision for single, married, and college whenever possible. Also separate provision for older and younger ages in age span.
Adults 30–55 or 60.	40 to 125 in departments; 15 to 25 in classes.	Wherever possible, the age span for a department should not exceed ten years, and the age range for a class should not exceed five years.
Senior Adults (56 to 61 up).	40 to 125 in departments; 15 to 25 in classes.	Wherever possible, the age span for a department should not exceed ten years, and the age range for a class should not exceed five years.
Adults who work on Sunday—week-time departments and / or classes.	25 in classes.	Department (designated as Adult III, IV, etc.) if enrollment justifies. If not, relate class organizationally to an existing Adult department.

DIVISION ORGANIZATION GUIDELINES (CONTINUED)

Adults who are physically unable to attend—*Homebound Department.**	8 members for each visiting teacher.	Fewer than 8 members for each visiting teacher.
Adults away from home temporarily—*Adult Away Department.**	4 members for each correspondent.	
*As an alternate approach for churches that cannot provide Homebound and Adult Away Departments, classes may assume responsibility for teaching and ministry.		

Figure 7.26

ORGANIZATION PLANSHEET FOR SMALLER SUNDAY SCHOOLS

Age Division	Enrollment			Number of Units			Number of Workers	
	1	2	3	4	5	6		
	Now	Goal for___	Now	Needed to Grow	Now	Needed to Grow	Now	Needed to Grow
Preschool (birth through age 5)								
Children's (ages 6–11 or grades 1–6)								
Youth (ages 12–17 or grades 7–12)								
Adult (ages 18–up)								
Total								

Guide to Use of Chart

Column 1: Record the number of *pupils* in each age division and the total. Notice that workers will show up in column 5.

Column 2: Write in your goals for the coming year or whatever date is appropriate. They should take into account the number of prospects available. Again, these goals are stated in terms of *pupils*.

Column 3: List the present number of classes and departments in each age division and the total.

Column 4: Indicate the number of units you need if you expect to grow. Remember that an additional unit is needed to start with three pupils and one worker. An adult class may have only five or six members.

Column 5: Show the present number of workers in each age division and the total.

Column 6: Enter the total number of workers you will need after you form the new units.

Figure 7.27

Grouping Patterns for Small Sunday Schools

	Pattern 1		Pattern 2	
Preschool Division	B–1 1 2 3 4 5	May have all these in one teaching unit (department)	B–1 1 2 3 4 5	May have two teaching units for all preschoolers
Children's Division	6 (Gr.1) 7 (Gr. 2) 8 (Gr. 3) 9 (Gr. 4) 10 (Gr. 5) 11 (Gr. 6)	May have all these in one teaching unit (department)	6 7 8 9 10 11	May have two teaching units for children's departments
Youth Division	12 (Gr. 7) 13 (Gr. 8) 14 (Gr. 9) 15 (Gr. 10) 16 (Gr. 11) 17 (Gr. 12)	May have all these in one class	12 13 14 15 16 17	May have one youth department with two classes
Adult Division	18 (high school graduate and up)	May have only one class for adults	18 (high school graduate and up)	May have one adult department with two or more classes
Pattern 1 will usually accommodate a Sunday school with up to forty to fifty enrollment. Pattern 2 may be used in one or two of the age divisions, while Pattern 1 is used in other divisions.				

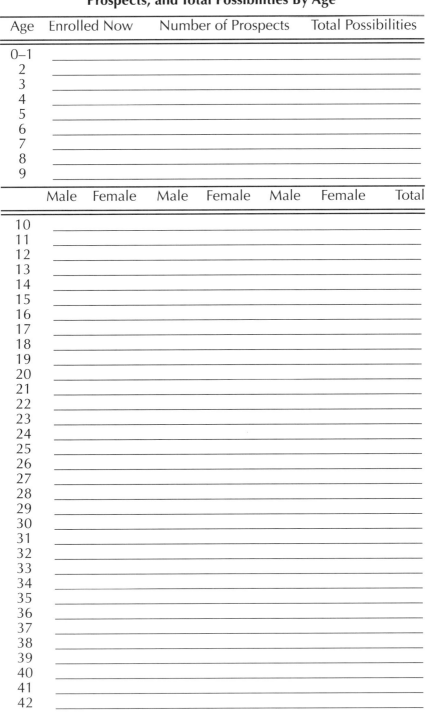

Figure 7.28
Work Sheet for Listing Enrollment,
Prospects, and Total Possibilities By Age

Age	Enrolled Now		Number of Prospects		Total Possibilities		
0–1							
2							
3							
4							
5							
6							
7							
8							
9							
	Male	Female	Male	Female	Male	Female	Total
10							
11							
12							
13							
14							
15							
16							
17							
18							
19							
20							
21							
22							
23							
24							
25							
26							
27							
28							
29							
30							
31							
32							
33							
34							
35							
36							
37							
38							
39							
40							
41							
42							

Age	Enrolled Now	Number of Prospects	Total Possibilities
43			
44			
45			
46			
47			
48			
49			
50			
51			
52			
53			
54			
55			
56			
57			
58			
59			
60			
61			
62			
63			
64			
65			
66			
67			
68			
69			
70			
71			
72			
73			
74			
75			
76			
77			
78			
79			
80			
81			
82			
83			
84			
85–up			

Figure 7.29
Sunday School Grouping-Grading Plan[a]

Division Titles	Divisional Grouping Patterns			
	I.	II.	III.	IV.
Preschool Division	Birth–1 1 2 3 4 5	B–1 1 2 3 4 5	B–1 1 2 3 4 5	B–1 1 2 3 4 5
Children's Division	6 (Grade 1) 7 (Grade 2) 8 (Grade 3) 9 (Grade 4) 10 (Grade 5) 11 (Grade 6)	6 7 8 9 10 11	6 7 8 9 10 11	6 7 8 9 10 11
Youth Division	12 (Grade 7) 13 (Grade 8) 14 (Grade 9) 15 (Grade 10) 16 (Grade 11) 17 (Grade 12)	12 13 14 15 16 17	12 13 14 15 16 17	12 13 14 15 16 17
Adult Division	18 (high school graduation and up)	18 (or high school graduation) Young Adult 34 35–64 (or retirement) Adult 65 Senior Adult	18 (or high school graduation) Young Adult 1, 2 34 35 Adult 1, 2 64 (or retirement) 65 (or retirement) Senior Adult 1, 2	18 (or high school graduation) Young Adult 1, 2, 3, 4 34 35 Adult 1, 2, 3, 4 64 (or retirement) 65 (or retirement) Senior Adult 1, 2, 3, 4

a. The size of your Sunday school is a factor in your use of the four patterns shown. The smallest Sunday school would begin to use column one with all members of one age group in one unit. The Sunday school next in size would probably use pattern two with one age group divided into two units. (Example: In pattern two, children would be in two units instead of one because of the number enrolled.) Larger Sunday schools would select the pattern for each age group that provides for the enrollment.

Figure 7.30

WORKERS NEEDED WORK SHEET

GENERAL OFFICERS
Sunday school director _____

Assistant director_____

Outreach director _____

Secretary _____

CRADLE ROLL DEPARTMENT*
Director _____

Visitor-teachers _____

_____

PRESCHOOL DEPARTMENT* (BABY-AGE___)
Director _____

Outreach leader _____

Teachers _____

_____

PRESCHOOL DEPARTMENT * (AGES___)
Director _____

Outreach leader _____

Teachers _____

_____

PRESCHOOL DEPARTMENT* (AGES___)
Director _____

Outreach leader _____

Teachers_____

CHILDREN'S DEPARTMENT* (AGES___)
Director _____

Outreach leader _____

Teachers _____

_____

CHILDREN'S DEPARTMENT* (AGES___)
Director _____

Outreach leader _____

Teachers _____

_____

YOUTH DEPARTMENT* (AGES___)

Director _____

Outreach leader _____

Teachers _____

_____

YOUTH DEPARTMENT* (AGES___)

Director _____

Outreach leader _____

Teachers _____

_____

ADULT DEPARTMENT* (AGES___)

Director _____

Outreach leader _____

Secretary_____

Teachers _____

_____

ADULT DEPARTMENT* (AGES___)

Director _____

Outreach leader _____

Secretary_____

Teachers _____

_____

*Note: Fill in ages as appropriate for your organization.

Figure 7.31

WORKERS' MEETINGS

PLAN 1

(for small Sunday schools)

GENERAL PERIOD (all workers together)   15 minutes

- Administering School Concerns
- Planning for   . . . Reaching
                  . . . Witnessing
                  . . . Ministering
- Praying Together

PLANNING PERIOD   45 minutes

- All workers together for directed planning of age-group units and lessons (about 30 minutes).
- Special age-group preparation time to prepare room or area of building for Sunday's session (about 10 minutes).

PLAN 2

GENERAL PERIOD

(all workers together)   10 minutes

DEPARTMENT PERIOD   50 minutes

Administering Department Concerns

- Planning for   . . . Reaching
                  . . . Witnessing
                  . . . Ministering
- Planning for Teaching-Learning
- Praying Together

OUR WORKERS MEETING SCHEDULE

Agenda/Activities   Time   Location(s)

(List items on your schedule: general period, department/division periods, teaching-learning period, supper)

_____	_____	_____
_____	_____	_____
_____	_____	_____

See the suggested plan 1 and plan 2 for a possible agenda/schedule for your Sunday school. Write in the plan that you will be following for your meetings.

Figure 7.32
Sunday School Budget Planning Worksheet

LITERATURE

Formula for determining cost:

Cost of last literature order	÷ Current enrollment	+ Anticipated Inflation	=	Cost per person enrolled

Enrollment Goal:

First quarter	x	Cost per person	=	Total cost per quarter
Second quarter	x	Cost per person	=	Total cost per quarter
Third quarter	x	Cost per person	=	Total cost per quarter
Fourth quarter	x	Cost per person	=	Total cost per quarter
				Cost for year

As a result of our worker training program, we anticipate funds needed for additional teaching aids, such as kits, cassette tapes, teaching pictures and leadership magazines:

	TOTAL Literature budget requested	$

SUPPLIES (examples: record books and forms, paper, art materials, refreshments, laundry)

Preschool   _____

Children's   _____

Youth   _____

Adult   _____

Special Education   _____

General Officers

	TOTAL Supplies budget requested	$

FURNISHINGS AND EQUIPMENT (examples: chalkboards, pictures rails, cabinets)

Preschool   _____

Children's   _____

Youth   _____

Adult   _____

Special Education   _____

General Officers

	TOTAL Equipment budget requested	$

MEDIA RESOURCES (examples: filmstrips, videos, books, maps)

Preschool   _____

Children's   _____

Youth   _____

Adult   _____

Special Education   _____

General Officers

	TOTAL Resources budget requested	$

NEW UNITS

New Space (footage   )   _____

Remodeling of Existing Space
(footage   )   _____

Sunday School Budget Planning Worksheet (Continued)

Portable Walls

TOTAL New Units budget requested	$

WINTER BIBLE STUDY

Books

Refreshments

Guest teachers (expenses and gifts)

Other expense

TOTAL Winter Bible Study budget requested	$

VACATION BIBLE SCHOOL

Books

Supplies

Refreshments

Backyard Bible Clubs

Mission Vacation Bible School

Other VBS expense

TOTAL VBS budget requested	$

SUNDAY SCHOOL COUNCIL ANNUAL PLANNING

Lodging, Meals

Transportation

Materials

TOTAL Annual Planning budget requested	$

PREPARATION WEEK

Books

Kit and other materials

Refreshments

TOTAL Preparation Week budget requested	$

WORKER TRAINING

Event, Date

Book

  Books

  Publicity

  Guest teachers (expense and gift)

Event, Date

Book

  Books

  Publicity

  Guest teachers (expense and gift)

Glorieta, Ridgecrest, Green Lake, or state assembly

  Transportation

  Lodging, meals

  Materials

TOTAL Worker Training budget requested	$

Sunday School Budget Planning Worksheet (Continued)

OUTREACH-EVANGELISM PLANNING

Outreach events and supplies

Promotional materials, postage

Outreach meals, fellowship
refreshments

TOTAL Outreach-Evangelism Planning budget requested	$

OTHER NEEDS

Worker appreciation
or training banquet

Fellowships

Other

TOTAL Other Needs budget requested	$
GRAND TOTAL SUNDAY SCHOOL BUDGET REQUESTED	$

Figure 7.33

SUNDAY SCHOOL GROWTH SPIRAL

One effective plan for increasing enrollment is the Growth Spiral. (See figure 7.34.) The Growth Spiral is not a project, but a structure for planning for ongoing Sunday school enrollment. You can plan for twelve months or twenty-four months, or even longer if you wish. It is set up to be planned on a quarterly basis so that as you set goals for increasing enrollment, you can see on the spiral what you need to do to reach that goal in terms of starting new classes and departments, enlisting and training new workers, finding space, and doing visitation. Many churches have found that the spiral provides an excellent framework for growing a Sunday school.

1. You begin at the inside of the Growth Spiral and work outward.

2. On the inside set of squares record the present figures for your Sunday school.

   a. Under date, record the date today.

   b. Under the goal, write in your present Sunday school enrollment. (This figure should be the total number of persons on the roll, not the number attending each week.)

   c. Units means the total number of adult and youth classes plus children's and preschool departments. Put in the total number of teaching units you now have.

d. Beside workers, write in the total number of workers (teachers plus general officers).

e. "Space" means the number of places available for classes/departments to meet. Record your present total.

f. Under "contacts," record the average number of contacts made per week. Contacts include visits, phone calls, letters, cards, and casual contacts, inviting absentees or prospects to Sunday school.

g. Under "visitors," write in the average number of persons from your Sunday school who do personal visitation each week to reach people for Sunday school.

h. Beside "S.S. Att.," place your Sunday school average attendance for the past quarter.

i. Beside "W. S. Att.," record your worship service average attendance for the past quarter.

j. "Offerings" means the average weekly total of tithes and offerings through the Sunday school for the past quarter.

k. Beside "baptisms," write in the total number of persons baptized by your church during the last quarter.

3. Now look back at the "Date/Goal" column. This spiral is designed to help you set growth goals for twelve months.

a. At the very top of the column, write in what the date will be and your goal for the growth of your Sunday school at the end of twelve months.

b. Subtract your present enrollment from your goal. Divide the difference by four and you get quarterly enrollment goals.

c. You are now ready to fill in both of the Date/Goal columns. Under "date," write in from the bottom up the dates of the first day of each quarter. Under "goal" write in the quarterly enrollment goal totals.

4. You have set some challenging enrollment goals. The rest of the work suggested on the Growth Spiral serves to help you reach and maintain your enrollment. One essential action will be to create new classes and departments. If you divide your present enrollment by the number of units (classes and departments), you will discover the ratio of units to pupils. To be in a position to grow, that ratio needs to be 1 to 16 or less. To find out how many units you will need to reach your enrollment goal, divide your enrollment goal by 16 and enter the result for each quarter.

5. Divide the present number of workers into your enrollment and you will get your ratio of workers to enrollment. For your Sunday school to grow, that ratio needs to be 1 to 8 or less. To find out how many workers you will need to reach your enrollment goal, divide that number by 8 and record it in the last block. Divide that number by 8 and you learn how many new workers you will need each quarter.

    By now you can see the planning value of the Growth Spiral. Since you know you will need, for example, four new workers in six months, you can begin enlisting and training them now. Enlist and train at least one extra worker to compensate for drop-outs and persons moving away.

6. You will need a place for each unit to meet. If you see that in a year or eighteen months, your units will exceed available space, you can begin now to plan for that space. It may mean rearranging classes and departments; remodeling your building; or finding adjacent space like homes, vacant buildings, or movable units. More space may mean new construction. You can begin now to plan for your future needs.

7. The total number of contacts per week to members and prospects needs to equal or exceed one half of your enrollment.

8. In order to have consistent growth, the number of visitors (persons doing visitation) must be at least equal to the number of units. That is a minimum number.

9. Calculate the percentage of your enrollment now attending Sunday school. If, for example, your average attendance is fifty percent of your enrollment, you can expect that percentage to remain about the same as your enrollment increases. This assumes that you start the new units, add workers, provide space, make the contacts, and enlist persons for visitation.

10. Your worship attendance also should continue to increase as your Sunday school attendance increases.

11. Offerings usually increase along with attendance, although there often is some lag time before new members grow to the giving level of others.

12. Often a church experiences a much more rapid increase in the number of baptisms as the Sunday school starts to grow, since a large proportion of the new enrollees usually are not Christians. One church that enjoyed a net gain of 50 percent in enrollment in a year had a gain of over 100 percent in baptisms.

Figure 7.34

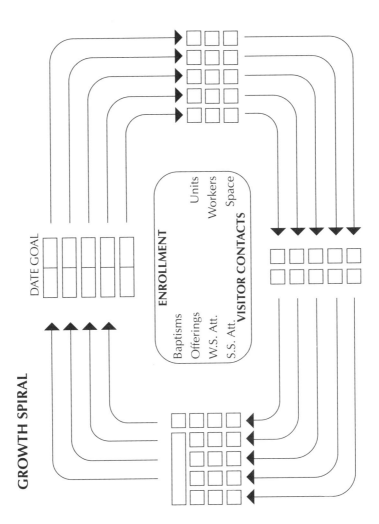

GROWTH SPIRAL

DATE GOAL

ENROLLMENT

Baptisms
Offerings
W.S. Att.
S.S. Att.

Units
Workers
Space

VISITOR CONTACTS

Figure 7.35
Determining Space in Age-Division Rooms

Organization and Space Needs for Division Grouping and Grading

Division	Age	For Each Department			For Each Class			Suggested Floor Space Per Person — Department		Assembly	Classroom	
		Maximum Enrollment	Average Attendance[a]	Capacity of Space[b]	Max. Enrol.	Aver. Attend.[a]	Cap. of Space[b]	Min.[c]	Recommended	Recommended	Min.[c]	Recommended
Preschool	B-1	12	5-8	7-10								
	2-3	20	9-13	12-16	NA			20 sq. ft.		25+	None	None
	4-5	25	11-16	15-20								
Children	6-8	30	14-20	18-24	NA			20 sq. ft.		25+	None	None
	9-11[d]											
Youth	12-14	50	23-33	30-40	10	5-7	6-8	8 sq. ft.		10		
	15-17	60	27-39	36-48	15	8-10	9-12				10 sq. ft.	12
Adult	18 up	125	56-81	75-100	25	12-16	15-20	8 sq. ft.		10	8 sq. ft.	12

Space is provided for each person expected to be in the rooms of the building. Determining the number for which to plan this space is a result of a careful analysis of projected enrollment, organization, and attendance. In determining the total number of square feet of educational space required, the church should add to the floor space mentioned above enough space for offices, corridors, stairways, rest rooms, storage, service space, and other accessory areas. This will require a total square footage from 35 square feet to 45 square feet per person in the educational building. Many churches provide even more space.

[a] Average attendance in churches ranges from 45% to 65% of enrollment.

[b] Capacity space to provide is figured at 60% to 80% of enrollment to be adequate for high expected attendance. Percentage to be used should be determined by the individual church's record of enrollment and attendance.

[c] Minimum square footage may sometimes be necessary in smaller churches and mission buildings.

[d] Existing assemblies with classrooms may be used by departments in the Children's Division. Provide additional tables, chairs, and chalkboards as needed.
Church Architecture Department, The Sunday School Board of the Southern Baptist Convention, Nashville, Tennessee.

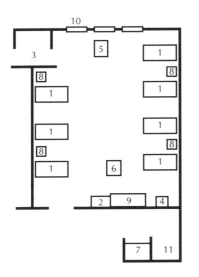

Department for Babies and Creepers

1. Beds (hospital cribs, 27 by 42 inches)
2. Diaper bag shelf
3. Diaper rinsing provision (with flush bowl)
4. Record player
5. Rocker (adult)
6. Safety chair
7. Sink-refrigerator combination (28 inches wide, 30 inches long, 40 inches high)
8. Tables (utility)
9. Wall supply cabinet (mounted 50 inches from floor)
10. Windows (clear glass; sills 22 to 24 inches from floor)
11. Adult toilet

   Note: In the Creeper Department it will be desirable to have fewer beds and substitute a playpen.

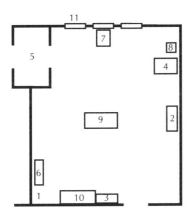

Department for Toddlers

1. Area for cardboard blocks
2. Bookrack with slanting shelves (11 inches deep, 28 inches long, 27 inches high)
3. Diaper bag shelf
4. Doll bed (16 inches wide, 28 inches long, board supporting mattress, 8 inches from floor
5. Adjoining toilet (child-size fixtures)
6. Open shelves with closed back (26 inches high, 30 inches long, 12 inches deep)
7. Record player
8. Rocker (child size)
9. Rocking boat and steps
10. Wall supply cabinets (mounted 50 inches from floor)
11. Windows (sills 22 to 24 inches from the floor)

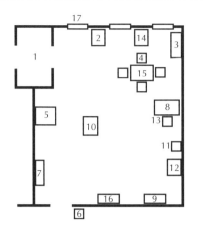

Department for Two- and Three-Year Olds

1. Adjoining toilet (child-size fixtures)
2. Bookrack with slanting shelves (11 inches deep, 28 inches long, 27 inches high)
3. Cabinet sink (32 inches high, 34 inches wide, 18 inches deep, 24 inches from floor to top of work surface)
4. Chairs (seat is 10 inches high)
5. Clothes drying rack (for wet paintings)
6. Coatrack (for adults, outside room)
7. Coatrack (for children; 40 inches high, 40 inches wide, 14 inches deep)
8. Doll bed (16 inches wide, 28 inches long, board supporting mattress 8 inches from floor)
9. Open shelves with closed back (26 inches high, 30 inches long, 12 inches deep)
10. Painting easel (45 inches high with 25-by-20-inch painting surface)
11. Puzzle rack
12. Record player
13. Rocker (child size)
14. Stove (24 inches high, 18 inches wide, 12 inches deep)
15. Table (24 inches wide, 36 inches long, 20 inches from floor)
16. Wall supply cabinet (mounted 50 inches from floor)
17. Windows (sills 22 to 24 inches from floor)

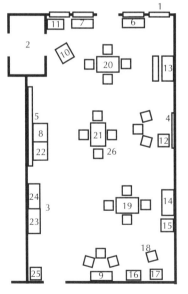

Department for Four- and Five-Year Olds

1. Windows (clear glass; sills 22 to 24 inches from the floor); draperies and blinds not necessary, unless needed to prevent glare
2. Rest room may serve two adjoining departments for four- and five-year-olds; two commodes 10 inches high; two lavatories, faucets 24 inches from floor; desirable to have drinking fountain attachment on one faucet
3. Wall supply cabinet units hung on wall side by side (bottom 50 inches from floor; picture file desk and rack for children's wraps under supply cabinet)
4. Picture rail (about 6 feet long, near middle of longest unbroken wall)
5. Tackboard (not as essential as some other items; beginning 20 inches from floor; 8 to 12 feet long; 18 to 24 inches wide; on wall other than front wall)
6. Block shelves (30 inches wide, 26 inches high, 12 inches deep)
7. Nature shelves
8. Art shelves

9. Bookrack (with slanting shelves, 14 inches deep, 33 inches high, 36 inches wide)
10. Painting easel (45 inches overall height, 25 inches wide, painting surface 20 by 25 inches)
11. Small clothes drying rack (for drying paintings)
12. Record player (three-speed with turntable visible to children and easily operated by them) or table cabinet (for record player and recordings; 24 inches long, 18 inches wide, 20 inches high)
13. Piano (studio type, approximately 44 inches high)
14. Cabinet-sink (34 inches wide, 24 inches to working surface, 18 inches deep, 32 inches overall height)
15. Stove (18 inches wide, 24 inches high, 12 inches deep)
16. Doll bed (16 inches wide, 28 inches long, 16 inches high, board supporting mattress 8 inches from floor)
17. Chest of drawers (for doll clothes and dress-up clothes, 18 inches wide, 12 inches deep, 24 inches high)
18. Child's rocking chair (seat is 12 inches from floor)
19. Table for home living (24 by 36 inches)
20. Art table (30 by 48 inches)
21. Puzzle table (24 by 36 inches)
22. Puzzle rack (9 inches wide, 12 inches long, 9 inches high)
23. Picture file desk (for teaching pictures and reports, 38 inches long, 22 inches wide, 30 inches high)
24. Rack for children's wraps (40 inches wide, 40 inches high, 14 inches deep)
25. Rack for adult wraps (18 inches wide, 60 inches high, 14 inches deep)
26. Chairs (wooden; formfitting, two horizontal back slats; seat 10 inches high for four-year-olds; 12 inches high for five-year-olds or for fours and fives together; one chair for each child and each worker; same chairs used by activities and group time)

*All tables are ten inches higher than the seats of the chairs; plastic tops are desirable.

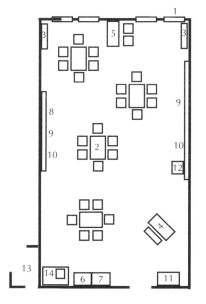

Department for Children

1. Chairs (one chair per child for largest organization using the room; seats are 12 inches high for ages 6 and 7; 14 inches high for ages 8 and 9; 16 inches high for ages 10 and 11)
2. Tables (waterproof tops; 36 by 54 inches or 30 by 48 inches; height is 10 inches above chair seat height; one table for every six children)
3. Two or three portable shelves with closed backs (42 to 46 inches high, 3 feet wide, 4 feet long, 12 inches deep, 12 to 14 inches between shelves)
4. Piano (studio size)
5. Bookrack (slanted shelves on one side and flat shelves on other side; 42 to 46 inches high, 2 1/2 feet wide, 3 1/2 feet long)

6. Coatracks (portable; 4 feet, 4 inches high for children; 5 feet, 8 inches high for adults)
7. Storage cabinets (18 inches deep; hung on wall; adequate size for material and for separate storage needed by each organization using the room)
8, 9, 10. Combination chalkboard, tackboard, and picture rail may be permanently installed so as to make the surface tilt with the top against the wall and the bottom about six inches from the wall; (lengths for younger ages would be minimum of 6 feet of chalkboard and 18 feet of tackboard, both 30 inches high and mounted with the bottom 28 inches above floor; lengths for older ages would be a minimum of 8 feet of chalkboard and 24 feet of tackboard, both 30 inches high and mounted 28 inches above the floor)
11. Cabinet (for pictures—12 by 18 inches; for posters—24 by 36 inches)
12. Record player (3- or 4-speed; record storage cabinet 26 inches high, 24 inches wide, 14 inches deep)
13. Rest rooms nearby on hall for all children
14. Sink

Department for Youth or Adults
1. Movable chairs (stacking or folding; seats are 18 inches from floor)
2. Small table (or lectern) for use by director
3. Table for secretary or outreach leader
4. Piano (studio size)
5. Movable rack for coats and hats
6. Chairs with tablet arms (folding arms recommended)
7. Small table and/or tablet-arm chair for teacher
8. Folding tables (30 by 72 inches; for class members to sit around)
9. Movable chalkboard (freestanding)
10. Chalkboard-tackboard (fixed to wall)
11. Tackboard (fixed to wall)
12. Shelves (open and adjustable; for Bible study aids, books, etc.)
13. Easel
14. Wastebasket

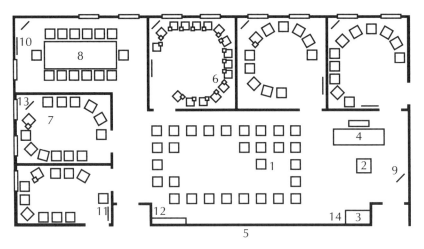

Figure 7.36

Discipleship Training Organization

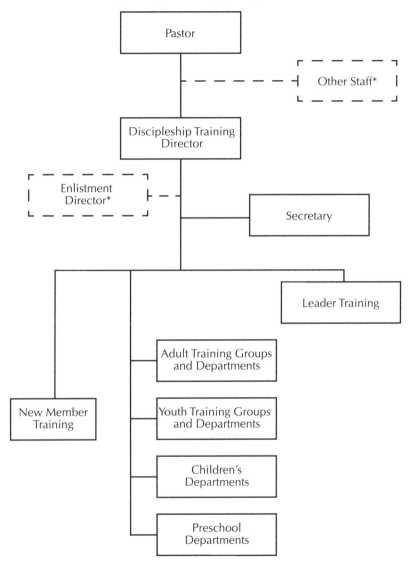

*Optional Leaders

Figure 7.37

New Member Training Organization

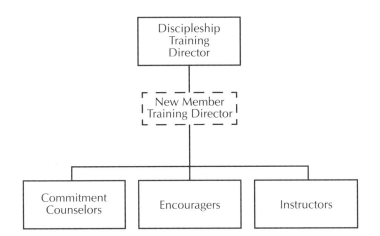

From Commitment to Responsible Church Membership

Stage 1: Counseling	Stage 2: Training in Christian Basics	Stage 3: Training in Church Membership

Types of Commitment
• Salvation
• Baptism
• Church Membership
• Reaffirmation
• Commitment of Life
• Toward Christian Maturity
	Choose an Approach
	• Individual Study
	• Encourager Plan
	• One-to-One Plan
	• Group Study
	• Combination Plan
		Choose an Approach
		• Four-Session Study
		  —Group Study
		  —Individual Study
		• Thirteen-Session Study
		  —Group Study

Figure 7.38
Training Group Organization Chart

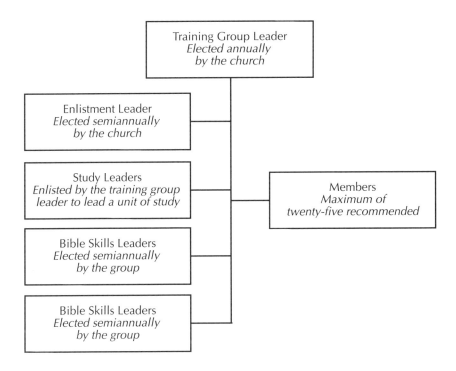

Training Group Leader
*Elected annually
by the church*

Enlistment Leader
*Elected semiannually
by the church*

Study Leaders
*Enlisted by the training group
leader to lead a unit of study*

Members
*Maximum of
twenty-five recommended*

Bible Skills Leaders
*Elected semiannually
by the group*

Bible Skills Leaders
*Elected semiannually
by the group*

Figure 7.39
Leader Training Project Plan Sheet

Priority Rating _____

Date Prepared _____

Training Event: _____

Objective: _____

Number of persons needing this training

(Minimum_____   Maximum_____)

Schedule: _____

Meeting place: _____

Cost: _____

ENLISTMENT PLANS

Who should participate?   Leaders needed

_____   _____

_____   _____

Program leaders to help with enlistment: Materials for trainees:

_____   _____

_____   _____

_____   _____

Other assignments: Supplies:

_____   _____

_____   Equipment:

_____   _____

_____   Other special concerns:

_____   _____

_____   _____

Figure 7.40

LEADER TRAINING EVENT PLAN SHEET

Title of course: _____

Names of persons who need this training (attach list of names, if necessary): _____

_____

_____

Training plan: ____ Introduction   ____ Basic   ____ Advanced

____ Specialized   ____ In-depth

Training approach: ____ Group Training ____ One-to-one Training

____ Individual Study ____ On-the-job Training

Date to begin: _____   Date to Conclude: _____

Day of the week:_____   Time: _____

Schedule approved: _____   Assigned Space: _____

Person enlisted to train leaders: _____

Person assigned to enlist participants: _____

Study resources needed: Date ordered:

_____   _____

_____   _____

_____   _____

Equipment and supplies needed: Date requested:

_____   _____

_____   _____

_____   _____

Costs for training: _____

Amount from church budget: _____ From participants: _____

Promotion/enlistment activities: Date:

_____   _____

_____   _____

_____   _____

Date of recognition for completion of training: _____

Figure 7.41

PROJECT PLANSHEET

Unit title _____

Activity _____

Persons helping   _____   _____

                     _____   _____

                     _____   _____

                     _____   _____

Questions to be answered _____

_____

_____

_____

_____

_____

Possible sources of information _____

_____

_____

_____

_____

_____

Jobs to be done   Person responsible

_____   _____

_____   _____

_____   _____

_____   _____

Materials needed

_____ _____ _____

_____ _____ _____

_____ _____ _____

Method of reporting_____

_____

Follow-through_____

Figure 7.42

Training Group Functions

	PLAN	CONDUCT	EVALUATE
COORDINATION (Training Group Leader)	1. Identify needs and concerns of group members. 2. Lead the group to evaluate and select resources to be studied. 3. Coordinate the planning of the total work of the group so that all functions operate in the life of the group.	1. Coordinate the work of training group officers and assist them in performing their duties. 2. Assist each member in participating in group activities and in sharing group responsibilities. 3. Lead the group to determine its organization, to elect its officers, and to assign responsibilities for the work of the group.	1. Evaluate the effectiveness of the group in terms of purpose, goals, and objectives. • How were members involved in the work of the group? • How well did other group officers plan and carry out their responsibilities? 2. Make suggestions for group involvement.
FELLOWSHIP (Enlistment Leader or Training Group Leader)	1. Lead group members in planning meaningful social and fellowship activities. 2. Encourage other group officers to plan activities that foster and reinforce openness, sharing, and mutuality among group members.	1. Create an atmosphere in which members feel "this is a good group and I am accepted." 2. Encourage members to be sensitive to one another's support needs and to minister to one another.	1. Evaluate the level of fellowship in the group. • How do members feel about the group and their place in it? • To what degree do members minister to one another? • Are group members growing in their ability to be open, accepting, and supportive of one another? 2. Make suggestions to other group leaders about how they can help foster a spirit of fellowship among group members.

Training Group Functions (Continued)

	PLAN	CONDUCT	EVALUATE
ENLISTMENT (Enlistment Leader or Training Group Leader)	1. Determine enlistment and publicity needs. 2. Maintain a list of prospective members. 3. Prepare plans and assignments for maintaining and increasing group membership.	1. Publicize the group's activities. 2. Coordinate enlistment efforts. 3. Involve group members in publicity and enlistment activities. 4. Greet visitors and new members and introduce them to the group.	1. Evaluate publicity and enlistment activities each quarter in terms of: • Average weekly attendance • Number of visitors • Number of new members • Number of members involved in publicity and enlistment activities.
STUDY (Study Leader)	1. Plan to involve members in the study of assigned units and sessions of study.	1. Lead training group study sessions.	1. Evaluate group study. • How did members respond to the subject? • How did members respond to group process? 2. Make suggestions to training group leader and other study leaders for improving group study.
APPLICATION (Study Leader)	1. Identify areas of concern about which the training group might need to study. 2. Lead in planning activities and projects through which members practice or apply what they are studying.	1. Lead members to participate in planned application activities. 2. Lead members to share ways they have used training received in group study.	1. Evaluate effectiveness of application in terms of: • Completed projects in home, church, and community • Projects now in progress.

Training Group Functions (Continued)

	PLAN	CONDUCT	EVALUATE
BIBLE SKILLS DEVELOPMENT (Bible Skills Leader or Study Leader)	1. Plan to lead group members to develop skills in using and interpreting the Bible and in using different Bible tools.	1. Lead members in Bible skills activities related to topics being studied. 2. Conduct Bible features when the group has chosen to use such features. 3. Encourage personal Bible study.	1. Evaluate Bible skills activities. • How well do members respond to Bible skills activities? 2. Are members engaging in personal Bible study?
RECORD KEEPING (Secretary)	1. Plan to use the Simplified Church Training Record System.	1. Maintain department/group records. 2. Give your group's request for curriculum materials to the person in your church responsible for ordering literature each quarter.	1. Study group/department records and share findings with the group.

Figure 7.43
Discipleship Training
Growth Potential Chart

Continuing Church Member Training		S.S. Enrollment NOW	C.T. Enrollment NOW	Potential for Growth
Division	Age			
Preschool	Birth–1			
	2			
	3			
	4			
	5			
Children	6 (Grade 1)			
	7 (Grade 2)			
	8 (Grade 3)			
	9 (Grade 4)			
	10 (Grade 5)			
	11 (Grade 6)			
Youth	12 (Grade 7)			
	13 (Grade 8)			
	14 (Grade 9)			
	15 (Grade 10)			
	16 (Grade 11)			
	17 (Grade 12)			
Adult	18–34 Young Adult			
	35–64 Adult			
	65–up Senior Adult			
General Officers				
Totals				

Notes:

_____

_____

_____

_____

_____

_____

_____

_____

_____

_____

_____

_____

_____

STOP AND DO—5

Compare your present training group and department enrollments with the saturation charts.

Units Maximum Enrollment
Adult Training Groups   25–30
Youth Training Groups   15
Children's Departments   25–30
Preschool Departments   12–16

Comparing each training unit's enrollment with the potential, what additional units do you need?_____

_____

Figure 7.44

Small Music Ministry

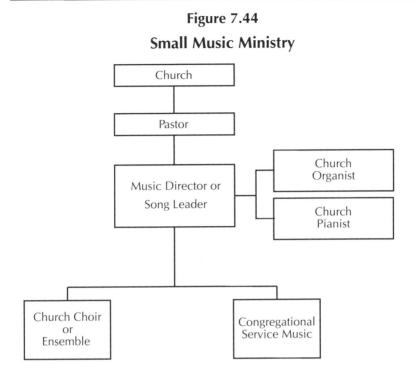

Figure 7.45

Medium-Sized Music Ministry

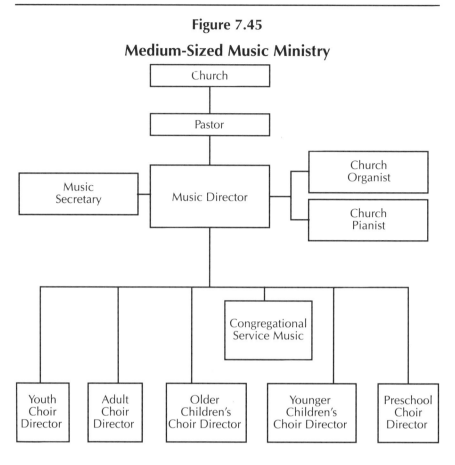

Figure 7.46

Large Music Ministry

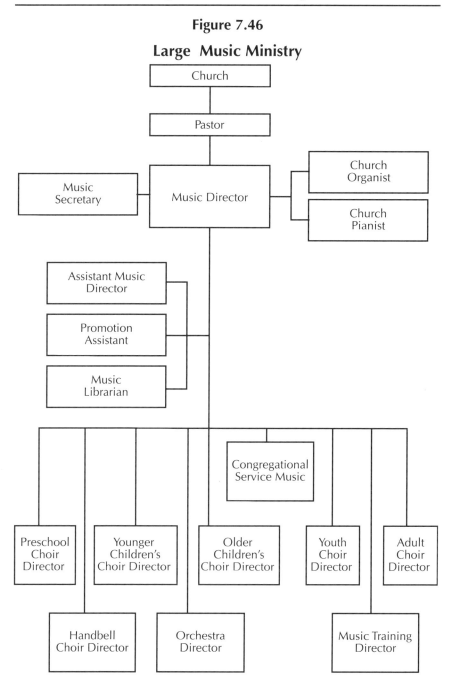

Figure 7.47
Guidelines for Organizing Preschool and Children's Choirs

Division	Age Grade	Average Attendance Range	Number of Choirs	Number of Workers Needed	Space Needed	Span	Leader Member Ratio	Space Ratio
Preschool Choir	4 years to 5 years	8–18	One Choir	2 to 3	450 sq. ft., approx. 15' x 30'	2 yrs.	1-6	25–35 sq. ft. per person
		18–24	Two Choirs	4 to 6	2 Rooms, 450 sq. ft. each	1 yr.	1-6	
		25–54	Three Choirs	6 to 9	3 Rooms, 450 sq. ft. each	6 mo.	1-6	
Children's Choir	Grades 1–6	6–12	One Choir	2 to 3	300 sq. ft., approx. 15' x 20'	6 grades	1-7	25 sq. ft. per person
		6–21	One Choir	2 to 3	450 sq. ft., approx. 15' x 30'	3 Grades	1-7	25 sq. ft. per person
Younger Children's Choir	Grades 1–3	18–42	Two Choirs	4 to 6	2 Rooms	1 1/2 Grades	1-7	
		42–54	Three Choirs	6 to 9	3 Rooms, approx. 450 sq. ft.	1 Grade	1-7	
Older Children's Choir	Grades 4–6	6–48	One Choir	2 to 6	450 sq. ft. to 1,200 sq. ft.	3 Grades	1-8	25 sq. ft. per person
		48–100	Two Choirs	6 to 13	2 Rooms, approx. 1,200 sq. ft. (30' x 40')	1 to 2 Grades	1-8	
		100–150	Three Choirs	13 to 19	3 Rooms, approx. 1,200 sq. ft. ea.	1 Grade	1-8	

Figure 7.48
Brotherhood Organization

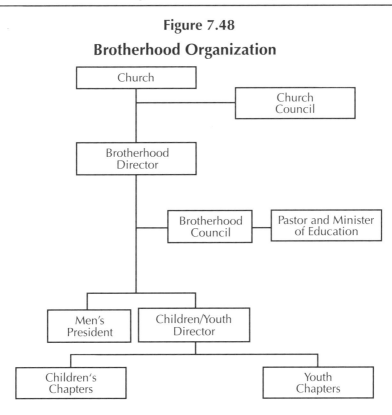

Figure 7.49

THE BROTHERHOOD DIRECTOR

Brotherhood leadership begins with the director. He is elected by the church through its nominating committee as are directors of Sunday school, Discipleship Training, and Woman's Missionary Union. He is responsible to the church for his work.

A Brotherhood director should be elected regardless of the type of work to be started, whether it would be the mission action unit, prayer unit, children's chapter, or other kinds of approaches.

The Brotherhood director is to lead in providing organization, leadership, and resources to carry out Brotherhood work.

The director:

1. Leads total Brotherhood planning, coordination, and evaluation.

2. Leads in establishing Brotherhood age-division units.

3. Serves as leader of each unit until he secures additional leadership.

4. Works with Brotherhood leadership in discovering mission needs and in discovering and channeling member gifts in ministry.

5. Leads men and boys to participate in mission learning experiences and mission activities in age-division units and church wide activities.

6. Develops a plan for training Brotherhood workers.

7. Recommends Brotherhood budget, policies, and procedures.

8. Leads in coordinating the selection of mission areas to be taught and the ordering of curriculum materials and supplies.

9. Reports the progress of Brotherhood work to the church and church council regularly, working with the Brotherhood secretary.

10. Leads in implementing special projects of the church as assigned and in helping members to understand the work of the church and denomination.

11. Works with WMU director in planning and conducting church-wide projects such as graded series mission studies, weeks of prayer, mission offerings, mission action.

12. Leads church to participate in World Mission Conferences as they are planned by the association.

13. Serves on the Search Group for Lay Renewal.

14. Represents Brotherhood on the church council.

In summary, the Brotherhood director performs his duties in four areas: planning, delegating, coordinating, and evaluation.

Figure 7.50

MISSIONS ACTIVITIES TARGET GROUPS

The aging	The military
Agricultural migrants	Minority groups
Alcohol/drug abuse	Inmates
The bereaved	Illiteracy
Moral problems	Resort areas
Divorced persons	The sick
Language groups	Troubled families

Persons with physical disabilities

Victims of disaster

The economically disadvantaged

Food centers and other mission agencies

Internationals, refugees, and international seamen

Figure 7.51
Woman's Missionary Union

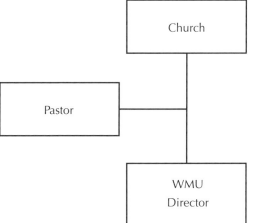
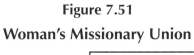

Figure 7.52
Woman's Missionary Union
with one organization each in one or more age levels.
Mission action director, enlistment and enlargement director,
and secretary are optional.

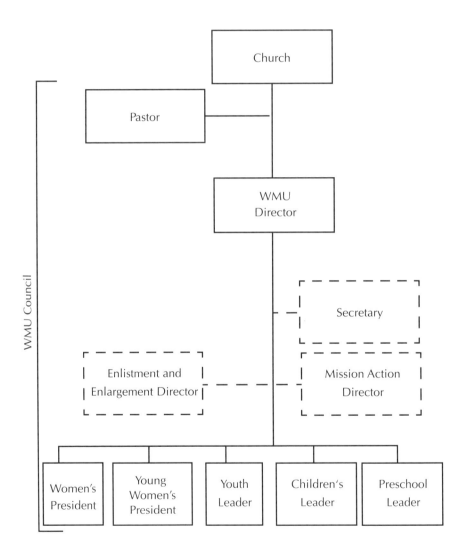

Figure 7.53
Churchwide Missions Projects
Coordination of WMU-Brotherhood Joint Action

Essential Actions	WMU/ Brotherhood Age-Level Organizations	WMU/ Brotherhood Councils or WMU and Brotherhood Directors as Representatives of Councils	Church Council
1. Suggest church-wide projects (on an annual basis).	Suggest projects for year.	Suggest projects and assignments of over-all initiative for each project during year.	
2. Approve projects and assignment of overall initiative for each.			Approve projects to be conducted and assignment of initia-tive for each project. Add additional projects and make other suggestions if desired.
3. Suggest work to be done in con-ducting a project and the assign-ment of responsi-bility (to be completed nearer time when project is to be conducted).		Suggest work to be done and assignment of responsibility to WMU and/or Broth-erhood.	
4. Approve work to be done and assignment of responsibility.			Approve work to be done and assignment of responsibility.
5. Make work assignments.		Assign work to be done to officers, council, and age-level organizations.	(Some assignments may be made to church council mem-bers such as Sunday school director, Dis-cipleship Training director).
6. Make detailed plans (with reviews as neces-sary).	Make detailed plans for work as assigned.	Make detailed plans for work as assigned.	
7. Conduct activity.	Conduct activity.	Conduct activity.	
8. Evaluate work.	Evaluate work com-pleted by age-level organization.	Evaluate work com-pleted by the organi-zation.	Evaluate total project.

Figure 7.54

MARKS OF A MISSIONARY CONGREGATION

• The congregation is to be centered around the mission of God in the world.

• Every believer in the congregation has a ministry.

• The ministry of every believer is to be expressed in the world. The ministry of the members grows out of their gifts.

• A deep, daily inward walk with God prepares members for their services.

• The congregation provides a supportive fellowship for ministry.

CHAPTER 8

Administering Specialized
Educational Activities

Jerry M. Stubblefield

All educational activities do not fit under existing church educational organizations. When existing organizations can support and administer specialized educational activities, they should. However, a special organization is needed when objectives and goals for an area of ministry cannot be fulfilled by existing organizations.

Specialized educational concerns include activities for youth, senior adults, single adults, family life, Vacation Bible School, kindergarten, Christian schools, child care ministries, and day camps. These activities usually meet on days other than Sunday and require more than the one hour to one and one-half hours normally given to program organizations. Some activities occur while the church's adults are participating in other church educational activities.

Activities may be daily, weekly, monthly, quarterly, or annually. The frequency is decided by the nature of the programs and the needs and numbers of persons who participate. Some function at special times of the year, such as Vacation Bible School and day camps in the summer.

For any program to be effective, someone must be responsible. Though a church may have a staff member charged with this responsibility, volunteer leaders often provide leadership and the administrative functions vital to an effective program.

Information below is applicable for any size church where there is need for a particular specialized educational activity. For any effective program, four ingredients are necessary: (1) the need for such a ministry, (2) a dedicated person who believes that this ministry needs to be done, (3) a minister and church leaders who are supportive, and (4) the church's decision that "this is *our* ministry."

This chapter seeks to answer these questions: What specialized educational activities or organizations are needed? How do you decide between short-term and ongoing programs or activities? How do you develop short-term and ongoing programs? What are suggested objectives and goals for specialized educational activities? What organizational pattern is needed?

Specialized educational activities are grouped according to appropriate age divisions—preschool (birth through age five), children (ages six through eleven), youth (ages twelve through high school), and adults. Some activities include all ages; these will be listed under the primary target group.

HOW TO DECIDE WHAT MINISTRIES
TO HAVE OR NOT TO HAVE

Does your church need to begin a specific ministry? Consider these two warnings before initiating new activities. First, an activity need not be started because a neighboring or influential church is doing it. The other group may be doing it effectively and may be willing to do it for all the community. Because of their involvement, your church may become sensitized to a need that you should be meeting. If so, do not try to duplicate what they are doing; this must be your own program to meet the unique needs of your congregation and community. In talking with the other church, you can learn from their mistakes and their successes.

Second, be careful about starting programs you read or hear about. Such a ministry usually is presented in idealistic terms, implying, "Do it the way we do, and success is guaranteed." The difficulty is that success usually is not instantaneous nor without its problems; remember, that church began a specialized ministry because it had a special *need* and appropriate *resources*. Programs cannot be transferred from one location to another without study of needs, resources, and necessary modifications.

Before beginning a new activity you need to discover what other churches are doing in these specialized educational activities and read about as many as possible. You must recognize that programs in your church are there because you had a need, the program was designed to meet those needs, and it was done your way.

WHAT SPECIALIZED ACTIVITIES
OR ORGANIZATIONS ARE NEEDED?

First, you should decide that there is a need for a particular program. Ask questions such as these:

- What needs would this meet for church members? for people in the community?
- How many persons are potential participants in this activity?
- What other churches and/or community organizations have programs or activities for this target group?
- What facilities and equipment are needed?
- Who has the best facilities and/or equipment? the church? the community?
- What organizational structure is needed?
- How many volunteers are needed?
- What specialized skills must volunteers have?
- What financial resources will this activity require?

Figure 8.1 on p. 198 provides a work sheet that can be used for this activity.

After answering these questions a church must ask these questions: Are we able to do this activity? Do we have the necessary resources—facilities, volunteers, finances, and so forth?

How do you gather such information? Interviewing community organizations will reveal if a need exists. Visits to organizations that have special interest in persons in need are helpful. Needs are also discovered by ministers or members who are sensitive to people. Personal needs may be known to the minister through pastoral counseling and visitation. Programs cannot be started because a community organization confirms that there is a need. More information is necessary before you begin a new program.

What specific persons could benefit from this activity? Names and addresses—*people*—are necessary to ensure success. Specialized ministries can be publicized through regular church channels and also newspapers, radio, television, posters, handbills, and other ways. People must know that a program exists before it can fulfill their needs.

HOW TO DECIDE BETWEEN SHORT-TERM AND ONGOING PROGRAMS

What kind of program should it be—short-term or ongoing? What factors determine whether it is a short-term or ongoing program? A *short-term program* meets a specific need through a one-time event or a series of activities held over a set time or number of meetings. It could have a narrow objective or similar objectives. It could be an annual emphasis or done only once.

Religious organizations have tendencies to repeat activities indiscriminately year after year. Church leaders frequently announce, "This is the

Figure 8.1

SPECIAL MINISTRY PLANSHEET

1. What needs would this meet for church members? for people in the community?

2. How many persons are potential participants in the activity?

3. What other churches and/or community organizations have programs or activities for this target group?

4. What facilities and equipment are needed?

5. Who has the best facilities and/or equipment? the church? the community?

6. What organizational structure is needed?

7. How many volunteers are needed?

8. What specialized skills must volunteers have?

9. What financial resources will this activity require?

first annual. . . ." Some events need to be held only once. Evaluation of each activity answers the following questions:

- What was the objective or purpose? (Why did we do it?)
- Was the objective achieved? How? If not, why?
- For whom was the event planned? Who was the target audience?
- Who participated in the activity? Who came?
- Does the need still exist?
- What other needs were revealed during the session(s)?
- Should this activity be done again? Why? Why not?
- Is there another event that should be done?
- Did the response justify the cost?

Short-term programs that meet occasionally are scheduled in conjunction with other activities. Such events are vital to a comprehensive educational ministry and should be well-planned and promoted.

Ongoing programs are those that have multiple objectives or needs that cannot be accomplished in a set period. Needs are diversified and cannot be fulfilled in a few sessions. Each activity or event is critically analyzed, using the questions listed above. Obviously, ongoing programs require more planning, administrative organization, and finances than most short-term projects.

SPECIALIZED EDUCATIONAL ACTIVITIES[1]

PRESCHOOLERS

CHURCH WEEKDAY EARLY EDUCATION

Weekday activities conducted for preschool children are called collectively church weekday early education. For such a program to be more than "baby-sitting," it must be an extension of the church's educational ministry. Before mentioning specific activities, a brief description of the values of weekday early education is in order.

- Weekday education is a function of the church, like Sunday school. It is financially supported by the church. Church members and other participants pay fees for this ministry.
- It is ministry in action. Christian teachers show Christ as they teach and care for the children.
- Weekday education includes Christian teaching that is not found in other public and private programs. It is a holistic approach to education.
- It seeks to relate to the child not only in the classroom but also in the home. The home is an integral part of the learning process.

- It is family-oriented. Workers make follow-up visits to witness to families who need to know Jesus Christ or to minister to whatever needs the family may have.

- It achieves maximum uses of the church buildings. The church becomes an activity hub. People begin to see the church as more than a place for Sunday activities.[2]

The values of such a program are important; however, decisions should not be based on what such a program can do for the church. Instead, weekday early education is to be viewed as a service to children and families. The information described in figure 8.2 on p. 201 must be considered before beginning a weekday program.[3]

Following a decision to proceed, administrative decisions must be made. Figure 8.3 on p. 202 lists the questions to consider and can be used as a worksheet.[4]

What is taught during the sessions of early weekday education? Some churches prepare their own curriculum materials, but this takes lots of time and expertise. Curriculum resources that can be adapted for your situation are available from denominational and independent religious publishers.

MOTHER'S (OR PARENT'S) DAY OUT

This program usually operates one day each week, enabling the primary caregiver to relax, shop, visit friends, or do other things. Modest fees defray some operational expenses. Children engage in educationally sound activities on their developmental level. Children are supervised and taught by church volunteers or paid workers. This is an educational activity, not baby-sitting. One worker is needed for each six to eight children attending. The objective is to provide educational activities for the child while the parent has some personal time.

DAY-CARE

This is an all-day, five-days-a-week program involving teaching, rest, and at least one meal plus snacks. This ministry helps working parents provide for their children while they work. It is open to children ages birth through five. Fees are charged, and the program is under professional supervision. Licensing is required in most states. Each teacher has up to ten students and there are separate rooms for each class. Day-care programs require more equipment than that usually provided for the church's regular educational activities. Some churches also have after-school care for kindergarten children who attend public kindergartens. Plenty of activities are needed to keep this from becoming baby-sitting. A schedule of varied activities at the children's developmental level helps them enjoy the sessions. Suggested activities are available through denominational and independent religious publishers.

Figure 8.2

MYTHS ABOUT
CHURCH WEEKDAY EARLY EDUCATION

1. *Weekday activities automatically bring unsaved and unenlisted parents into the church.* Evangelistic outreach comes by deliberate efforts to reach those who are without Jesus Christ. Church leaders must be sensitive to the needs of parents and family members of children enrolled in the program. Family information is secured and used in an appropriate way. The primary objective is to provide authentic educational activities for preschoolers.

2. *It will guarantee religious education.* Weekday education ministers to the total child. Children are approached in their wholeness. Religious instruction is part of their total educational experience. The teaching of religious values and ideas is done in a natural manner as part of the child's learning processes.

3. *Weekday education provides additional income for the church.* Unless fees are set exceptionally high, the church will subsidize weekday education activities. Fees normally cover personnel and supply costs. Weekday programs require additional lights, air-conditioning, heat, janitorial services, and more frequent painting due to heavy use. A weekday early education program is a ministry, not a source of additional revenue.

4. *Every church should consider having a weekday education program.* Begin only after the need is established, not because you believe it should be done. Not every church has the facilities, personnel or financial resources to have an effective program. Unless your church can have a quality program it should not have one. It does not need to be extravagant, but it should be equal or superior to that offered in the community.

5. *All church members approve of the program.* A public relations program should be directed to the community-at-large and to the church. Keep members informed of what is going on. Volunteer leaders frequently believe that their work is the most important. Sharing of rooms and supplies can cause friction. Help each church program see that all are engaged in a ministry that is significant to the advancement of the church and the gospel.

Figure 8.3

WEEKDAY EARLY EDUCATION PLANSHEET

1. What type of program or activity is anticipated?

2. What is the purpose of this program or activity?

3. What administrative structure needs to be developed? (All activities should be under one church-elected committee to help eliminate friction and rivalry.)

4. What kind of staffing is required? (Paid? Volunteer?)

5. How will this program be financed? (Fees? Church support? A combination?)

6. Does this program require state licensing? What has to be done to meet state standards, requirements?

7. What are the space and equipment needs for this activity?

8. Will remodeling and/or additional equipment be required? If so, how is it to be done, attained, financed, etc.?

9. What are the anticipated objectives and goals of this program or activity?

NURSERY SCHOOL

This program meets one-half day, with the children coming two, three, or five days per week. It is for children ages three and four. Each teacher works with up to ten children. The emphasis is on teaching and educational activities, with socialization stressed. Some churches include two year olds one day a week. The sessions are usually two hours in length. Costs are offset by fees. The program is directed by professional teachers. Churches that have ministers of music and recreation/activities could use these ministers to strengthen their programs. The nursery school schedule follows closely that of the community public schools. Activities at the developmental level of the children are essential for a successful nursery school.

KINDERGARTEN

This is a program for five year olds that meets for one-half day, with a major emphasis on teaching. Some churches include four year olds in their kindergarten program. Most states now have public kindergartens that children are required to attend; however, many churches continue to have quality programs that meet state requirements. Much that describes the nursery school applies to the kindergarten. A teacher may teach up to fifteen children because of their maturation and the activities in which they engage. The total growth of the child is considered, especially in relation to preparation for first grade.

CHILDREN

Specialized educational activities for children occur primarily in the summer when they are out of school: day camping, resident camping, and Vacation Bible School. Weekday education functions as an after-school activity operating concurrently with the school year.

DAY CAMP

Day camp is a program in which children are daily transported to a nature setting. This program may operate five or more consecutive days, or it may be a one-day experience repeated several weeks in the summer. Primarily, this program is for children ages six through eleven or grades one through six. Some churches have one-day camp experience for fours and fives, with a shortened schedule. John LaNoue states the four goals of day camping:

1. To reach children and their families for Christ.

2. To help children develop new friendships, good life habits, and sound ecological practices; to present a concern and appreciation for

nature; and to provide an understanding of God's plan for all of life
and for their own lives.

3. To prepare children for participation in resident camping when they
   reach the proper age.

4. To give children a solid experience with nature that will provide
   them with the background and ideas that will help them better understand the Bible's teachings which are heavily immersed in nature illustrations.[5]

The staff includes a director, a Bible study leader, a craft leader, a cook,
a nature study leader, a lifeguard if swimming is available, and unit leaders
and counselors. Older youth can be enlisted to work in day camp. Careful
attention must be given to site selection, transportation coordination, and
the safety of the campers. Each staffer should be trained before beginning
activities with the children.

How will day camp be funded? Various ways of handling it include the
church budget, camping fees, and a combination of the two. Registration
in advance helps in planning for the number of persons attending, the necessary staff, and transportation needs.

Day camp can also be used to minister to special groups of children who
cannot participate in ordinary day camps. Such groups include those who
need assistance due to physical, emotional, or social impairment. Persons
possessing professional skills are needed with these groups.

RESIDENT CAMPING

Resident or church camping takes the camper away from home for several days and nights. The focus is on camping which uses the natural environment for fellowship, Christian education, personal development, and
spiritual growth.

Camping experiences begin in the early morning or early afternoon.
Recreational activities help campers become acclimated to camp life. Administration of the camp is under the leadership of the camp director, who
is helped by the camp pastor, the camp missionary (camping is an excellent time to teach missions), camp counselors (one for every eight campers), a nurse, an activity director, cook, and other kitchen personnel.
Depending upon the nature and objectives of the camp, persons possessing
special skills may be needed.

Camping objectives are to share the gospel of Jesus Christ with the unsaved and encourage Christian growth for believers. Evangelism takes
place through the clear presentation of the good news of Jesus Christ.

Camping is an extension of the church's educational activities. It is
more concentrated and, like other educational activities, allows for development of personal relationships.

The camp pastor participates in various activities, thus gaining additional information on the campers' spiritual experiences. Non-church children become a part of the church's prospect file and become objects of the church's outreach program. Care must be taken to see that each decision is genuine and not the product of emotionalism or peer approval.

Many details go into preparing for a camp. Figure 8.4 on p. 206 shows a plansheet that can be used by the camp director.

Camping is part of the church's educational program for children. Activities for children are appropriate to their developmental stage. The age span is restricted so that objectives are attainable. Usually, a resident camp experience begins with children age nine or with those who have completed the third grade. Several counselors are provided. Older youth make excellent counselors. The older youth must understand, however, that the camp is for the children, not the counselors. Caution is needed so that too many adults and youth do not overpower the children, and add greatly to the cost.

VACATION BIBLE SCHOOL

Vacation Bible School is an age-graded, Bible-centered activity conducted during vacation time. Until recently, Vacation Bible School was a preschool, children, and youth activity. In many congregations, it now includes adults. Children comprise the largest age group enrolled in it. It is a significant part of the church's Bible teaching program. The prepared curriculum is sometimes for ten sessions, lasting three hours each. Most churches meet for five sessions or a total of fifteen hours.

The purposes of Vacation Bible School correspond closely to those of the Bible study ministry of the church. Efforts focus on the following:

- Reaching and involving persons
- Teaching the Bible
- Worshiping
- Learning about missions
- Developing skills in Christian living and witness

Vacation Bible School is a vital part of the church's educational program. Its leadership is church-elected. Its budget is provided by the church. Offerings taken during the school are usually donated to a mission project or program, not used to defray expenses.

A successful Vacation Bible School is dependent upon six primary factors:

1. early election of the faculty;
2. faculty training sessions;
3. general and departmental faculty meetings;

Figure 8.4

CAMP PLANSHEET

1. Where will the camp be held?

2. What will the program emphasize?

3. For whom is the camp designed? Members? Non-members?

4. Who will be the camp pastor? the missionary? other key leaders?

5. What is the total camp budget? How much of this cost does the church provide? How much does each camper pay?

6. What are the criteria for selecting counselors? Age? Special skills? Training needed? Persons to consider?

7. What will the daily schedule be?

8. Decide the schedule for planning, preparing, and promoting the camp.

4. adequate publicity within the church and community;

5. provision of curriculum materials and other learning aids; and

6. planned follow-up of non-church members and their families.

The chief administrative officer is the director, who usually is a teacher or minister in the church. The director is helped by other persons in the total operation of Vacation Bible School. A refreshment committee chair and a secretary are necessary to complement the teaching staff.

Each department (age group) has a director who functions as a lead teacher. Workers are enlisted in the same teacher/student ratio as the Bible teaching program. Each department needs at least two adult workers. Older youth can help if they are available.

Extensive resource materials are available for administration, teaching, projects, and promotion of Vacation Bible School. Information is available from your denominational publisher or religious bookstore. Be sure to inquire five to six months in advance to allow sufficient time to secure and review sample materials, make plans, and place orders.

A schedule is drawn up for the entire Vacation Bible School and for each individual department. Each activity is listed showing the amount of time allotted to it. Failure to abide by the schedule creates confusion and frustration. All faculty members should know the time of the joint worship service, playground time, and when and where their group is to have refreshments.

The pastor and other church staff persons participate in the various activities as possible. They are supportive even when not in a leadership role. All faculty persons should receive evangelistic training so they can deal individually with children in the normal process of the day's activities. Commitment services are kept simple, not highly emotional. The child is encouraged to respond to Jesus Christ but not pressured.

Nonmembers are visited and invited to participate in the activities of the church. Unsaved persons need to hear the gospel and to know how to become a Christian. The fact that persons attend Vacation Bible School is no assurance they will attend either Sunday school or a worship service. Good information secured through registration may reveal other family members who are prospects. To be effective, follow-up visits should be made soon.

Vacation Bible School is a part of the church's Bible teaching program as is Sunday school. Depending upon when it is held, many Sunday school workers also work in Vacation Bible School.

CHRISTIAN DAY SCHOOLS

In recent years Christian day schools have greatly increased in number. What factors should churches consider in establishing and operating Christian day schools? What should be the objectives of such schools?

The basic idea is that each child should be afforded the best education possible. The quality of education should not be sacrificed. Education in the Christian day school should be equal or superior to public education. Teachers should possess academic credentials besides their spiritual qualities. Schools exist to aid each child to discover and develop his or her God-given gifts. The mission of the Christian day school, ultimately, is the development of the future leadership of the community, the state, the business and professional groups, and the church.

Besides a principal, an office staff, and faculty, the church needs to elect a committee charged with the responsibility of operating the school, much like public school trustees. This committee decides policies, elects faculty and administrators, sets tuition fees, and gives general oversight to the school activities.

The school should be licensed by the state board of education and meet all state requirements. Other important considerations include transportation, a lunch program, and provision of textbooks. The committee meets regularly and has the authority to make decisions. One member of the church staff works in liaison with the committee. Sometimes, a church designates an associate minister to be principal. If so, this should be his/her major responsibility, to ensure that the Christian day school functions effectively and adequately.

Administering a Christian day school can be complicated and is beyond the purview of this book. Complete guides are available. If your church is interested in this area of Christian education, a visit to a Christian school can be made to discuss your interest with the principal or director, or information can be requested from a seminary.

MISSIONS EDUCATION

Missions education is a program to teach children about missions and lead them to participate in mission activities. Many denominations have children's missions education programs and materials. A recent pattern is for churches to turn to parachurch groups to provide missions education for their children, though they have denominationally-sponsored programs. Churches are free to choose programs they want, but they should do so with certain cautions. They should enlist and train those who work with the children. Parachurch groups emphasize *their* missionaries and mission projects, leading your children to support and give to *their* causes. If you are a denominational church, you should support and pray for your missionaries and mission projects.

YOUTH

Youth ministry is popular in most evangelical churches. Some churches have professional youth ministers; others rely upon lay volunteers. Youth are ministered to through the regular educational activities of the church, such as Sunday school, discipleship training, missions education, and music ministry.

"Youth ministry" is a comprehensive term that includes all efforts a church might make because of a concern for this age group. More than fun and games, youth ministry is an integral part of church programs and a variety of complementing activities for fellowship, learning, and serving. Objectives such as those listed in figure 8.5 are included in most church programs.

Figure 8.5

OBJECTIVES OF YOUTH MINISTRY

To help youth:

- make a commitment to Jesus Christ as Lord and Savior.
- experience meaningful church membership.
- grow in Christian discipleship.
- experience worship.
- increase their knowledge and understanding of Bible truths.
- learn to apply Christian principles in every area of life.
- witness to Jesus Christ and seek to lead others to Him.
- recognize and respond to the will of God in all decisions.
- participate in Christian ministries and missions.
- practice good stewardship of money, time, talents, and skill.
- grow in understanding and acceptance of self.

A ministry to youth is a team endeavor. It involves the pastor and staff of the church, parents of the youth, youth workers in the youth-related program organizations and services, and the youth.

Mission and ministry options are open for the youth locally and on mission trips. Successful mission trips require training the youth in how to do the projected ministry—musical, mission work, and so forth. Many activities are possibilities for youth ministry. Church resources and location greatly influence and decide youth activities.

Administratively, the youth program functions under the leadership of a youth council. Each church must decide its representative base and the specific functions of the youth council. Representatives are selected from church members, adult youth leaders, youth from the various program organizations, age-group representatives, and the youth minister/youth coordinator. Youth activities are planned according to church objectives and church policies.[6]

Resident camping is also popular with the youth. Some churches have a camp for their youth only. Others may join denominational camps where they interact with youth from different locations.

ADULTS

Specialized educational activities for adults may be developed in a great variety of areas. Many are offered through existing organizations, primarily as projects and activities of classes, departments, and other groups. Three areas of specialized work are examined here due to their wide use in churches: family ministry, single adult ministry, and senior adult ministry.

FAMILY MINISTRY

With the increased fragmentation of the family, the church has been forced to consider the needs of the family. Family ministry involves all ages. Adults hold the key to wholeness for younger family members.

A family ministry program usually offers a variety of services and activities that will enrich life from a Christian perspective. The purpose is to meet needs such as those listed in figure 8.6.

Figure 8.6

FAMILY MINISTRY OPPORTUNITIES

- Help family members learn to talk with one another and to understand and solve family problems.
- Help couples to enrich their relationship.
- Help those who have experienced loss or separation to find acceptance in the church and to grow in their personal lives.
- Help parents as they try to understand and cope with problems they encounter in rearing children.
- Help persons to grow in self-understanding and to assume responsibility for making their lives worthwhile.
- Help persons to form wholesome friendships and to enrich their lives.
- Help families in times of crisis.
- Help people learn the biblical bases of sexuality, marriage, and family life.
- Help young people prepare for their future roles in marriage and family life.

Family ministry is administered differently from church program organizations, like Sunday school. It is not under any organization nor is anyone assigned the responsibility for family ministry. The church council or Christian education committee could assume this responsibility, since they are charged with planning for the total needs of the church. No program of family ministry should be initiated before the needs of the congregation are known. Identified needs are listed in priority order. Instead of assuming that all family ministry needs can be met during a special week, you should project a year's plan of action. These proposals should be presented to the church for adoption.

Family ministry activities could include marriage enrichment workshops, parenting conferences, grandparenting seminars, courses designed for blended families. Some are one-night activities and are designed for a target group, such as couples, singles, seniors, or grandparents. Other activities include retreats for target groups or special study/workshops that meet for two hours each week for several weeks.

Family ministry activities are for the entire family. They include teaching preschoolers, children, and youth about meaningful family relationships. Some activities are targeted to one group; others are more integrative, such as helping youth and parents have positive relationships.

Churches do family ministry differently. Some do it through special events and activities; others do it through their ongoing educational programs, such as Bible teaching or discipleship training. To do an effective job, more is needed than a Christian Home Emphasis. Several events or activities should be offered each quarter.

Activities with singles and seniors may be part of family ministry programming. However, when needs are great and there are many participants in these categories, separate programs are provided.

SINGLE ADULT MINISTRY

Many single adults participate in the church's educational program. Churches that have a singles ministry usually have an ongoing Bible teaching program for them. Some have discipleship training, missions education, and music activities for single adults. Attention will be focused on developing a weekday ministry with and to single adults.

Singles are now more than fifty percent of the American adult population; only a few years ago they were about one-third of the population. This is a significant group with whom the church has an opportunity to minister. They are found in many varieties—never-married, divorced, deserted, separated, single parents, or widowed. They are also found in every part of America. In metropolitan areas singles may approach seventy-five percent of the adult population. An emerging trend is for more single males to participate in the church's single adult ministry.

Before beginning a single adult ministry, several questions need to be asked:

- Who are the singles? How many singles are presently members of or attending your church? How many singles are in your community?
- What needs of singles can your church meet?
- What types of activities, programs, and organizations are required to meet these needs?

Some needs of single adults include self-worth, companionship, acceptance, financial assistance, help with children, sexuality, the desire to know the will of God, and loneliness. Meeting these and other needs requires a plan, a program.

Single adult activities are carried out and evaluated by a single adult council. The council is composed of the single adult minister (or other staff member), a lay coordinator, and representatives from each of the church program organizations ministering to single adults (Sunday school, discipleship training, missions education, music, etc.). The single adults plan and execute their own program and activities, not the staff member. Elected representatives are members of the various unit organizations and members of that local church.

The council is responsible for planning, organizing, coordinating, and evaluating all single adult activities, and for reporting directly to the church or through the church council.[7] Council members carry the primary responsibility for the single adult ministry but should not attempt to do everything themselves. They should enlist other single adults or qualified persons to work with them.

An effective single adult ministry has a variety of activities meeting the multiple needs of singles in its area. Some target a narrow group such as single parents; others focus on ministering to the separated and divorced. Some activities are for a special target group; others are more general in nature, addressing common needs of all single adults.

The church cannot be all things to all people; therefore it should focus on meeting the spiritual needs of single adults. Every time there is a single adult event or activity, fellowship or relationships are a part of the process. Singles' ministries built around social activities only are not successful over time. Another church will give bigger or better parties, and the singles will go there.

A church that is serious about its ministry to single adults provides childcare each time the singles meet. That would include childcare for retreats and some outings not appropriate for children. However, some activities are family oriented and are planned with children and single adults in mind.

A singles ministry should not have activities every day in the week. Singles need time to do laundry, shop for groceries, and attend to personal needs. Not all singles should attend every singles event sponsored by the church, only those that meet their needs.

The singles ministry seeks to speak to the unique and special needs of single adults. This ministry is further strengthened when the single adults also have opportunities to minister in the church and outside the church. These adults lead independent lives, making decisions for themselves; some also have significant management or administrative positions in the work arena.

SENIOR ADULT MINISTRY

The number of senior adults is rapidly increasing; we are experiencing a senior boom. People over sixty-five now outnumber the youth. Estimates are that by 2050 Americans over sixty-five will outnumber teens two to one. By the year 2050 one in four Americans will be over sixty-five. Senior adult clubs and other activities are organized to meet the unique needs of adults, beginning as early as age fifty.

The purpose of senior adult ministries is to enhance all areas of life, related especially to the spiritual, emotional, and physical needs of participants. Through various activities centered about a weekly or monthly meeting, a senior adult ministry can provide the following:

- A way for the church to show love and concern for senior adults in an environment that leads them to feel they are wanted in the worship and life of the church
- A way to use their natural and learned abilities by providing opportunities for service
- A way to combat loneliness through Christian fellowship, new interests, and a sense of belonging
- An opportunity to contribute actively to society through the church

The senior adult council provides the administrative structure for this ministry. The group has a coordinator and representatives from each church organization that has senior adult participants. The council discovers the needs of senior adults, plans and implements activities, coordinates the calendar of activities, reports to the church or the church council, and evaluates the program. Senior adults are in charge of their own activities. They may need help in some areas but should primarily provide their own leadership.

The senior adult weekday ministry is usually called a senior adult club. Officers needed include a president, program chair, enlistment chair, and a secretary. Additional committees are added as the activities and needs expand.

Churches that have a large senior adult population may need two different groups. Those sixty-five and over could be one group. The other could be the new category of senior adults composed of those who retire early—the "in betweeners." Their needs and interests are far different from those over sixty-five. There can be some joint meetings, but many activities will be done differently.

Some churches provide funds for the senior adult ministry, especially to defray transportation and meeting costs. Senior adults have fixed incomes but want to feel that they are paying their own way, so most activities will involve a fee or contribution from participants. Care should be given to costs and making everyone feel included. Senior adult activity funds should be planned and administered just like the allocations for youth activities.

Senior adult ministry is primarily to the older citizens in your church and community. There are special needs of this age group that a congregation can and should meet. However, many seniors are in the prime of life and can contribute significantly through volunteer service in the church and community. Possessing valuable knowledge and experience, they can provide major help in committee work, teaching and fellowship activities, church office tasks, visitation, and even by serving as surrogate grandparents. Many are good with mechanical or physical things and can do minor repairs around the church or for those in need. Others might choose to minister to those in convalescent homes or visit members who are homebound.

CHAPTER 9

Christian Education and the Small Church
Jerry M. Stubblefield

I served as pastor of two small churches. The first had only an adult Sunday school class. The second church had age-graded Bible study and discipleship training programs, plus missions education for women and children. This church had a strong heritage of quality teaching and congregational support for Christian education. They worked hard, attended training opportunities provided by the denomination, and took pride in the church's educational ministry.

On the back wall of the sanctuary were many banners signifying they were a *standard* Sunday school. To achieve this distinction, their Sunday school had to comply with eight or ten specific items each year. It was at Victory Baptist Church that I learned how to do church. On a good Sunday there were thirty-five in the worship service. Years later when I became minister of education at a church with 2,500 members, I did what I had done at Victory, only more of it.

Many feel that the way you work in the small church is do what you do in the larger church but divide it. My experience is just the opposite. You do in the large church what you did in the small church, but multiply it. The same principles work in both large and small churches.

Over the years I served several small churches as interim pastor. I find that like large churches, some smaller churches have quality Christian education programs, others have modest programs, and some have weak ones. The small church, because it is small, however, should not have an inferior or weak Christian education program. It depends upon the leadership of the pastor and lay persons.

There are different definitions for the small church. Usually this is a church with less than 200 members. Those who have a graded Sunday school define the small church as having 150 or less enrolled in their Bible teaching program. Either church setting has 75 to 125 attending on a given Sunday. Two thirds of evangelical churches in North America are small churches. Most have some kind of Bible study or teaching ministry, which is Christian education.

It is not the purview of this chapter to explore the characteristics of the small church; the concern here is how the small church can have quality Christian education.

WHAT IS CHRISTIAN EDUCATION?

What is the purpose of Christian education? What should happen in the lives of people as they participate in Christian education activities? A simple statement is that Christian education is to help persons respond to God.[1] An expanded statement is that the purpose of Christian education "is to love and be loved; to know and to be known; to live and forgive within the context of a single cell, culture carrying, history bearing primary group."[2] Donald L. Griggs and Judy McKay Walther see the broader scope of Christian education as learning: what it means to be Christian, what the Bible says and its relevance for daily faith and life, understanding and responding to the needs of people, and learning to love God, neighbor, and self. This, they say, is a lifelong process.[3]

D. Campbell Wyckoff asks, "What do our people (at various ages and stages of life and experience) need to know and become in order to come to maturity in Christ and understand and undertake the church's mission?"[4] His idea is that Christian education should help the participants mature in Christ and engage in the church's mission, in Christ's mission. Carolyn C. Brown, in contrast, notes that "Christian education describes all our efforts to enable people to grow in their faith."[5]

Each statement helps us examine the purpose of Christian education and how what we do can affect the lives of those in our churches. Christian education is not an activity, an event, or a program. It is an attempt to influence the lives of the participants so they can be mature in Christ and engage in the mission and ministry of Christ through the church and in the world.

Take a moment and reflect on the ideas of Foltz, Griggs and Walther, Wyckoff, and Brown. Can you identify some key words that describe how you see the purpose of Christian education? You may want to write out *your* purpose statement for Christian education in the small church.

Many churches depend upon their *Bible teaching program* to provide all their Christian education. When this is done, it is primarily for children. My religious tradition seeks to do Christian education through three different vehicles. One is Bible study, often called Sunday school, church school, or Sunday church school. It also includes Bible conferences, Vacation Bible School, and other concentrated studies of biblical books. Bible study is for Christians and non-Christians. An effective Bible study program seeks to reach unsaved and unchurched people so they can hear the gospel and respond to God's offer of salvation.

A second emphasis is *discipleship training,* which some churches focus at the time of conversion or when decisions are made. Discipleship training, however, is needed throughout the Christian life. This phase of Christian education should help Christians better understand their faith. Study areas include Christian doctrine and history, ethics, and church polity. Discipleship training should help the believer mature in Christ and learn how to minister and witness to others. It seeks to provide three kinds of training—new member training, leader training, and member training. This requires a specific plan to achieve these three ends. Adults need discipleship training as do children and youth.

The third emphasis is *missions education.* Christians need to know their heritage and how the gospel is spread around the world, beginning at home. Missions education involves studying about missions but also missions involvement—the *doing* of missions. Missions education is not for children and women only but is needed by adult men as well. Missions education focuses on supporting missions. We support missions by praying for missionaries and mission endeavors, giving to missions, and encouraging missionaries and their families.

These three aspects of Christian education—Bible study, discipleship training, and missions education—should be a part of the program and activities of *all* churches, large or small. Most churches have an ongoing Bible study program. Discipleship training and missions education can be special events or projects but are essential for the growth of Christians and the application of the gospel to all of life. I have conducted Christian education activities in small churches on Sunday evenings, during the worship time, for several Wednesday evenings, or on Friday nights. When we used a time other than Sunday, it was also a time of fellowship and was for the entire family.

Education takes place in all that the small church does—worship, mission, and fellowship; this is also true in larger churches. Brown writes, "Good Christian education is not limited to classes of the same age. Good Christian education happens whenever people are challenged to explore some part of their faith."[6] The church educates through all its activities of being the church.

DEVELOPING CHRISTIAN EDUCATION
IN THE SMALL CHURCH

Effective Christian education programs and activities are customized to fit a particular church. Denominational programs are generic, geared to meet the needs even of small churches in a variety of settings. Griggs and Walter share a good guideline: "The development of effective Christian educational ministries in small churches is related to the ability of the congregations to look at themselves, to discover the needs that must be addressed, and to find ways to communicate the gospel among themselves and to those who live in their communities."[7]

All churches, denominational or nondenominational, must adapt and adjust their Christian education activities to meet their special needs. Otherwise, the program is ineffective or weak in meeting local needs found in the church and community.

Pamela Mitchell underscores this need, quoting from an early book on Christian education in the small church: "A basic principle to keep in mind is that a program of Christian nurture must be worked out in each particular church, allowing for the character and needs of its members, the place of the church in the community, its tradition and heritage, and its resources and opportunities. If this principle is followed, it will mean that the small church will not try to imitate the large church."[8] The key, Mitchell says, "is to recognize, recover, and honor the character of the small membership church."[9] The small church has integrity in what it is and its mission, not by trying to imitate the large church or trying to be a large church.

Self-esteem is an issue for many small churches. If they approach their ministry with the idea that they are doing God's work, they have a significant ministry in the kingdom of God. They should do whatever they do with integrity and a sense of fulfilling God's mission and plan for them.

Our culture says that "bigger is better." That is not always the case. Although much attention has been given to several megachurches, not all churches can or should do what these large churches are doing. What small churches can and should do is to have a quality program that meets their needs and has integrity.

All Christian education programs must meet local needs. The small church must do what it does best. It is relational and offers a sense of intimacy and warmth not always found in a larger church. The small church should not mimic or pattern itself after the larger church. It must be true to what it is and the setting in which it exists.

Thus, organizational patterns begin with the character of the church. A characteristic of the small church is that it is lay owned and lay operated. This is also true in its educational ministry. Lay members must have ownership and leadership of the educational program. Bob I. Johnson feels that the following questions are critical to an effective Christian education program in the small church: "Who designs the religious education program, who invites religious education leaders to serve, who takes care of the leaders, who takes care of the rooms, who keeps the records and pays the bills, who orders the curriculum and the supplies, and who leads the opening exercises?"[10]

Your answers to these questions reveal who the Christian education leaders are in the small church. Often Christian education is in the hands of laypersons, and it should be. The pastor is involved in the Christian education program but more as equipper, trainer, and consultant, rather than the dominant head.

Christian education is primarily relational. That is why small classes are recommended for Christian education activities. The small class gives persons an identity; they are important as individuals. In the small church Christian education is an all-church endeavor, and each time the people gather there is a potential opportunity to learn and to teach.[11]

The small church functions much like a family. Its entire life is part of Christian education. Christian education occurs in informal, not formal educational activities always. People learn much by personal observation, sometimes as much as they do in teacher-directed classes.

ORGANIZING CHRISTIAN EDUCATION
IN THE SMALL CHURCH

The small church will have broadly graded classes, like the old one-room school house. There are still many one-room schools in America, and many provide quality education. Broadly graded classes have many advantages. Brown identifies the following: "The church is a community or a family. The 'family setting' allows for some close-to-home heroes, and it forces people to share their faith in informal, less academic ways."[12] Teachers present material but also interpret and discuss their experiences with Christ. With the small church intimacy, learners know their teachers and the way they live.

For teaching effectiveness, each class or group needs at least two people who plan together and are in the classroom. They must know the learners and what each can gain from being part of the class.[13] Classes normally will be divided into preschool, children, youth, and adults, with age or grade ranges assigned if necessary. One worker will be the teacher and the other will assist, substituting when necessary.

If there are more than eight regular attendees in any class, consider dividing when an additional leader can be enlisted. An assistant usually will become the new teacher and two assistants can be named. Adults and youth may be divided according to age or gender, whereas children and preschoolers should be divided into younger and older.

The pastor or an interested lay leader should serve as Sunday school director, coordinating activities and promoting Bible study in the congregation.

STAFFING THE CHRISTIAN EDUCATION PROGRAM

People are willing to work in the Christian education program if they feel they are needed, if they have responsibilities that match their interests and abilities, if they have meaningful assignments, and if their efforts are appreciated. Lyle Schaller says that 30 to 65 percent of the members are willing to be teachers and leaders. In smaller congregations, a larger proportion of members is willing to serve as volunteers.[14] In the large church there are more "spectators," those who will not accept leadership places. People in the small church are more "participants" as they share places of leadership and responsibility.

How do we recruit people to work in Christian education? Brown has a high view of the task of recruiting workers:

> Recruiters are asking people to share their faith with other Christians. Teaching is a calling ranked high among the spiritual callings by Saint Paul. To be asked to teach is an honor, as well as a challenge. These teachers are going to be given carefully prepared and selected materials to work with and will have the support of the entire church. All of this is being done because the church places a very high value on Christian growth. So, set aside the cloud of doom, and approach the task of recruiting teachers for the church's education ministry with the prayerful energy it deserves.[15]

Beginning the recruitment process early helps people feel that the church takes seriously its task of finding people to serve in its Christian education program. Last-minute recruiting has the feeling of panic and desperation.[16] The process of staffing should begin several months ahead of the new church year. (The ideas in chapter 6, "How to Staff and Motivate," also apply to the small church.) This allows time to train those who are new to this ministry. It also gives them time to feel more confident about this job.

Turnover in leadership positions plagues churches of all sizes, including the small church. Brown suggests that teachers in small churches need three kinds of care and feeding to survive:

Encouragement. Teaching can be a lonely job. Teachers often are given their books and must do the best they can. Some feel that the job is more than they can handle and that they are spending too much time on it. "Besides, no one cares about it." Discouragement is avoidable if you keep in touch with the teachers and share student compliments, ask how things are going, and express appreciation. Teachers can lead in public prayers in worship services. "Teachers need to know that their work is valued by the church and that the church supports them as they teach."[17]

Skills. A teacher must have some specific skills to do a good job. If unable to perform adequately, a person will quickly become discouraged and likely drop out from teaching. Through its training program a church can provide opportunities for teachers to develop needed skills.

Inspiration. Volunteer teachers in the church usually see their work as a commitment to do God's work. The church should honor and develop this sense of commitment. Illustrations and biblical references to teaching and teachers in sermons and on special occasions can be used to encourage workers. An effective workers meeting also helps stimulate and support teachers. Such efforts will help them grow in their understanding of what it means to be a teacher for Jesus Christ and also increase their teaching effectiveness and the personal pleasure they find in their work.[18]

Worker appreciation and recognition help teachers feel that what they are doing is important and appreciated by their church. These can be a part of a worship service, a banquet, or other celebration. Having a covenant-sharing time at the beginning of the church year highlights the importance the church places on its Christian education program.

SELECTING CURRICULUM MATERIALS

Selecting curriculum materials is a difficult task for church leaders, especially for those in small churches. Two issues small church leaders face are (1) keeping up with what curriculum is available, and (2) selecting material appropriate for their particular situation.[19] Fortunately, churches have many good choices of curriculum resources.

If you already are using effective learning resources, you will need only to supplement for special studies or events. If you are dissatisfied with current resources or are starting a new class or program, you can contact the educational consultant at your state or regional office. In the event this does not work, you can request a church materials catalog from your denominational publisher or religious bookstore. Review of resources should be based on the needs of your people.

If you cannot find appropriate resources produced for churches of your denomination, materials from publishers with compatible doctrinal and educational standards can be considered.[20] Christian education leaders should make a long-term commitment to curriculum change only when the material does not meet the needs of the people.

Griggs and Walther give the following caution concerning the selection of curriculum: "What is needed to respond to these concerns is a sense of direction, the affirmation of some basic goals for Christian education, and a recognition that curriculum involves more than ordering materials for teachers."[21] Curriculum, even good curriculum, is a tool, a way to help a church achieve its purpose in Christian education. It must always be adapted or customized for that specific church.

Churches sometimes choose curriculum materials for their attractive format or because teaching procedures are simple and easy to use. Brown gives some sound advice: "Any material that offers an unacceptable message must be discarded, no matter how teachable or attractive it is. Generally, it is more important for material to pass the message test and be teachable than it to be attractive."[22]

Curriculum materials for ongoing programs such as Sunday school are written in sessions, which make up units of study. These units are sequenced over quarterly and yearly plans to cover specific content or study areas. Thus, any curriculum needs to have continuity. Brown says, "If people are to grow in their faith, they need to explore and be challenged by all parts of it over the years."

Topical studies offered as part of a cafeteria approach may be popular but may not help people mature and grow as much as a planned, annual curriculum. For example, preschool and children's curriculum materials deal with specific topics at certain times in the child's life. Skipping around or using different materials may mean the children are not taught these important issues.

THE CONGREGATION AS TEACHER

Effective teaching uses a variety of learning activities. A wise teacher once said, "There is only one wrong teaching method, the one you always use." Learning activities, by the nature of what they are trying to help the learner do, must use different approaches. Wyckoff points out some areas covered in Christian education: "The subject matter covers the necessary knowledge of the Bible, the faith, and the personal and social demands of discipleship."[23] Each subject requires different teaching approaches as it covers knowledge, attitudes, and skills for applying what is learned. Following only one approach will be ineffective in helping the learners incorporate these truths into their lives.

Different learning aims require different methods or teaching approaches. The learning aim decides the teaching methods that are available to the teacher. Wyckoff notes, "The choice of learning activities is guided by the principle that persons learn the Christian faith and life by rich and reflective involvement in the worship, witness, and work of the church in its various ministries."[24] If worship, witness, and work of the church are important educational opportunities, some reflection, interpretation, and debriefing must occur after these activities so that maximum learning will take place.

The small church functions more like a family so "appropriate learning activities are more like informal learning in the family than formal learning in a school. There is an atmosphere of closeness, warmth, intimacy, and informality, difficult to achieve except in the small membership church."[25]

David R. Ray, summarizing The Search Institute's research on churches that are highly effective in promoting maturity of faith, says these are the desirable characteristics: "A climate of warmth, people experience receiving care from others, a climate of challenge, worship that touches the heart as well as the mind, lay and pastoral leaders of mature faith, and a strong and vibrant educational ministry."[26]

TRAINING CHRISTIAN EDUCATION LEADERS

Providing adequate training for its workers is a hard task for the small church. Doing local training has many hazards and problems to overcome. To do age-group training, there are sometimes only one or two people. In working with small churches I have tried several approaches.

If there are several small churches near yours, you could combine your training efforts with them. By pooling your workers and resources you could find a competent person to lead the training. (A pastor should not attempt to do all the training for the various age groups. You cannot be a specialist in every area.) Some denominations have volunteer teams that are willing to help train leaders for specific educational ministries. These teams will come to one church for this.

Denominational training events offer good opportunities to train educational workers. The small church should take advantage of these when they are in your area or your workers can attend. An advantage of this kind of training is that your workers are with people from other churches who are experiencing the same problems you are. There is a special dynamic that takes place at these events that motivates and inspires your workers. There are also interdenominational training events that can benefit your workers. These are usually in the area of Bible teaching or Sunday school work.

When I pastored a small church, we offered some local, in-house training opportunities. I would give workers a book that would help them. They were asked to read portions of the book, and then we would meet for an hour or so to review and discuss what they had read.

Another effective way to train new Christian education workers is to assign a new worker to an experienced worker. This works like an apprenticeship in that the novice learns from the experienced worker. The novice should take a turn at teaching or leading a group and then discuss what was done well and areas that need improving. Most small churches have excellent teachers and workers in every age group who should be used to train others.

RESULTS OF EFFECTIVE CHRISTIAN EDUCATION

What should happen to people as they become involved in Christian education? As people participate in activities and events, they should grow in Christian maturity and in the ability to influence their world for Christ. Griggs and Walther summarize the desired goal of Christian education as, "all will be of little value in the end if persons have not been invited to make choices, challenged to commit themselves to significant actions, encouraged to be in dialogue with one another, and nurtured and nourished to grow spiritually."[27]

Small churches are effective in nurturing mature faith. Through its quality Christian education ministry, the small church influences its local and larger community with the gospel of Jesus Christ.

CHAPTER 10

Training Teachers and Leaders

Edward A. Buchanan

Teachers and leaders in a local church require an effective Christian education program of training. Without trained volunteers a church would be unable to conduct its programs. Teachers need *content knowledge* in the areas in which they provide instruction, and *process skills* to teach and work with persons in small- and large-group situations. Other church leaders need content and skills to make them productive in fulfilling their offices as well. In Ephesians 4:12, the apostle Paul said that the purpose for providing church leaders is to *equip* members of the body of Christ to carry out their tasks of ministry. That equipping function requires trained teachers and leaders.

Evangelical Christians have stressed several important beliefs. Among these are the *priesthood of the believer,* which means that an individual Christian has direct access to God through the Holy Spirit. Another doctrine is the *soul competency of the believer.* This involves the ability of a believer to understand the biblical revelation and apply it appropriately under the guidance of the Holy Spirit. A third essential belief is a *regenerate church membership.* This means that each member must have a personal experience with Jesus Christ as Savior and Lord. Under the guidance of the Holy Spirit the work of the church is conducted by regenerate church members.

To practice these doctrines, a believer must have some biblical and theological understanding. It is important for an effective church that leaders understand, practice, and teach these doctrines. Therefore, leadership training is essential.

Teachers and leaders may be taught how to teach, administer, and interact with other church members. But there are basic, personal qualities that need to be considered in their selection. Being a teacher in Sunday school or ministering as a deacon requires that an individual exhibit personal faith, maturity, and integrity. These traits are not taught and should be present when the person is recruited for training and service.

There are several other desirable qualities: a teachable spirit, spending time in personal devotion and intercessory prayer, openness, honesty, self-control, humility, and maturity. Important spiritual traits include discerning the hand of God in everyday life experiences and demonstrating the inner peace of God. Together, these qualities assume a high standard for church leaders, but they are necessary for church effectiveness. Note that the requirements differ markedly from qualities expected of leaders in the business world.

In this chapter we will identify those persons for whom leadership training would be desirable, and we shall consider the elements of administration for an effective leadership training program.

SELECTING LEADERS FOR TRAINING

Because we live in a technologically advanced culture, many business organizations emphasize annual training and updating of their personnel. The only way that a business can compete in the contemporary world is by ensuring that its employees are knowledgeable and competitive in today's market. When one considers the myriad of activities conducted within American churches today, can there be any less emphasis upon leader preparation? The three groups of persons who need training are the paid professional staff, volunteer educational staff, and other volunteer church leaders.

TRAINING FOR PROFESSIONAL STAFF

The complexity of church organizations places heavy demands upon the pastoral staff. Continuing education for doctors, dentists, and lawyers is mandatory to remain licensed to practice in most states. While most churches do not require updating, they can encourage and reward ministers for seeking to improve knowledge and ministry-related skills. Studies show ministers are keenly aware of their educational needs and desire to participate in activities that will provide increasing competence in ministry.

A minister is expected to be spiritual leader, counselor, educator, discipler, administrator, teacher, motivator, worship leader, gifted communicator, and trainer. Also, a minister may be called upon to engage in the more specialized tasks of fundraising and directing a building program.

Another major responsibility is that of providing training for laity. Even if a minister has a seminary education, however, that person may not have the expertise to conduct specific types of training that may be required. For example, some seminary students become so enamored with preaching or counseling that they fail to prepare themselves adequately in courses for teaching. But running an active Bible study program will require specialized skills in teaching and leading. It is important for a church to recognize its responsibility to provide the ministerial staff with further preparation to carry out these vital roles. The expenditures will be well repaid in increased competence, ability to perform ministry, and more effective training of lay leaders for their tasks.

There are many ways by which a church can help its minister(s) increase useful knowledge and skill. Budgeting for books, journals, and membership in denominational and professional organizations is one way to increase effectiveness. Providing time and funds for workshops, denominational conferences, visits to other churches that are doing effective ministries, and paid sabbatical leaves are other means for rewarding service and increasing professional competence.

Another way to foster increased competence for ministers is through formal education. College, seminary, and extension programs are some possibilities.

TRAINING FOR EDUCATIONAL STAFF

A wide range of workshops, conferences, and materials is available for instructing the educational staff. The importance of this kind of training cannot be overemphasized. Teachers who know how to teach and what to teach can greatly help a church to fulfill its ministry purpose.

The vital role of teachers places them at the top of the list for receiving additional training. In leading teacher workshops the author has often been impressed with the many persons who have been affected by the ministry of a Sunday school teacher. The care and personal involvement of a teacher with a student have often made a difference in the student's commitment to Christ and the church.

A minister can multiply outreach and ministry by investing time and effort in instructing members of the teaching staff. Even if a pastor's time commitments prevent personal involvement in this teaching, the pastor should encourage, support, and strengthen the education of the teaching staff. If a church has a minister of education, he or she should either engage in teaching the staff or train other persons for such activity.

The content of teacher training usually focuses on methods. They are important but also must be balanced with knowledge of subject matter in theology, biblical foundations, missions, music, evangelism, and an understanding of Christian education in the church.

Other educational or semi-educational ministries require specialized training for workers. These include, for example, day-care, recreation programs, newcomer visitation, clubs, prison ministries, student ministries,

and meals-on-wheels. Family-centered ministries are increasingly important, requiring trained volunteers who can teach and counsel. Media and
library personnel need to receive training for their unique areas of ministry. Training for these specialized tasks should be sought from local, state,
and national denominational sources. It is unlikely that a local church will
have all the needed internal resources to prepare persons for all these tasks.

TRAINING FOR OTHER VOLUNTEER LEADERS

Along with the pastoral staff, deacons are most deeply involved in the
spiritual growth and welfare of the congregation. They need to receive special training, usually from the pastor, to carry out their duties. The same is
true for trustees. Their responsibilities require management of the physical
and financial resources of the church, but they should not be isolated from
the spiritual leadership. The pastor needs to help deacons and trustees to
accomplish their tasks of ministry as well. A portion of meeting time
should be set aside for training each month. Deacons and trustees should
also be involved in the more general training for church leaders toward
deepening their knowledge of Scripture and skills for leadership.

Ushers should receive specific training for the performance of their duties. Since ushers are often the first persons to meet a visitor, their attitudes
can encourage or discourage future involvement in the church. Their training needs to include meeting people and effective discharge of their responsibilities.

Central to church life are committees. Even a small church has many
committees that function to carry out its work. Team building, agendas,
conflict resolution, decision-making, and working to accomplish tasks are
all part of the training for persons who work on church committees. For
efficiency and effectiveness committee members need training. A small
portion of the time that committees meet may profitably be used in such
training.

Church officers, such as the financial secretary, church clerk, or church
chairperson, may require both specific training and an apprentice program
to develop skills. These positions require an individualized approach to instruction. Electing a new person to serve under the one who is already doing this ministry may be a helpful means for training. These leaders should
also receive more general leadership training as well.

In a church the list of training requirements and opportunities is almost
endless. As a byproduct, many learned skills can be used in other contexts
outside the church. Following the instruction of Jesus, leadership in ministry requires servant leadership. This leadership depends upon God
through prayer and seeks the welfare of both the individual and church.

ADMINISTERING A CHURCH LEADER TRAINING PROGRAM

Effective churches have found that there is no substitute for having leaders who are effectively trained for their tasks. The remainder of this chapter will focus on training these volunteer church leaders.

As listed in figure 10.1 and described below, there are nine steps in preparing and conducting an effective church leadership training program. At each step in the development of the program, there are choices that must be made. Careful attention must be focused upon needs in the local church situation.

STEP #1: FORECAST LEADERSHIP NEEDS

Knowing how many workers are needed for the church year can help you avoid the panic of not having enough teachers and leaders. You will need to anticipate enrollment changes and work to supply adequate support for the various ministry programs. As a church grows, the need for teaching and leading personnel will increase.

One growing church has had problems in the deacon Family Ministry program. As the church grew, the number of families for whom each deacon is responsible has exceeded reasonable limits. As new families entered the church, there was growing discontent because families did not receive packets of materials about ministry opportunities, nor were they invited to participate in the new member class. As a result the church enlisted the help of several husband-and-wife teams to minister in this manner. This freed the deacons to manage the tasks that could not be delegated and allowed more families to become involved in ministry. It also required training for the teams to assume their responsibilities.

In teaching activities such as Sunday school and Vacation Bible School, many educators recommend desirable teacher-to-student ratios at each age level. For preschoolers and kindergartners, a ratio of one teacher to five students is optimal. In childhood through high school, a one-to-eight ratio is preferred. At adult levels, the ratio will vary depending on the type of activity and your church's organizational patterns. You will also want to consider the number of departmental directors and other support staff personnel needed. After examination of your current teaching staff and any additional persons needed for turnover among teachers, you can anticipate the needs that will occur through growth of your church.

Churches need to employ a variety of means to discover potential leaders. Pastoral support through pulpit preaching about the role of laity in ministry is an important part of motivating people toward willingness to teach or lead. Through Bible teaching and discipleship programs, a church may sponsor an emphasis upon finding and using personal spiritual gifts. Some churches work with their new members to aid each to find his or her spiritual gift and exercise that gift in the ministry of the church. Following

Figure 10.1

9 STEPS FOR LEADERSHIP TRAINING

1. Forecast leadership needs

2. Identify training needs

3. Prepare a budget

4. Select training leaders

5. Schedule programs

6. Provide program support

7. Implement training

8. Recognize course completion

9. Evaluate the program

a churchwide emphasis upon the importance of ministry, an interest inventory may be used to locate persons who have experience and those who have interest but little experience in teaching and leadership.

An up-to-date computer file listing of membership interests and experience should be developed and maintained. Regularly teachers and other church leaders need to suggest the names of persons who seem ready to grow into positions of teaching or leading. To be effective all these potential leaders need to be trained!

STEP #2: IDENTIFY TRAINING NEEDS

A primary purpose for a church training program is to equip leaders for effective service. Throughout the church's organizations there should develop some uniformity in the knowledge and skills of leaders. All leaders should have general knowledge of the Scripture, doctrine, denominational distinctives, and personal Christian witness. Specialized training should also be provided as needed.

Each type of training will require a different approach. The Sunday school council should serve as the coordinating group to plan and oversee the kind and quality of training for Sunday school personnel. The church council should give oversight to plan and train general church leadership. A minister of education should be involved in coordinating a total program for improvement in teaching, training, and organizational administration. An associate minister might also be involved in these tasks.

In smaller churches the approach to training should be adjusted to meet local conditions. For example, the pastor, Sunday school director, and a knowledgeable member might assist in developing the necessary training. Someone needs to assume the responsibility for the program, however. It is important for the planning group to examine carefully the total training effort and avoid duplication. Some training may be useful for both general church leadership and for workers in the educational ministries.

Since time, money, and personnel resources are limited, a congregation will not be able to provide all of the training that it might wish to do. Priorities will need to be established, and some needs may have to be postponed. How does the planning group know which needs should be addressed this year? One way may be to determine where weaknesses, caused by faulty understanding, exist in the program. The pastor and pastoral staff can alert the committee to areas of need. A second way to gain insight into needs for training is through observation and assessment of the work of the Sunday school staff. A third way to accomplish this is by comparing job descriptions with the ability of workers to do the tasks listed. If there are gaps in understanding or doing a job, there are training needs.

A fourth means for deciding the leadership approach is prioritizing the knowledge and skills needed to serve and teach. Figure 10.2 on p. 232

Figure 10.2

TEACHER TRAINING NEEDS ASSESSMENT

Directions: Rank order items from 1 to 10, with 1= most needed to 10 = least needed.

___ Lesson planning

___ Classroom management

___ Growth and development across age levels

___ How to understand and use curriculum materials

___ Evaluating the lesson

___ Meeting needs of singles

___ Meeting needs of the elderly

___ Local church organization for Christian education

___ Methods for teaching

___ How people learn

Figure 10.3

TRAINING NEEDS ASSESSMENT INVENTORY

Directions: Rank order items from 1 to 10, with 1 = most needed to 10 = least needed.

___ Bible Introduction: Old and New Testaments

___ Administrative skills for church leadership

___ Interpersonal skills

___ Personal spiritual growth

___ Personal evangelism

___ Helping skills for counseling hurting persons

___ Strengthening the family

___ Christian beliefs

___ Missions

___ Developing a ministry of small groups

Figure 10.4

BUDGET PLANNING WORKSHEET
CHURCH LEADER TRAINING

Estimate costs for the following items to submit for the annual church budget:

1. Administrative costs:
   Paid outside speakers
   Other
   Total

2. Student materials:
   Books
   Other literature
   Duplicating costs
   Total

3. Instructors' resources:
   Books
   Instructional media
   Printing and duplicating
   Supplies
   Total

4. Publicity:
   Total

5. Recognition:
   Total

6. Miscellaneous expenses:
   Total
   TOTAL EXPENSES

presents a "Teacher Training Needs Assessment" form that can be used to evaluate the educational needs of church teaching personnel. The Sunday school council and pastoral staff may rank the items from "most needed now" to "least needed now." After each member of the group has finished ranking the items, the rankings for each item are added and divided by the number of participants. Then, the items are placed in priority order according to the *group* ranking, from the lowest score (most needed) to the highest (least needed). Then training activities are planned in the areas that the group has identified as most needed. Figure 10.3, Training Needs Assessment Inventory, presents a similar list for general church leadership. Following the same procedure, the pastoral staff and church council can also rank the items.

STEP #3: PREPARE A BUDGET

After deciding what kind of training is needed, the costs involved are considered. The financial costs of training may be determined by using the "Budget Planning Worksheet" in figure 10.4 on p. 233. Prices of materials may be found in a church literature catalog or obtained from a religious bookstore. The cost of printing noncopyrighted materials can be discovered through the church office. The means for recognition of participants—and the estimated cost of dinner, certificates, or other means that the church will provide—must be discussed. Miscellaneous costs will also need to be estimated. The course leader and the pastoral staff may also have additional costs. The budget should be submitted at the normal time for developing the annual church budget.

Besides financial costs, there is the time and personnel required. If a significant portion of the time for a minister of education is spent in training, this may necessitate curtailment or elimination of some other tasks. For the laity, the cost may include time away from family by attending training sessions and engaging in home study.

If the cost for training seems high, what about the lost opportunities that can occur if leaders are not trained? For those who are taught by untrained persons, it may mean failure to find a meaningful and eternal relationship with Christ. For others, it may mean going to another church where the volunteer staff is trained and displays greater understanding of Scripture and compassion for persons. In other situations, it may mean a church fight because leaders do not know how to work effectively with persons or do not adequately understand church doctrines. To determine the importance of your training program, the costs must be weighed against the benefits to be gained.

STEP #4: SELECT TRAINING LEADERS

A typical responsibility in the job description for a minister of education is that of leader training. Lacking a minister of education, the church may want to seek help from a qualified lay person to be program director. The trainer of leaders must be a good example to those who are trained. The qualities of an effective leader, discussed earlier, should be present in the program director—including skills in program and administration. He or she should be relieved of other responsibilities to devote adequate time and energy to this very important assignment.

The program director should be effective in planning church training events that will meet the needs determined by the Sunday school council or the church council. This includes organizing an effective program and staffing it with teachers who can instruct the various courses. Above all, the director should be well respected and an effective motivator.

Coordinating the entire program will require major effort by the director. Besides planning, organizing, and directing activities, the director will need to oversee publicity for the program, manage the training budget, and report progress of the program to the congregation. Finally, the director will guide the council to evaluate the effectiveness and suggest revisions for training efforts.

Selecting qualified course instructors will be a major responsibility of the director of training. Instructors should be skilled in selecting and using appropriate resources to guide leaders. Planning sessions should include the development of a teaching plan for optimal use of training time. This is especially important in modeling behavior for persons in the educational programs. The course instructor should also show skill in the performance of teaching. Both content and methods should reflect a high quality of church training. Each course should be evaluated for its effectiveness in meeting needs.

STEP #5: SCHEDULE PROGRAMS

The first consideration in scheduling the programs is setting the calendar for training events. If the church chooses to conduct short-term training events for new workers or programs, sessions may be scheduled several weeks before the time when duties will begin. For general leadership courses, such as a study on age-group needs or hospital visitation, the middle of the fall and/or spring works well.

If training will be provided in quarterly, thirteen-session cycles, the same schedule used by other church organizations should be followed. If only two cycles will be offered, you can consider September through November and February through April. However the church chooses to schedule programs, it is wise to avoid meetings that would interfere with Advent and Easter. Short-term events might be scheduled around the 13-week cycles or even during the summer.

The second consideration involves whether training will be done *before* service or *during* service. Educator and psychologist Robert Havighurst enunciated the principle of the *teachable moment*, the moment when persons are most apt to be motivated and learn.[1] The teachable moment is that point when the learner is called upon to teach or minister but may feel inadequate or overwhelmed by the task. The teachable moment may mean that training should be conducted at any of three times during the cycle of leadership: preservice, inservice, or advanced training, which provides deepened understanding.

Preservice Training. Preservice training is a means for enlisting and equipping persons who are interested in teaching or leadership but who do not yet possess the knowledge and skills needed to do these tasks. Identify persons for preservice training who have shown interest and are found in

Figure 10.5

BIBLICAL/DOCTRINAL FOUNDATIONS

WEEK	TOPIC
1.	Understanding the Old Testament Books of the Law
2.	Understanding the Old Testament Books of Poetry and Wisdom
3.	Understanding the Old Testament Books of Prophecy
4.	Understanding the Old Testament Books of History
5.	Understanding the New Testament Gospels
6.	Understanding the New Testament Church in Acts
7.	Understanding the New Testament Letters of Paul
8.	Understanding the other New Testament Writings
9.	How we got our Bible
10.	What we believe—Basic doctrines
11.	What we believe—Basic doctrines
12.	How the Church grew from the early Church to the present
13.	How our denomination developed and what it believes

TEACHER TRAINING

WEEK	TOPIC
1.	Personal Christian growth for the teacher
2.	Organization of our church's educational programs
3.	How people learn
4.	Understanding children
5.	Understanding youth
6.	Understanding adults and senior adults
7.	Understanding special groups, as singles, divorced, handicapped
8.	Lesson planning
9.	Understanding your curriculum
10.	Presentation methods for teaching
11.	Interactive methods for teaching
12.	Evangelizing the persons with whom you work
13.	Evaluating your teaching

LEADERSHIP PREPARATION

WEEK	TOPIC
1.	What is church leadership?
2.	Examples of leaders from the Bible—Nehemiah, Jesus, Paul
3.	Developing skills and working with people
4.	Effective personal witness to faith
5.	Developing ministry skills of caring, counseling, and relating
6.	How our church is organized and conducts its work
7.	Leadership principles: planning and organizing
8.	Why programs are necessary for effective ministry
9.	Developing and managing resources of people and money
10.	Directing and coordinating programs for ministry
11.	Reporting and evaluating the work of the church
12.	Effective work on committees
13.	Developing your personal Christian life

the computer file, as suggested under step 1, "Forecast Leadership Needs." Preservice courses are designed to introduce a person to the teaching or leading ministries. General knowledge of the Bible, doctrine, and church ministries are among the topics that should be included for all persons who are interested in positions of teaching or leading.

Interpersonal skills are essential for all church leaders. A course in this area is important before a person enters a leadership role. The prospective teacher may be given opportunity to observe experienced teachers and to teach part of the lesson as familiarity with content and methods is gained. For other leaders, preservice training may include development of administrative skills. Planning, leading, communicating, involving, budgeting, and evaluating are possible topics.

Preservice courses have a distinct advantage over inservice courses, since they prepare persons in advance for their leadership tasks and teaching may be extended over a quarter or more.

A suggested schedule for three thirteen-week preservice courses is in figure 10.5. The first, "Biblical/Doctrinal Foundations," will prepare persons to understand the biblical and doctrinal foundations of their faith and may be taken by all leaders and teachers. The second, "Teacher Training," is for teachers and leaders in the educational programs. A third course, "Leadership Preparation," is designed to present material that will help develop all potential leaders.

While the preservice model for teacher/leader training is ideal, many potential workers do not feel the need to engage in training until they are pressed into service. Therefore, we turn next to the inservice model.

Inservice Training. The inservice model is the most popular form for training teachers and leaders for church ministries. Training events may be scheduled in a variety of formats, such as one-on-one tutoring, small-group workshops, and large-group sessions/denominational conferences. The most common approach involves teachers and leaders in small- to medium-sized groups for a specified time.

Self-study is another format for inservice training. Under the guidance of a manual or syllabus, the learner engages in the study of written and audiovisual materials in the privacy of one's home or in designated rooms at specific times in the local church. The advantage of self-study lies in its flexibility to fit the specific needs of the learner. The disadvantage is that self-study requires the learner to be a self-starter and highly motivated. If either of these qualities is missing, the learner may have good intentions, but the learning may be displaced by more immediate concerns. The use of audiovisual materials, such as well-produced videotapes, may help to alleviate some of these disadvantages by engaging the learner through a delivery system that is contemporary and effective.

Figure 10.6

PREPARING LEADERS:
INSERVICE TRAINING COURSES

1. Self-directed study courses

2. Local church workers' conferences

3. Regular meetings for officers and teachers

4. Curriculum preview and planning workshops

5. Curriculum resources clinic

6. Short-term courses and study courses

7. Skill development clinic

8. Media center

9. Denominational workshops

10. Telelectures/teleconferences/computer assisted instruction

In a small-to-medium-sized group, one can combine group study with personal study. Accountability to the group can help to motivate the learner. Having a set time for meeting will alleviate the necessity to be a self-starter.

Several formats appropriate for inservice training are listed in figure 10.6. Weekend workshops, retreats, and Sunday or Wednesday evening meetings are popular. Regional or associational meetings have the added advantage of cost effectiveness by involving several churches in the training program.

For Sunday school training, a weekly or monthly workers meeting provides an excellent opportunity for teachers and officers to gather and share common concerns. They can use this time to plan teaching and outreach strategies, understand the curriculum, develop skills for teaching, and pray together. For other organizations, periodic sessions or a portion of regular group meetings may be used to develop needed knowledge and skills.

A church's media center is an excellent location for training sessions, with audiovisual aids and learning resources easily available. A byproduct of meeting here is that teachers and leaders will become familiar with helpful resources for future use.

Large-group sessions and denominational conferences may also be used for inservice training. (Refer to fig. 10.5 for several outlines of topics that might be covered in large-group sessions.) These sessions will be relevant for inservice teachers and also those in preservice.

The key for the pastor or minister of education is the maintenance of contact with a variety of resources for workshops and seminars. A schedule of events and training conferences may be obtained from local, state, or national offices. Also, many church-related colleges, seminaries, and conference centers sponsor training events and conferences for church workers. Increasingly, religious publishers are providing training for those who use their curriculum materials.

One unique program available for lay church leaders is the Church Study Course. Leadership training for every phase of church life is represented, with several hundred courses available.[2] Certificates are available in a variety of categories upon completion of a prescribed course of study.

Another approach to instruction involves the use of new technologies for teaching. These include telelectures, teleconferencing, microwave and satellite transmission, and cable television. For example, the insignificant cost of a phone amplifier will often be adequate to provide the participation of an expert in a training session for the cost of a long distance telephone call. Cable television stations often sell time at reasonable rates, especially during off-hours, and some public channels will even train personnel to run the cameras and edit tapes for local use. Computer-assisted instruction (CAI) is another avenue that is available. New technology offers a host of possibilities that were unavailable until recently.

Advanced Training. Both general and specific competence may be enhanced by taking courses through recognized institutions of higher education. These would include correspondence, Bible college and seminary courses. Many church-related colleges and seminaries offer programs to help lay persons to enhance their ministry skills.

Another opportunity is through volunteer work related to internships, fellowships, and missions. Well-trained lay leaders and pastoral staff often are the best prospects for short-term assignments that involve the use and development of skills in an advanced way or in mission settings. Training is attained through working at a different or higher level, studying topics related to the assignment, and working with highly skilled colleagues. For example, many special workers are used in denominational offices to help with leadership training conferences, Sunday school conventions, and church growth consultations.

STEP #6: PROVIDE PROGRAM SUPPORT

To run a successful program it is essential to secure the commitment of the pastoral staff and other church leadership. Lack of support or only half-hearted support from church leaders will quickly squelch enthusiastic participation among church members. Leaders may affirm the program and encourage involvement by announcements from the pulpit and by personally contacting prospective participants. With all of the discussion about church growth, training for teachers and leaders is one tangible means to affect the quality of church experience for newcomers and older members alike.

There are topics that should be considered for inclusion in the curriculum for leadership training. Examples of content for general leadership training might include administrative skills, interpersonal skills, Christian beliefs, denominational history and polity, Bible content, personal spiritual growth, evangelism, and missions. Beyond the general leadership content, teacher training might include lesson planning and methods, age-level specializations, music education, church educational ministries, and developing Christian disciples. These resources can be located by consulting persons from association, state, and denominational agencies, or by examining catalogs of training materials, including the bookstore and especially the study course catalogs. For most training situations the available resources will satisfy needs. If they do not, state or local resource persons may help custom design a training package for specific situations.

This support needs to extend as well to time and place of meeting and financial backing. If the program is assigned a meeting time that is inconvenient or unlikely to attract the best prospects for training, then the church will show that it does not place a high priority on teacher training. The largest number of persons will be reached on Sunday mornings. Sunday evenings and times congruent with a midweek service are probably the next most desirable times.

Place of meeting is another concern. If the facilities are dingy and unattractive, the church is telling current or prospective leaders that it does not value them or the training that they are receiving. The training facilities should be the best that the church can provide. The same principle applies to the financial support for the program. If a miserly approach is taken, the church will reap proportionate results. One must assume that help with providing textbook materials and duplicated materials are important to the success of a training program. Since leaders are donating their time and effort to become prepared, the church should be willing to provide the materials for training.

Publicity is another ingredient to a successful program. Teachers and leaders are not likely to respond to one or two general announcements. A personal request for participation is desirable. When the planning group has decided the kind of training and the time and place of meeting, an attractive brochure should be developed. It should clearly state the purpose and specific benefits that will be gained from the program. It should clearly state the requirements. The next step is sending the brochure to persons likely to benefit. Copies of the brochure are then prominently displayed in the church foyer. But brochures are no substitute for the personal contact by a church leader, who asks for participation and gives a copy of the brochure with the details of the program.

STEP #7: IMPLEMENT TRAINING

The training must be undergirded with prayer in advance and throughout the program. One or two weeks before the first session, members of the leadership team should initiate a personal contact by letter and follow up the contact with a telephone call before the first session. In our culture people are so bombarded with competing requests for time and energy that they are unlikely to respond unless they are reminded and can see the potential benefits.

Teachers should be encouraged to develop goals and lesson plans for each session. Many programs have a teacher's manual with prepared goals and lesson plans. Even these will need to be modified to meet local conditions. If the participants do not know each other, the first session should be devoted to developing acquaintance and beginning relationships. Throughout the course, the director should be in touch with the class instructor to provide encouragement and assistance.

STEP #8: RECOGNIZE COURSE COMPLETION

Members who have completed the course should be recognized for their accomplishment. The ministries of the church will be furthered because of their diligence. A service of recognition provides one expression of the church's appreciation for their work. The service might include video-taped highlights from the training sessions, a prayer of dedication for the persons who participated, and presentation of certificates of achievement. It is important for the pastor to have high visibility in the service and with the persons who finished the course. The pastor's involvement will help in enlisting participants for future educational endeavors. Certificates are available at most religious bookstores, or churches may prepare their own with the assistance of a desktop publishing program.

STEP #9: EVALUATE THE PROGRAM

The final step in this model is evaluation of each course and the total program for the year. Participants in the course should be asked questions like the following: What did you learn from this course? How has this course helped you to become a more effective leader in our church? What did you like best and least about this course? What could be done more effectively in this course?

The course leader should write his or her reflections upon the course and, with the program director, discuss and record findings. Suggestions for improving the course should be recorded for future training events.

At the end of training for the year, the director should gather all of the evaluations for the courses and examine what has been accomplished during the year. The training is then compared with the purposes that were originally established, as suggested under step 2, "Identify Training Needs." Were the purposes of the course(s) realized? Did our church achieve its goals for training during this year? If we did not, how might we improve? What should be our priorities for next year?

In reporting to the Sunday school council and the church council, the program director will want to offer guidance for working through the nine steps of the cycle for the next year. The cycle begins anew.

CHAPTER 11

Guiding Outreach and Enlistment

Bruce P. Powers

Outreach and enlistment are major activities for evangelical churches. Along with their educational endeavors, these churches stress reaching and involving new persons in their activities, with the hope of making and maturing Christian disciples.

WHY COMBINE EDUCATION AND OUTREACH?

Efforts to involve more people in an organization must be viewed from two perspectives: individual growth and corporate growth. *Individual growth* focuses on providing experiences that will enable people to discover their existence as children of God and grow to their full potential as part of a loving, supportive community of faith. This type of growth might be selfish and self-centered, however, unless complemented with a commitment to *corporate* growth.

Corporate growth relates to the spiritual growth of a group or congregation; to the development of a maturing, caring, cohesive body; to the process of discovering, developing, and using spiritual gifts; and to reaching the multitudes for Jesus Christ.

Some people dichotomize individual and corporate growth, usually at the point of meeting personal needs *versus* reaching the masses. This is unfortunate because neither can be fully accomplished without the other. Each supports the other and makes the other more effective.

The Great Commission (see Matt. 28:19–20) focuses on four action words that bring individual and corporate growth together: *go, make* (disciples), *baptize*, and *teach.* It is this *mandate* that calls leaders to seek growth not only for each person but also for the entire body of which individuals are a part.

GUIDING OUTREACH

Ongoing visitation that is a natural outpouring of personal conviction and concern is central to reaching people. For many persons, such contacts are a natural part of daily life, whether telling others about Jesus, visiting a sick person, or inviting newcomers to visit a Sunday school class. Others, however, find it helpful to have planned outreach activities, and most congregations find a regular program increases the quantity and quality of visitation.

A TIME

There should be regular times for churchwide (or department, class, etc.) visitation. This might be weekly, biweekly, or monthly, in the morning and/or evening. The key is to make it regular and to provide all the encouragement and support necessary for the congregation to believe this is a priority. Promoting the time, not scheduling conflicting activities, and, if needed, providing childcare for those visiting are vital.

A PLACE

A regular meeting place can serve as an administrative center and rallying point. Often this will be the church building, but it could be any place that is convenient to visitation points and where parking and meeting facilities are available.

A VISITATION FILE

There should be a file of prospects and other persons who might be responsive to a visit. Persons can be classified in three categories—nonmembers, inactive members, and sick/shut-in members—and equal attention given to each group. Before each visitation time, priorities for visits should be set so that visitors will know exactly whom to visit, why, and where.

Information gathering. Channels can be set up to receive names and contact data for persons in each of the three visitation categories. A person (and place) is designated to whom outreach leaders, department directors, teachers, and other interested church members will send names. Cards are provided in pew racks or a tear-off slip in the bulletin which worshipers can use to indicate if they want a visit or to give the name of someone who does (see fig. 11.1).

Contact can be made through church members if possible, with realtors, newcomers clubs, and utility companies to secure lists of newcomers to the

Figure 11.1

Please fill in

DATE_____

YOUR NAME _____

ADDRESS _____ PHONE _____

CITY _____ STATE _____ ZIP_____

BUSINESS _____

YOUR HOME CHURCH   _____

WOULD YOU LIKE A VISIT FROM THE PASTOR?   _____

PLEASE CHECK AGE GROUP   ☐ Under 12   ☐ 18–29   ☐ 45–over
                           ☐ 12–17   ☐ 30–44

(Front)

Pastor's Card

NAME _____

ADDRESS _____

PHONE _____

BUSINESS _____

THIS PERSON ☐ IS SICK   ☐ IS NEW RESIDENT
            ☐ DESIRES PASTORAL CALL   ☐ WANTS OFFERING ENVELOPES
            ☐ PROSPECTIVE MEMBER   ☐ HAS CHANGED ADDRESS TO

_____   _____
(Name of person giving information)
PLEASE USE THIS CARD FREELY.   Place in offering plate.

(Back)

community. At least once a week, all names and contact information should be transferred to visitation cards or forms. Preliminary lists may be maintained in a computer data base or file folder, but for use by visitors, information must be transferred to cards or forms. (See fig. 11.2 for an example.)

Figure 11.2

Prospect File Card

Date | Prospect's name

Street address | City | State | Zip Code | Home phone no.

Mailing address (if different) | Date of birth | School grade

Church member? ☐ Yes ☐ No | Church to which prospect belongs | City

Additional information

Assigned to: | Department | Class/group/choir/etc. | Date

Visited by | Date | Results

Setting up the file. Cards are arranged in three categories: nonmembers, inactive members, and sick or shut-in members. In a small church, all cards might be kept together. If many cards are involved, different colors can be used to distinguish the categories. In large churches or in urban areas, it would be helpful to maintain a separate set of files according to area of town, community, or zip code.

Maintaining the file. Comments recorded on visitation cards should be reviewed periodically to reclassify the card if appropriate, channel it to a class outreach leader or other responsible person, recycle for another visit, or place in an inactive file.

A LEADER

Effective visitation requires a committed leader who will promote and coordinate activities. This person reviews the visitation file; arranges and distributes assignments; supports, encourages, and participates in visitation; and helps in collecting, evaluating, and reporting results. A church staff member or a highly motivated layperson could provide this leadership. If visitors gather at several meeting places, a coordinator for each location would need to be enlisted by the leader to assist with leadership responsibilities.

Figure 11.3

ENLISTING MEMBERS IN EDUCATIONAL ORGANIZATIONS

A. Distinguish between publicity and enlistment.

What is publicity?

What is enlistment?

Notes:

B. Evaluate your group's publicity.

1. What image is your group conveying to the church through its publicity?

2. What are some ways your group has made people aware of study opportunities available to them?

3. What types of publicity are used most often?

Is there good variety?   Yes   No

4. Where are some places that would be good to locate publicity?

5. What other channels for publicity are available to your group?

C. Evaluate your group's enlistment.

1. Who is responsible for enlistment in your group?

2. What methods of enlistment are used most often? How are these related to the topics studied?

3. How effective has your enlistment been?

4. What are some suggestions you would make to your group?

D. Application

The worksheet on the following page is based on the information given above. Select a coming unit of study and work through it as if you were planning activities for enlistment and publicity.

Figure 11.4

PUBLICITY AND ENLISTMENT WORKSHEET

STUDY TOPIC _____   **LEADER(S)**_____
DATE(S) OF STUDY _____   **PUBLICITY CHAIR** _____

1. **Decide on target groups or persons.**

    (List in column one groups or individuals who need this study or might be interested.)

2. **Select publicity and enlistment locations.**

    (Figure out the best places to find and influence the groups or persons listed above and write the locations in column two. This might be in Sunday school departments, at meetings, at homes, bulletin boards, newsletters, etc.)

3. **What specific methods and plans will you use?**

    (For each group or individual, decide the exact way the publicity or contact will be made, such as letter, visit, phone call, announcement, or posters.)

4. **Assign responsibility for each of the publicity or enlistment actions.**

    (Write names next to each of the actions listed above. Each person should know exactly what is to be done, when, and by whom. The publicity chair should retain a copy of the plansheet and follow up as necessary. Be sure to evaluate the effectiveness of these efforts so that you can learn what works best for your group.)

GUIDING ENLISTMENT

Closely related to outreach is enlistment. Rather than having a general purpose, however, the aim of enlistment is to secure participation in specific organizations or activities. Although usually administered by leaders at the department/class/group level, persons with churchwide educational responsibilities often are called on to provide assistance.

To help you give guidance in enlistment, here are the basic principles involved in reaching and involving new people in educational organizations. Included in this chapter are a training session worksheet (fig. 11.3, p. 247) and an enlistment plansheet (fig. 11.4, p. 248) which could be used in training workers.

WHY DO PEOPLE RESPOND?

People are need-oriented; that is, they respond to needs they feel or can be caused to feel. The greater the need they feel, the stronger their desire to satisfy that need. For example, if a person wants a more active social life, the tendency is to try to satisfy this need. If a person feels a need for training in how to witness, he or she will try to meet this need.

People usually respond to invitations that they believe promise some satisfaction or benefit. For example, if you were to invite some couples to join your group, they would think, "Why?" The appeal must answer this question if the expectation is to reach and involve them in that group.

HOW ARE PEOPLE REACHED?

Prospects ask themselves, "Why should we?" To reach them, you must do two things: (1) determine and/or help them recognize a need that they have; and (2) offer a *benefit* that, in the prospects' opinion, will meet their need. People have needs; a group must offer benefits. When needs are matched with appropriate benefits, the potential is greatly increased for reaching and involving prospects.

WHAT IS ENLISTMENT? WHAT IS PUBLICITY?

Most people are familiar with the word enlistment, but if you had to describe what it means, what would you say?

We must also be concerned about publicity. What does this word mean? How are enlistment and publicity related?

Basically, enlistment is reaching and involving someone in an activity. It may involve informal contacts, personal visits, telephone calls, or a personal note. But the contact is usually person to person.

Publicity, on the other hand, is designed to provide information, to create awareness or an image, or to develop a desire by the person receiving the message. Publicity may involve posters, announcements, skits, signboards, and mass mailings. Usually the contact is impersonal in that the message is intended to reach many people.

Once enlistment and publicity are distinguished, one can tell that they have similar purposes—that is, to reach people. Yet, strangely, they do not accomplish similar results.

Publicity does not guarantee a response. It provides information or creates an image, but this merely increases the potential for response. It does not "sell" anything unless the person receiving the message feels or can be caused to feel a need related to the "product" offered by the publicity. If the publicity offers a benefit that will meet a need felt by the receiver of the message, then the potential for positive response is present.

Here is the problem: Most of what is done in enlistment efforts is really publicity. How do most churches try to reach new members? They use posters, bulletin announcements, announcements from the pulpit and in Sunday school departments, skits, newsletters, and various other types of mailings. All are publicity, and publicity never enlists anyone unless a person feels a need that can be met by the "product" offered.

Enlistment, however, can build on a potential for response. Prospects can be reached through personal contact, attention to their needs and concerns, and by showing them the benefits that would meet their needs. Enlistment is always person-to-person and can relate benefits and needs.

PLANNING FOR AND CONDUCTING ENLISTMENT

The key to reaching people effectively is to match a prospect's need with the needs a particular unit of study or a particular group will meet. For example, a person who feels the need for a study on witnessing could most easily be reached when the group is studying witnessing.

Here is how to plan for effective enlistment and publicity:

1. Determine the needs a particular unit of study will meet.

2. Answer these questions:

    • Who has these or similar needs (may be individuals or groups)?

    • Where can these people be reached?

    • What methods will be most effective in reaching these people? (Keep in mind a balance between publicity and enlistment activities.)

    • Who will be responsible for each publicity or enlistment action?

The important thing in this plan is to be specific and to involve the group in making enlistment and publicity plans. (fig. 11.4 shows a plansheet that could be used with classes and groups.) The teacher, director, or enlistment leader should lead members in this planning at least two weeks before a new topic or program. An intensive enlistment effort based on a unit of study that will meet specific needs should be made at least once a quarter.

CHAPTER 12

Nurturing and Teaching New Christians

Edward A. Buchanan

A husband and wife recently joined a local church. The Bible study class of their age level invited the couple to attend a social function at a recreational center on Saturday morning. In advance of the event the couple drove to the location in order to assure themselves that they would not have difficulty finding the center. They were excited about the opportunity to make new friends in their new church. But on the day of the event, they were unavoidably delayed. As a result they arrived at the center after the function began. It was obviously crowded and they would have been embarrassed to enter late. The couple left disappointed. Their attendance on Sunday became more sporadic. Within a few weeks they stopped going to the church altogether. Even though this couple had recently made a profession of faith, the church lost its opportunity to nurture them.

How different this scenario could have been if the church had paid a little more attention to the welfare of the couple. A person from the class could have called the couple and arranged to meet them and involve them in this social event and, later, in the life of the class and the church. It would not have involved a lot of effort, just a little planning. It might have changed the entire involvement of this couple in their relationship to the church and the church's relationship to them. Even more importantly, it probably would have had an impact upon their personal relationship with God. God has entrusted to the church an awesome responsibility for the guidance and spiritual welfare of persons.

NURTURING AND TEACHING FOR GROWTH

The Bible speaks often of the need for nurturing and teaching new believers. The early church nurtured and taught its converts. Teaching new believers is still an important function in the church today. Many contemporary churches, however, are giving less attention to this vital objective.

DEFINITION OF NURTURE AND TEACHING

Before examining the use of these terms, it may be helpful to define them as they will be used in this chapter. Both terms appear in the New Testament. The applicability of each term is significant to the growth and development of the church. Each individual believer has responsibility before God for spiritual growth within the community of faith. In a congregational form of government, the effectiveness of the church depends on a regenerate church membership for leadership and carrying out the ministries of the church. Hence, the role of nurture and teaching is important.

Nurture. Nurture was originally derived from a Latin word that meant to provide nourishment for a child. Over the centuries this definition expanded to encompass the idea of educating or training any person. Its use in the New Testament (see Eph. 6:4) carries the idea of "bringing up a child." The classical Greek concept included the idea of striving for the good. In other words, it included a moral element. Nurture also includes an affective dimension of emotional support. In adult education in the church, the term applies to the caregiving, encouragement, and emotional support of persons as they grow in their understanding of their new faith in Christ.

Teaching. The word *teaching* is derived from an old English word that means to impart knowledge or to instruct. It also means to learn by example or experience and to fit a person for a desired role. As it is used here, the desired role is that of functioning as a mature Christian in the home, work, church, and the world. Teaching also carries the idea that it is done in a systematic manner. In the New Testament the term appears ninety-five times. It includes educating the whole person, not just the intellect.

BIBLICAL BASIS FOR NURTURE AND TEACHING

Several examples of the ideas encompassed by these concepts will illustrate their importance in preparing persons for growth in the Christian life.

Deuteronomy 6:4–9. This Old Testament passage exemplifies the importance of family-centered teaching of the covenant relationship between the people of Israel and God. Godly persons are instructed to impress the message upon children in a continuing rehearsal of their relationship with God.

In the Feast of the Passover, for example, the father and son carry on a dialogue and recount the deliverance of the people of Israel from bondage in Egypt. But the telling and retelling of the story is not limited to the feast days. The command to love God is to be told while the family is at home and when they are traveling. It is to be rehearsed in the morning and at night. As the text indicates, teaching symbols are to be used to keep God in the forefront of the thoughts of the people.

Matthew 9:35. This verse describes Jesus' teaching in the synagogues. Years later the apostle Paul did the same. The synagogue was a learning center designed for teaching and learning. The teaching was not so much theoretical learning but especially practical learning for everyday life. There is a need to call the church back to this perspective as a significant part of its mission.

Matthew 28:19–20. Jesus commissioned his disciples in his final words. He commanded them to go and make life-long learners of those to whom they brought the good news of the gospel. The life-long nature of the command would allow the learners to have their lives molded and refashioned from a worldly approach to life into a godly lifestyle. Baptism symbolizes the significance of this change. Jesus commanded that his disciples teach new Christians. The teaching was to be done in a systematic manner.

Ephesians 4:11–16. Leaders of the church should guide and equip church members to reach a high level of maturity. The church should practice caregiving. A leader should seek to shepherd an erring member back into the way. The leader has the responsibility to build up or perfect the believers in his or her charge. The goal involves helping the believer reach the stature of the fullness of Christ.

Nurture is implicit in the admonition to maintain a level of understanding that will not allow a believer to be turned to false doctrine or religious fads. Rather, the body of believers, the church, is most effective when it is healthy and directed by the head, which is Christ. Each believer must maintain an intimate attachment to Christ. Teaching is important, but it must be accompanied by the nurture in love.

Colossians 1:3–14. In this prayer for the Colossians, Paul states that to love without the truth will result in mere sentimentality. To have faith without love can only end in a dead orthodoxy. Both extremes may be found in the church today. Any discomfort and suffering that a believer may suffer for fidelity to Christ will be repaid in the hope of the ultimate fulfillment of redemption in heaven. This kind of mature understanding only comes through nurture of faith under the teaching of their leader, Epaphras.

The apostle continues by praying that the believers will be filled with knowledge, wisdom, and understanding. It should result in application to practical living. Paul prays that they will conduct their lives in a manner that will please God. Finally, he prays that they will receive strength and power to accomplish this in life.

1 John 1:5–7. Fellowship is identified as a significant part of the life of the church. But the fellowship is not simply good friendships. Rather, fellowship in the church is determined by members' common commitment to Christ. They share a very special relationship through the Spirit of God.

TWO EXAMPLES OF CHURCH NURTURE
AND TEACHING FROM THE PAST

Several approaches to teaching and nurture from the history of the church have affected religious instruction. These have implications for Christian initiation and spiritual formation today. One comes from the early church and the other from the Reformation. In each case, a crisis needed to be addressed.

Catechumenate from the ancient church. The ancient church had to deal with an influx of converts, who did not understand the meaning of their new faith or how to incorporate their faith into a Christian lifestyle. It is evident from the church writings as early as 125, like the *Teaching of the Twelve Apostles* or the *Didache*,[1] that the church leaders wanted to carry out the biblical instruction to teach new believers. Since Roman society was very corrupt and immoral, it was necessary to find means not only to teach new converts but to ensure that their way of life was appropriate.

As a seeker or inquirer, and prior to conversion, a person could attend the preaching service. If a person wanted to join the church, however, he or she had to indicate this desire to the leaders and describe the conversion experience. If the person was accepted, he or she would enter a period of spiritual formation through the *catechumenate*. (The word originated from the Greek word, *katecheo*, which means "to instruct.") As the word suggests, this was a period of learning and growth. A sponsor was appointed to help with teaching, caring, and moral scrutiny. Following conversion, a person remained in the *catechumenate* for two to three years. During that time the new believer had to give evidence of the transformation that had occurred.

Toward the end of the *catechumenate* the person would again be given a moral scrutiny and could move to the final stage in preparation for baptism. This happened during the period that became known as Lent. The believer would receive more intense instruction. The teaching usually included study of the ethical demands of Christianity, study of prayer through the Lord's Prayer, and study of baptism, communion, Bible history, church history, and simple theology. The writings of the church fathers suggest that the *catechumenate* was fairly standard practice.

On the night before baptism, the candidate would stay up all night in prayer and penitence. The candidate then memorized a creed. This provided a compendium of the Christian faith and belief. Baptism usually took place on Easter morning and symbolized the death, burial, and resurrection of Christ. It also symbolized identification of the believer with Christ and the church. The newly baptized believer would then receive communion and become inducted into membership.

The *catechumenate* was a very effective form of adult education. It combined teaching about the spiritual life and Christian lifestyle with learning the basic facts of Christian faith. As infant baptism increased in popularity, however, the *catechumenate* declined and eventually disappeared altogether.

Catechism from the Reformation. Eleven years after the Reformation began, Martin Luther realized that something had to be done to meet biblical illiteracy among his followers. In response, Luther preached a series of sermons which have affected Christian nurture ever since. These sermons became the foundation for both the *Large Catechism*[2] and the *Small Catechism*. Unlike previous catechisms, these catechisms stressed Scripture. To Luther, the catechism was a summary of Scripture. He taught the Ten Commandments to emphasize the way in which Christians should ethically behave. He taught doctrine through the Apostles' Creed, much as the Apostles' Creed had also been used for the same purpose generations earlier in the instruction of the *catechumens*. He taught prayer through study of the Lord's Prayer. He taught the sacraments of the Lord's Supper and baptism. (In the free church tradition, these are ordinances, rather than sacraments.)

In the introduction to the *Large Catechism*, Luther stated that all of his subsequent preaching was affected by this study. He attested to his own personal, daily use of the catechism. It became part of the pastoral role that he used with other ministers. It played a vital role in the spiritual nurture of his own congregation. Luther not only wanted people to learn the contents at the time they were converted, but also to live by the catechism throughout their Christian experience. Luther also developed another theme from the biblical context, the family-centered nature of Christian education.

John Calvin wrote a similar catechism for Reformed churches in 1537. Other denominations produced their own catechisms. In 1693 the first Baptist catechism appeared, and it was followed by a host of other Baptist catechisms. But by World War II, even the word catechism had disappeared from the vocabulary of most evangelical Christians.

CONTEMPORARY CONTEXT
FOR CHURCH NURTURE AND TEACHING

Study of Protestant churches in the United States shows a precipitous decline in membership among mainline churches. In response, many churches have turned to church growth strategies to try to alter what appears to be a bleak picture. With this commendable goal in mind, it is not surprising that some churches have taken the path of least resistance and resorted to methods that will attract new members, without engaging them in the less popular and more difficult process of nurture and instruction. The short-term numerical growth through easy access to membership often is offset by stunted Christian growth, instability in personal life, and little long-term involvement in outreach and ministry.

To succeed in the milieu of modern American life, a church program for Christian initiation and discipleship will need to face a number of constraints from the culture. By studying (1) biblical and historical data and (2) contemporary societal and personal constraints, parameters can be set for appropriate program goals.

Americans generally live frenetic lives. To catch and hold attention above the competing cacophony of noise in American culture, a program must be attractively packaged and effectively advertised. Such a program will need to be well-planned, organized, and systematic. There is decreased commitment to specific denominations and programs. Americans have many options from work and community that compete for their time and energy. The value of such a program must be demonstrated.

Americans are attracted by television. There has also been a notable decline in reading among Americans recently. Any effective attempt at a meaningful discipleship program will of necessity utilize effective communication media, especially video.

The median age of adults is increasing. A program of spiritual growth must take into account the developmental needs and concerns of church members of all ages. The society is highly mobile, requiring that any program must have time boundaries and achieve results within a specified time. A period of three to five years is reasonable, as demonstrated by the catechumenate. Time of meeting is also an important consideration. Usually Sunday morning is the optimal time, followed by Sunday evening and Wednesday evening.

People in our culture have a fascination with the spiritual dimension of life. For many, the interest does not necessarily extend to the organized church. A program of initiation needs to build upon the latent spiritual interest but must not allow it to languish at a vague and non-responsible level. People need to find fulfillment in the ministries of a Christian church for fellowship, family life, worship, service, and outreach.

A related characteristic of this culture is the emphasis upon the experiential, as opposed to the rational. While a program needs to deal with nurturing, it also needs to provide understanding and factual data as a foundation for decision-making that is practical and thoroughly Christian.

Another related trend is the phenomenal growth of other religions in America. Lack of solid understanding has led people into different cults or religions. America is a highly technical culture. In such a culture, people need the touch of persons whose lives have been transformed by Christ and who are committed and knowledgeable to reach out and express love to others.

New Christians need help in expressing Christian love in their families. Christian vocational concern, evidenced in business ethics and other areas, needs to be addressed for new Christians. This is also true in relation to the number of persons who are experiencing hurt and pain from abuses and addictions.

Small, face-to-face support groups need to be included among the priorities for such a program. Program content will need to provide a distinctively Christian alternative to the secular values of American society. Content needs to be directed toward commitment and involvement in the local church and its ministries.

Based on these factors, three areas of concern emerge that can guide the development of an effective discipleship program, as described in figure 12.1, "Objectives for Nurturing and Teaching New Believers." The questions that need to be answered include the following:

- How can a church help new believers understand and grow in spiritual maturity?

- How can a church assimilate new members into the life and ministry of the congregation?

- How can a church develop a program of Christian initiation and discipleship for new believers and also maturing disciples?

To respond to the needs suggested in figure 12.1, a church must design learning opportunities and select curriculum resources related to each objective.

Consideration must be given, however, to the special needs of families whose children need to be evangelized and nurtured in the Christian faith. For example, it would be helpful to tailor a program for parents who want to provide guidance and resources in spiritual growth for their children rather than depending on the church.

DEVELOPING A STRATEGY FOR NURTURE AND TEACHING

In order to carry out these three objectives, a church must develop a strategy for assimilating new believers. Assimilation is the process of incorporating believers into the life and ministry of the church. The strategy begins with a clear articulation of the stages from expressed interest in the Christian faith to maturity.

FIGURE 12.1

OBJECTIVES FOR NURTURING AND TEACHING NEW BELIEVERS

1. **Christian Initiation and Spiritual Formation**

   To guide each new believer toward personal and lifelong maturity in Christ through a thorough understanding of the Christian faith, and through personal piety and integrity in family life, vocational concerns, and leisure activity.

2. **Assimilation into a Local Church**

   To guide each Christian toward assimilation into the fellowship, involvement in worship, and usefulness through witness and ministry.

3. **Programming for Discipleship Development**

   To develop a curriculum for Christian initiation and discipleship development that will integrate outreach and education.

STAGES OF CHRISTIAN INITIATION
TOWARD MATURITY IN CHRIST

Although they were known by various names, the Bible and records of the early church give witness to the importance of Christian initiation and spiritual formation. Today, many churches consider this approach to be new, but in reality it is a return to earlier efforts to guide and nurture new believers. There are seven stages in the development of a Christian from inquirer to maturity. At each stage identifiable markers suggest the kinds of faith development that should occur.

Stage #1: Seeker. During this stage a person is interested enough to have some contact with the church. The most common experience is attending worship services. But seekers may also be touched by the church through counseling, small groups, or special events. Or they may desire to have religious education for their children and become loosely affiliated in that manner. Members of the church could contact the individual through an evangelistic coffee in their home and then extend the invitation to special events at the church. Or perhaps a member could invite a work associate or neighbor to church or a Sunday School class.

If a person visits a church service, there should be a plan to contact that person within twenty-four hours and continue the contacts with a Sunday school teacher, deacon, and others for a period of about two weeks. In whatever way it happens, the church needs to reach out to the seeker with loving care and, at some point, encourage the individual to consider the claims of Christ. There are many ways to accomplish this, from friendship evangelism to a series of evangelistic meetings. Using an evangelistic video is another means for confronting persons with the claims of Jesus Christ upon their lives. Parents can help their children by taking them to church and other places where they will be exposed to the love of God and the gospel. Pastors may want to visit children and discuss their relationship with God around the tenth birthday.

Stage #2: Evangelization. At this stage of development the person has heard the gospel and is confronted with the need to make a decision. This stage will likely occur when a person responds during an invitation at the conclusion of a service, or at the evangelistic coffee, or at the end of a video. Trained counselors should be ready to take the new convert through the steps of making a profession of faith in Christ. Those who respond should sign a decision card and be introduced to a member of the pastoral staff, asking that he or she describe the commitment that has been made.

Training for the counselor should include how to give a personal testimony and how to lead a person to find new life in Jesus Christ. Scriptures, such as Romans 6:23 and Romans 10:9–10, can be used. Or a tract, such as *The Four Spiritual Laws*, might be used. As for training persons for witnessing, a number of programs are available such as Evangelism

Explosion or Christian Witness Training. Parents also need guidance from the church in how to lead their children to a relationship with Christ. They need to understand the appropriate ages for such instruction and to be sensitive to readiness.

Stage #3: Baptism and church membership. After making a personal profession of faith in Christ, the processes of Christian initiation and spiritual formation formally begin. In the free church tradition, a person may come into the fellowship of the church by baptism, statement of faith, or transfer of letter from another church. Believer's baptism means that upon profession of faith a candidate will be immersed. The statement of faith means that a person has made a profession of faith and previously been baptized, but a letter from another church is not available. Transfer of letter means that a person is coming from another church of like faith and has been baptized. Churches from other traditions will want to follow their common practices. It is important to assess the spiritual development of the person, in order to help the new believer to find meaningful counseling, relational, and teaching opportunities.

If the person comes as a believer, the counselor will wish to make some assessment of the maturity level of the candidate. For example, a new believer is one who has been a Christian for six months or less. An immature believer is one that has shown little evidence of growth. Another might be classified as an average believer, one who has been a Christian for some time, can explain his or her faith, but shows little other evidence of maturity. A mature Christian is one who gives clear evidence of growth.

At the time of commitment, the person should be invited to a class for new members and assigned someone to shepherd the family or individual. A husband-and-wife team, deacon, or other trained person would do well. Touring the church facility and providing the newcomer with literature about the times and places of services are important means to assist this process. The responsibility for the new person then passes from the initial counselor to the person assigned to shepherd. The shepherd will want personally to invite and take the new convert or church member to activities in the church. A Sunday school class, church dinners, prayer meetings, and social events are good opportunities to involve the new person in the life of the church. This will help a person become assimilated into the congregation's regular activities.

Parents will want their children to be instructed about baptism, the Lord's Supper, and church membership when the children are in the middle to late childhood years. After services in which these events occur, parents should be ready to interpret and discuss the meaning. Parents need to encourage their children, but not manipulate them into church membership.

Stage #4: Healing and caregiving. Many persons come to the church with difficult situations at home and personal hurts. Others come with problems of abuse or addictions for which they need help. Persons who have recently experienced divorce will need help in recovery. Single parents will often need assistance in developing coping skills. Churches may provide opportunities for members to receive individual counsel. They may also provide study in classes to teach effective functioning. They may provide opportunities to engage in therapy groups.

To make this work effective, however, the needs of individuals should be discovered early. These persons should be placed into helping situations that will foster relief, comfort, healing, and restoration. This aspect of ministry is important since it is difficult for a person to become a fully functioning and mature Christian without first dealing with anguish and pain.

Children can be the victims of abusive situations. Emotional scars are very painful. Sunday school teachers and other workers with children and youth need to be sensitive and report potentially abusive situations. Pastors need to be aware of their legal and ethical responsibilities for such situations.

A church should provide spiritual care and opportunity for establishing meaningful Christian relationships for all believers. Many churches have found that dinners in homes for persons in a close geographical area help to facilitate the development of relationships. Others have discovered that small groups are one of the most important assets toward providing caregiving for all members. In some churches, Monday evenings are set aside for small group interaction. These groups often convene in homes of members.

A group should meet for a period of one to two hours, since it is difficult to have meaningful interaction in a shorter period of time. Each group should attempt to deal with only one topic for a set period of time, such as a thirteen-week quarter. It is wise for members to commit themselves to attend group sessions unless seriously hindered. Groups may be designed for fellowship, Bible study, evangelism, missions, prayer, study, or career (such as medical ethics for medical practitioners). Effective groups have a clearly defined purpose, resources for study, and a planned schedule.

Stage #5: Nurture and teaching. Living as a Christian often requires radical change for new believers. Purpose in life, personal values, behavior, ethics, love and allegiance to God, and love for persons are all affected by faith in Jesus Christ. These need to be shaped through nurture.

Discipleship classes are one means to achieve this result. Meeting on Sunday evenings or at other convenient times, small group interaction provides an effective means for shaping lives in a Christian direction. New attitudes and habits need to be fostered that will help immature Christians establish time priorities, immerse themselves in reading for personal spiritual growth, engage in prayer, and study the Scriptures.

Strong churches provide effective models for the behaviors and attitudes that they wish to develop. Mentoring and discipling persons will help new Christians to discover meaningful relationships and motivate them to deepen their relationship with God and members of the church.

Effective churches will also help new believers establish a Christian belief system that is founded upon a biblical and theological approach to life. To accomplish this, a church will need to reclaim the synagogue and early church tradition of a learning center.

A core curriculum should provide the content knowledge necessary for maturing faith. Specialized courses should be available to deepen and expand interests of learners with special needs and interests. The church will engage the new believer in studying topics such as an orientation to the Bible, church history, doctrine, and Christian ethics.

While much of the learning in the church is closely tied to nurture, teaching plays an essential role also. Christians cannot face the difficulties of the world if they do not have adequate understanding of the Christian faith and what is expected of them as believers.

Parents can help their children with Bible memorization. They also can help them learn Christian concepts, such as salvation, sanctification, grace, and faith. Parents can assist as children develop their understandings of and reasons for prayer, Bible study, witnessing, and missions. The church should provide a class to prepare parents for these tasks and also to teach them how to assist their children in developing skills, like using the Bible, making moral decisions, praying, and finding new life in Christ.

Stage #6: Discovery of gifts and equipping for ministry. This stage may begin while the new believer is still in the nurture and teaching stage. It is important to have a new Christian solidly grounded in faith before attempting to empower that person for ministry. It is also essential that the new believer give evidence of Christian living. As one moves toward maturity, the Christian should be challenged to service. It is not necessary for a believer to be fully mature in order to minister. It is helpful to encourage a new Christian to engage in some ministry at his or her level of maturity. Assessment of one's spiritual gifts and abilities—and blending personality with those gifts—will help a Christian discover the kinds of ministries for which he or she is best suited.

Assessment is followed by equipping. Equipping involves preparing members for ministries both inside and outside the church. After members have been prepared, they need to exercise and test their new skills and knowledge in the crucible of life experience. They need the encouragement of a support group. If they are left to flounder, they may become discouraged and quit the ministry as well as the church.

New members who transfer from another church may be ready for ministry immediately or after some specialized training. It is important for the counselor in that first experience to begin to assess the spiritual development of the new member. If the person is well on the way toward maturity, it may be possible to involve him or her in ministry very soon. After helping the new member discover gifts, guidance to a meaningful ministry may follow.

As children move into the preteen and teenage years, parents can help their children understand how the love of God may be expressed through the church. Exposure to missions, poverty, social injustice, and other problems in the world are important for developing sensitivity. Helping youth find ways to act in opposition to social evils can assist growth.

Stage #7: Growing toward maturity. After conversion, life is a pilgrimage of spiritual formation for the believer. God is at work in shaping the life of a Christian toward fashioning a mature and godly person. The character, values, and lifestyle of a growing Christian are directed toward holiness; they stand in stark contrast to the character, values, and lifestyle held by the world. Jesus identified the character of a believer in the great commandment of the Law. He summarized this by saying we should love God and love our neighbor. The apostle Paul viewed maturity as allowing the Spirit of God to control a person's life. While it is not always easy to define maturity, one can identify some of its many facets.

The profile of maturity is observable. It begins with what Elizabeth O'Connor described as the journey inward, followed by a journey outward.[3] One may begin the inward journey with the relationship to God. Undergirding this relationship is a knowledge base. Knowledge of who God is and what God expects involves understanding of the Bible, the life of Christ, and basic doctrine. Knowledge and understanding are foundational to growth.

Growth involves more than knowledge, however; it is reflected in a deep and continuing relationship with God. This relationship builds character. Character is described in the Beatitudes (see Matt. 5:3–10), in the fruit of the Spirit (see Gal. 5:22–26), and in the obedient servanthood of Christ.

Maturity continues with self-understanding. Stewardship of time and talents is part of this inner search. Personal piety through prayer, study of the Scripture, practice of spiritual disciplines, devotion to God, and self-discipline provide other ingredients. All of these characteristics relate to a Christian lifestyle that affects a person's outlook on life, moral integrity, and ability to face crises.

The journey outward involves reaching out to other persons. God created humans as social beings. Life was not meant to be lived in a self-centered manner. Maturity involves a life of leadership and service. This expresses itself in a number of significant areas. One area is that of personal witness to other persons that expresses the need for new life that is available in Christ.

Practicing servant leadership, whether in the service of the church or in one's business dealings, is another evidence of the outward expression of the inner change that has occurred. Speaking out and dealing with injustice from whatever source and expressing compassion, caregiving, healing, reconciling, and guiding are other signs of a changed life. Underlying all of these evidences is a true humility.

The preceding stages of growth are directed toward a changed life in Christ. During this stage of Christian growth, the believer becomes a guide to lead other persons in the same direction.

EIGHT FUNCTIONS OF THE CHURCH

In order to accomplish the three objectives for nurture and teaching set forth above, the church must develop a curriculum for new believers. From the Scripture eight basic functions can be identified for the church. Design of an effective curriculum entails the integration of the eight functions with the stages of growth in the life of an individual. The eight functions are the following:

Function #1: Worship. Worship is central to the life of the church. Worship is the heart response of a believer to God, ascribing worth and honor through praise, adoration, and thanksgiving. Related areas of study are preaching and music. Worship needs to be taught for both individual and corporate settings.

Function #2: Fellowship. Fellowship is composed of the shared relationships with persons who have a common bond in their faith and relationship with Jesus Christ. It occurs among believers in the church and may be expressed through hospitality, care, and sharing.

Function #3: Proclamation. Proclamation begins with developing friendships with persons outside the church and witnessing to faith in Christ. It also includes the witness of missions to persons around the globe. Beyond that, proclamation includes the church's witness to faith in Christ in the political and business spheres as well.

Function # 4: Nurture and training. Nurture and teaching are functions that teach the facts of faith, including doctrine, study of the Word of God, Christian lifestyle, and developing the disciplined spiritual life. They also include the caring nature of the church for the community of faith. Nurture and teaching are primarily done in the church, as Christians enter to learn, but go forth to serve.

Function #5: Spiritual formation. Spiritual formation is the process of committing one's life to Jesus Christ. It occurs through reading, classes, and study, as well as through relationships with other believers. Modeling, classroom instruction, mentoring, befriending, and personal devotion in prayer and study are all part of spiritual formation.

Function #6: Ministry. Ministry comes as a person grows in faith. It involves giving of one's time and energy to meet the needs of other persons through acts of mercy, love, and service. It is most important for those who are suffering, hurting, and in poverty. Ministry is done in the world as Christians go forth to serve.

Function #7: Family life. Nurturing family life is an important function for the church; it is essential to the spiritual well being of both young and old. The gospel works within the matrix of the family as well as in other areas of society.

Function #8: Leadership. Leadership occurs as one grows in maturity and responsibility. It is necessary for accomplishing the work of the church.

When these functions of the church are integrated with the stages of Christian initiation and spiritual formation, a structure and curriculum emerge, as illustrated in figure 12.2, "Curriculum and Church Functions."

COURSES FOR INITIATION AND SPIRITUAL NURTURE

Probably the optimal time for scheduling courses is Sunday evening. Other times may be effective also, such as for a new member class, which would probably be most effective on Sunday morning, during the Sunday school hour. This would take a person out of class for only a few weeks.

Your denominational publisher or religious bookstore has information about courses that will meet the needs of your program. Materials are available for a variety of topics, with many resources containing student materials, video resources, promotional materials, and a leader's guide. Figure 12.3 gives examples of courses that might be offered at different levels in several categories.

The ingredients for an effective program are beginning to come together, now, as the program is assembled. The last components for a program that will nurture and teach new Christians are structure and time.

PROVIDING STRUCTURE AND CURRICULUM
FOR NURTURE AND TEACHING

Structure for the curriculum involves the time of meeting and size of the group. At any stage of development a new convert must not be overloaded with any one type of structure, nor should the learner be overbooked for too many hours during the week. The optimal times for families are Sunday morning, Sunday evening, and Wednesday evening. For other special purposes, such as an aerobics group, a Thursday morning might be acceptable. While the schedule may appear full from the perspective of the

Figure 12.2

CURRICULUM AND CHURCH FUNCTIONS

WORSHIP	MINISTRY	FELLOWSHIP
Listening to God	Elderly	Hospitality
Loving God	Bereaved	Caregiving
Preaching	Poor/Sick	Counseling

SPIRITUAL FORMATION	NURTURE/TEACHING
Christian Lifestyle	Doctrine
Personal Piety	Bible-OT/NT
Prayer	Church History
Spiritual Gifts	Origin of the Bible

FAMILY LIFE	LEADERSHIP	PROCLAMATION
Marriage Enrichment	Leader Skills	Witnessing
Parenting	Interpersonal	Missions
Divorce Recovery	Teaching Skills	Visitation

Figure 12.3

COURSES FOR NURTURE AND TEACHING

Core Courses:
Church Orientation
New Member Class

BIBLE	DOCTRINE	MINISTRY
Overview of the Bible	Basic Beliefs	Witness to Faith
Bible Study Methods		

ADVANCED COURSES:

BIBLE	DOCTRINE	SPIRITUAL FORMATION
Old Testament Survey	Ethics	Prayer/Devotion
New Testament Survey		Christian Disciplines
How We Got the Bible		

EVANGELISM	PERSONAL GROWTH
Describing your testimony	Self-Understanding
Leading a person to Christ	Interpersonal Relationships

SPECIALIZED COURSES:

FAMILY LIFE	MINISTRY	WORSHIP
Marriage Enrichment	Ministry to Bereaved	Church Worship
Christian Parenting	Ministry to Elderly	Church Music
Single Parenting		
Divorce Recovery		

LEADERSHIP	MISSIONS
Leadership Skills	World Missions
Interpersonal Skills	Short-term Missions

Figure 12.4
Nurture and Teaching in the Church

Stages	Day/Time				
	Sunday	Monday	Tuesday	Wednesday	Thursday
	11 a.m.	7 p.m.	9 a.m.	6 p.m.	9 a.m.
Seeker	Worship	Friends	Aerobics	Prayer	
Evangelism	Worship	Friends	Aerobics	Prayer	
Baptism	Worship		Aerobics	Prayer	Bible Study
Care	Worship		Aerobics	Prayer	Bible Study
Teach	Worship	Parenting	Aerobics	Prayer	Bible Study
Gifts	Worship	Leadership	Aerobics	Prayer	Bible Study
Mature	Worship	Vistation	Aerobics	Prayer	Bible Study
Church Function					
	Worship	Fellowship	Proclama-tion	Worship	Nurturing and Teaching
	Nurturing and Teaching	Family	Fellowship	Spiritual Formation	Fellowship
		Leadership			
		Ministry			
Structure					
	Large Group	Small Group	Class	Large Group	Small Group
		Mentor		Small Group	

church, consider the three- to-five-year program through which a new convert will develop and grow. This permits a variety of courses and activities.

It would be advisable to develop a chart at each stage of new member development and examine the feasibility of the total profile for the individual and for the family. There needs to be balance in the learning structures. These include large group (as the Sunday morning worship service), small group (as a fellowship group), classes (as a parenting class), and individual discipleship/mentoring (as visitation in a person's home). It is essential that small, face-to-face groups be included, since they provide the close contact that will keep a person coming to church. Classroom experiences may provide better structure for learning. The result is that a member needs a multiplicity of experiences in small groups, classrooms, and even large group worship. Study figure 12.4 for an example of how a schedule might look.

At this point it is important to assemble the various components presented in this chapter and map a strategy for meeting the needs of new converts and new members in your congregation.

SECTION THREE:

Educational Leadership in the Local Church

I give you a new commandment,
that you love one another just as I have loved you.
John 13:34

CHAPTER 13

Renewing Educational Ministry

James F. Hines

Ghanaians, of the Mamprusi tribe of Ghana, West Africa, can often be heard expressing to missionaries with whom they work the following proverb: *Yoma yoma devela ama bala bala n-soa.* Transliterated, the proverb says, "Slow slow is much better than fast fast." This is good advice for leaders who want to build healthy foundations for an effective educational ministry in the church.

Slow slow can best be applied in the sense of being deliberate in the planning process. This challenges leaders to take the time needed to understand the unique approach each church uses when planning new work. The planning process must also build a team synergy that has as its focus a servant spirit, guided by a belief in and a commitment to the functions and program tasks of a church. The deliberate process of building team synergy requires that leaders develop congregational commitment to educational ministry and a desire to develop and improve as necessary. Establishing a strong foundation for effective Christian education is the purpose of this chapter.

SITUATION AUDIT: UNDERSTANDING
YOUR EDUCATIONAL STRUCTURE

Prerequisites for beginning an educational audit include (1) clear understanding of the assigned tasks for each program or area of work, (2) educational leadership's understanding of and commitment to the assigned tasks, and (3) the congregation's commitment to and belief in the programs and their value within the community of faith. If any one of these prerequisites is lacking, the educational benefits will be diminished. This allows programs to take on a self-sustaining life of their own—when people maintain traditional structures rather than make changes needed to fulfill the original purpose of the programs. A situational audit will ensure that program tasks, organization, and leadership are focused on enabling a church to (1) provide life-changing experiences for each learner, and (2) develop not just good programs, but appropriate programs.

A distinction, at this point, must be made between a *basic church program* and *church program design*. A basic program is an ongoing church organization that has specific tasks, church-approved leaders, established curriculum, regular meeting places and times, and appropriate staff and budget support.

Program design, on the other hand, can best be understood as developing a new program or adjusting a fixed program with the intent of fashioning a new or improved version. Church program design requires a church to reinterpret or establish new tasks, leadership, curriculum, staff, and budget support.

To assess educational programs, leaders must recognize common elements that sustain any church program structure: objectives, participants, program core, leadership support, and technostructure (the illustration in fig. 13.1 shows the relationships among these components).[1]

OBJECTIVES

Objectives, as studied in a previous chapter, are statements of intended outcome that give direction to our work. Educational objectives must be evaluated in relationship to (1) the church's mission and vision, and (2) the effectiveness of existing programs in achieving the specified objectives. This keeps a congregation from becoming narrowly focused toward existing programs and ambiguous objectives that appeal primarily to the faithful. Continual assessment binds members to the purpose of the church, while ensuring that educational programs serve the spiritual, social, and personal needs of those who participate.

Of course, educational objectives must produce *two delivery systems* for the church, one focused toward the *believer* and the second focused toward the *nonbeliever*. Both program systems must reflect divine, institutional, and personal objectives.

PARTICIPANTS

Situation audits must give considerable attention to the people for whom the program core is designed. You must determine participant response to key questions:

Figure 13.1

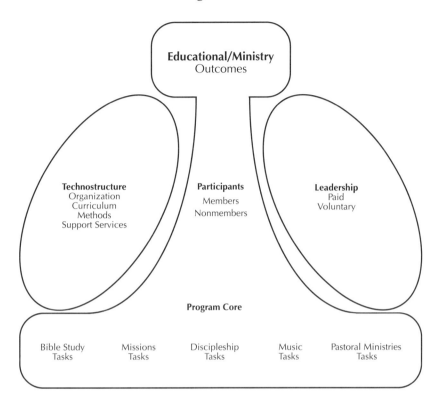

- Is the purpose of programs clear?
- Are there serious conflicts of interest among programs and/or program participants?
- Are there communication problems?
- Are there problems with responsibility for decision-making?
- Are participants adequately consulted when decisions will affect them?
- Are policies and procedures reasonable?
- Are there unresolved conflicts related to programs and/or participants?[2]

PROGRAM CORE

The program core contains basic programs considered critical to the life of the church and common to the church's denominational identity. Each program has responsibility for tasks that give shape to some aspect of Christian growth and development. Situation audits assess congregational commitment to, understanding of, and compliance with or resistance to each program task—and whether the church is benefiting from the program.

LEADERSHIP SUPPORT

Within each basic program, there exists the challenge of maintaining competent, committed leadership. An audit considers the following:

- Are clearly defined position descriptions used with current and potential leaders?
- Are time schedules and meeting expectations clear?
- Are gifts and skills identified and developed?
- Are training opportunities available?
- Are there problems that hinder the success of the program?
- Do leaders feel there is sufficient encouragement/affirmation?

TECHNOSTRUCTURE

A church's program core and leadership team must be complemented by a positive and empowering technostructure. The organization should show how programs are related and define clear lines of responsibility and accountability. Curriculum must be defined for each program and a range of acceptable teaching, learning, and performance methods decided.

Complementing the organization, curriculum, and methods of a program are support services, addressed in detail in chapter 7, "Administrative Church Educational Organizations." These enhance basic programs by providing administrative support, membership services, educational and promotional resources, supplies, and such. Support services may exist within a church by way of a media center/library, staff and secretarial support, supplies, or computer-generated information. Outside the church, support services might be provided by religious publishing houses, community service programs (food closets, counseling services, financial assistance programs, etc.), or denominational service groups.

GETTING STARTED

You must first have a clear understanding of what the church is to be and do. Churches that do not understand their mission will easily be swayed by every trend. Churches must find the unique vision that will guide them in fulfilling their role in God's will for the church.

Churches must be willing to assess their ministry situation, goals and objectives, programs, budget allocations and support, and implementation and evaluation methods. Churches that fail to commit to periodic assessments will, by omission, create hindrances to effective educational planning and design.

ENLIST AN EVALUATION COMMITTEE

This group can help you in blending new ideas and leadership with existing leadership and program structures. Membership of the evaluation team should include selected leaders and members from all programs, plus several respected members not currently involved in the educational ministry of the church. Balanced membership selection is crucial, not only for the success of the action team, but also to help reduce miscommunication and power control struggles. Church approval for this team will depend upon your church bylaws and/or policies.

This team would (1) serve as a catalyst in decision-making and in clarifying the purpose of and provisions for Christian education, (2) guide an ongoing process of planning and assessment, and (3) help the congregation understand and work within the mission of the church.

Before beginning work, an orientation should be planned for the committee. During an extended meeting or a weekend retreat, the following must be reviewed:

1. the church's mission/vision statement, and leadership organization;
2. a history of developments in educational program areas;
3. the team's stated tasks and its organizational structure;
4. an agenda for the work of the team;
5. the descriptions and task assignments for existing and planned programs; and
6. the human, financial, material, and physical resources available to the existing educational programs.

Before concluding, each team member should understand:

*   dates, times, and location of meetings,
*   persons who will plan and be responsible for agenda items,
*   the imperative of cooperative decision-making.

Once the committee is in place, an honest investigation and needs assessment must be conducted related to the two delivery systems (to believers and to nonbelievers) addressed earlier in this chapter. This assessment addresses needs and values related to participants, church organization, and the internal and external environments of the church. This includes a clear understanding of the beliefs and values of the congregation in relation to those of the church staff, community, society, and denomination—(as in fig. 13.2).

The committee must also analyze the heritage of both the church and the community. To understand the historical dynamics, the team should investigate thoroughly the suggested categories listed in figure 13.4 on p. 282.

The information secured will be helpful in these ways:

1. interpreting goals and objectives,
2. reviewing effectiveness of current program assignments,
3. identifying educational needs that could be met,

Figure 13.2

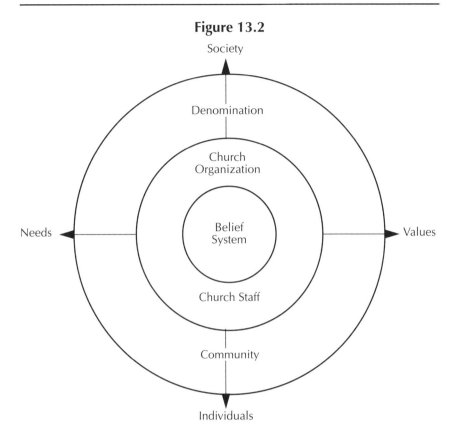

4. assisting program leaders in planning, budgeting, and scheduling, and

5. enabling team members to participate personally in the educational design of the church.

By securing the above information, you will be able to identify the strengths on which you can build and the problems that might prevent you from getting started or that might hinder effective planning.

As you discover the various inner workings of the church and community, you will discover common areas of service and ministries that are being provided. This will provide some avenues where your church might link with other worthy organizations to avoid replication of services. Such partnerships reduce strain on the church budget and leadership involvement.

CREATE PURPOSE STATEMENT
AND EDUCATIONAL OBJECTIVES

Once the discovery work has been researched, recorded, and distributed, it is time for the committee to study the information. What significant growth opportunities are being provided and need to be provided? Many types of educational growth opportunities exist, and the challenge is to discover those areas in light of the church's mission and vision. There must not be a hesitation to investigate growth opportunities that move the community of faith beyond thinking primarily of numerical growth or program/organizational changes. The more difficult and immeasurable areas like spiritual growth and development, value clarification, family relationships, and teaching for faith must also be addressed.

The committee should have sufficient time to digest information shared in the dialogue and study. Members should not feel rushed or caught up in a prescribed period that does not allow enough time for synergy to develop. You will also want to allow time for team members to process the findings with their network of friends, both in the church and in the community.

Once the committee has come to terms with the findings, a statement of purpose is developed for the educational ministry. The statement must interface with the church's mission and/or vision statement. Then the team is ready to develop objectives based on the purpose statement and the needs uncovered. These objectives should reflect information discovered in the needs assessment, addressing opportunities for improvement or growth. (See chapter 4, "How to Plan and Evaluate," for complete information on developing a mission statement, objectives, and goals.)

This is a good time for the team to share the educational statement and objectives with key leadership groups (such as deacons, church council, and program leaders not involved in the study), and then with the congregation. Depending on church policy, either secure formal approval of the purpose statement and goals must be secured or broad support available.

CONVERT NEEDS AND OBJECTIVES TO GOALS

Using the educational purpose statement as a compass and the objectives as a guide, the committee is ready to prepare educational goals, following the steps in chapter 4, "How to Plan and Evaluate."

Significant time spent preparing goals will involve as many individuals as possible in the process. Adults respond to significant challenges and high expectations, so failure to include them in establishing educational goals will stifle motivation and foster a lack of interest and enthusiasm. When you give appropriate leadership and significant time to preparing goals, you will conserve energy, save time, and limit confusion.

STRUCTURING THE PROGRAM AND CURRICULUM

The next step is to determine leadership possibilities for structuring the educational program and curriculum.

PROGRAM ASSIGNMENTS AND/OR NEW PROGRAM DESIGN

In light of educational objectives and goals, assignments are made for improvement in existing programs and/or for development of new program designs. Consideration is given to whether the newly developed goals can be accomplished through existing core programs, technostructure, and leadership support systems—for this is easier than starting anew. The focus at this point, however, is to ensure the best delivery system for the educational needs in your church. So, usually, a church must renew existing programs *and* develop new ones. A practical process for analyzing current designs and projecting future ones is illustrated in figure 13.3.

RESOURCE CONSIDERATIONS

Once the church's core program has been established, consideration is given to the resources necessary to accomplish the educational goals. This can be achieved by specifying all necessary resources important to the success of each program: leadership, materials/supplies, budget, church policy guidelines, facilities, equipment and furniture, and such.

BUDGET DEVELOPMENT

Once the core program is decided, an estimated budget should be developed for all components. Plans must be considered tentative until funding has been approved. A word of caution needs to be expressed concerning program budget support: the church should avoid the market mentality that says church ministry programs must pay for themselves. Effective ministry requires competent and efficient administration by leaders and sacrificial giving by church members.

A good educational program will involve budget forecasting. Figure 13.5 shows a worksheet for program budget planning.

PROMOTE, IMPLEMENT, AND EVALUATE

The last phase includes promotion of the new or revised programs, implementation of activities and organization, and evaluation of the changes to find out if they meet the identified needs.

If appropriate implementation is to occur, existing programs must be examined and redefined; the technostructure must be evaluated, and necessary changes made; leadership assessment must be undertaken and volunteers must be in place; and all anticipated outcomes must be accepted

Figure 13.3

ANALYZING CURRENT DESIGN
AND PROJECTING FUTURE DESIGNS

EXAMINE EXISTING CORE PROGRAMS

Review programs in relation to projected educational goals to determine which existing programs can best accomplish the desired outcomes. Goals that cannot be addressed through existing programs may either need new programs created or tasks of existing programs redefined. The purpose is to create the best core program structure that meets the challenge of your church while working within the educational program structure in place.

EVALUATE TECHNOSTRUCTURE

Align each element of the technostructure with the desired core program structure. Questions about all necessary core program adjustments must be raised and properly addressed concerning organizational structure, curriculum, methods (both teaching and ministry application), and support services.

ASSESSMENT OF LEADERSHIP SUPPORT

Securing spiritually gifted persons to use their gifts is a crucial and potentially difficult task. This requires helping individuals identify their specific giftedness, commit to ongoing development of these gifts, and use their gifts in Christian service within the church and community. Attention must be given to leadership development opportunities; number of leaders needed in relation to the persons available; support systems; core program position descriptions, leadership recruitment, and leadership expectations.

EFFECTIVENESS OF EDUCATIONAL MINISTRY

There is a high degree of objectiveness and subjectiveness in evaluation. It is objective in that you will be called upon to determine such things as: the number of persons touched by the core programs; effectiveness in providing for broad age groupings; and provisions for ensuring the church is achieving a balanced ministry to both church and unchurched individuals. Subjective outcomes must also be considered related to: change in values and behavior, improved family relations, commitment to the faith journey, and learner impact upon the church and community.

Figure 13.4

Analyzing Historical and Cultural Influences

Community History and Culture	Church History and Culture
Key Leadership: elected, city, clubs, ethnic	Church Minutes: read all minutes (to assess policy and procedure decisions)
School System: regional attitudes, regional prejudices	Church Policies: discover formal and informal policies
Community Events: parades, festivals, holidays, fairs	Leadership Patterns: related to programs, committees, deacons, trustees, spiritual giftedness
Community Places: restaurants, civic centers, community clubs, service centers/organizations, impoverished areas	Budget Patterns: spending, yearly & monthly giving patterns of church, financial obligations, financial stability
Economic Base: farm base, key business, industries (oil, mining, production, etc.), college, needs related to poor economic base	Prior Year Calendar: holiday activities, summer schedules, annual events
Communication Base: library, community newsletters, local newspaper, grapevine network, other church groups	Numerical Growth Patterns: last 10 years attendance (patterns of Bible study, worship , etc.), compare growth patterns with prior pastoral leadership, special promotions, transitions in community and/or church
Discover Resident Impressions: seek out community resident views (related to your church's image and influence), community ethnic relations, standing among business and community leaders	Discover Membership Attitudes: seek out membership views (related to personal visions, opinions, dreams, fears, etc.), ask charter members to tell their story of the church's history, discover membership understanding and commitment to program tasks

and supported. The greatest danger is that of becoming so satisfied with the planning that leadership never successfully implements the programs.

IMPLEMENTATION

Before starting any program, a strong support system should be developed that includes the following:

- Leadership groups: church staff, deacon body, church council, key committees, such as Stewardship/Finance, Committee on Committees, Nominating, and Publicity

Figure 13.5

Budget Projection Worksheet for Core Programs

	Program 1 Cost	Program 2 Cost	Program 3 Cost	Program 4 Cost
Leadership Paid Volunteer				
Materials and Supplies				
Equipment				
Furniture				

Curriculum Resources
  Teacher Materials
  Learner Materials
  Support Materials
    (Bibles, books,
    dictionaries,
    teacher guides,
    kits, etc.)
Sample Materials				

Leadership Training
  Workshops
  Speakers
  Consultants				

Miscellaneous
  Printing
  Postage
  Mailings
  Promotion
  Advertising				

Total Program Cost				
Less: Fees and Current Reserved Funds				
Project Cost				

- Program leadership: age-group coordinators, program directors, department directors, outreach directors, teachers, and workers

- Key participants: anticipated membership and nonmembership participation

Then a timetable should identify all advanced preparation important for starting of each program. This would include the following:

- Program schedules: start-up and stopping times for each program estab-lished; coordination with other activities to avoid program conflicts
- Control systems: goals assigned, responsibilities delegated, and lines of communication established, record systems in place (attendance, visitor information, committees, etc.), budget allocations made, and proce-dures for requesting support services established
- Leadership arrangements: recruitment, training, and preparation of all leaders completed
- Physical arrangements: rooms assigned and arranged, equipment in place, and educational resources/curriculum materials available
- Publicity arrangements: the mode of advertising decided, target times and dates established, and printing and distribution of public relation and promotional materials completed

Successful change requires the support and maintenance of an organi-zational climate that encourages personal and team efforts. Developing, using, and affirming personal skills in problem-solving, supporting and encouraging workers, and involving members in decision-making build confidence and boost morale within the educational organizations. Prob-lem-solving, as suggested in this chapter, is a proactive approach to admin-istration—anticipating needs, being ready to solve problems, and providing effective leadership to implement solutions. This requires lead-ers who seek to isolate the "real" problems and not just the "surface" prob-lems, who make observations without being intimidating or critical, and who examine options before acting.

Problem-solving alone, however, is not enough to ensure program suc-cess. It must be combined with encouragement that allows room for errors. Few workers within the church are professional programmers, teachers, or leaders; they need a redemptive atmosphere within which they can function.

The challenge is to find avenues of genuine support and encouragement throughout the year, not just during special events or when major goals have been achieved.

EVALUATION

Evaluation comes at the end, but it also is a continuing process. Results are monitored, needs identified, and corrective actions taken. Thus, evalu-ation identifies accomplishments but also points toward needed renewal—which starts the cycle over.

PLANNING PROCESS EVALUATION

These questions are part of the process:

- Was a thorough audit conducted?

- Were identified changes effectively implemented, or were the changes inadequate?
- Was data effectively collected and used?
- What changes in program statement and/or goals need to be made?
- Is there a need to reexamine core programs and/or structure?
- Are leadership positions continuing to function appropriately?
- Did the budget development process effectively work?
- Did leadership believe things were well organized, or disorderly and chaotic?
- What gaps existed in program implementation?

INDIVIDUAL PROGRAM EVALUATION

- Were the program goals accomplished?
- Is the content of each program continuing to address the educational goals established?
- Are the program methods appropriately supporting the program and/or curriculum?
- Does organizational structure aid communication and work commitment?
- Were support systems affirming?
- Are the support and delivery systems accomplishing their tasks?

PARTICIPANT PROGRESS EVALUATION

- Were personal goals identified and met?
- What attitudes of self-improvement were promoted and accomplished?
- Was consistent commitment to the program(s) evident?
- Did the methods used effectively relate to the individual/learner?

CHAPTER 14

Leadership in the Small Church

Bob I. Johnson

The call was both expected and welcomed. Western Hills Church would be the setting of Merle's pastoral ministry—according to search committee chair Dean Dennington—if Merle felt so led. Merle believed the Spirit was leading and accepted the church's invitation. This would be his first pastoral experience, and he would serve as the only paid staff member. He remembered a casual comment made by one member in the interview process: "Pastor, we'll do anything you can get us to do." He also remembered one of his teacher's saying, "A church calls you because they think you can lead them to be the church they want (or ought) to be."

The next question for Merle was, "How do I lead the church not only so that the people sense fulfillment but also so that God is pleased?" This chapter considers that question by focusing on how one full-time or part-time minister can help a small congregation develop its educational ministry. Since Christian education can be defined broadly to include all the church does, the focus is not so much on programs (as in large churches), as on the total life and ministry of the congregation. This often is referred to as a small church's *congregational curriculum*.

GETTING STARTED

It is beyond reason to expect that one small chapter can give the only paid staff member all the help needed to lead a congregation. There are, however, factors common to all such situations that can be studied. One is that there is always a *starting point*.

One way to get started is to make as many needed changes as possible in the first year, or "honeymoon" time. That doesn't work too well in marriage, and with few exceptions, it doesn't hold true in churches. Most situations call for the steady, long-term process of change—the exception being a church with a history of failure and/or turmoil that calls a pastor specifically to make rapid changes.

ASSESS THE SITUATION

These questions are important: Is it a newer parish? An older congregation? Rural? Urban? Does it have a history of *destructive* conflict? Have pastors served long or short tenures? What are the capabilities and commitment of lay leaders? What are the resources available?

Does it appear the church needs to remodel existing buildings and/or provide new space? What are other congregations in the area like? How effective are these churches' ministries? Has the church done formal planning? If so, what were the results? How does the church make decisions, budget its resources, nominate and choose its official leaders? Who are the power brokers? Are they among the elected leaders? After other similar questions, you must ask, "Who am I? Am I the person who can lead this parish to be the people of God, on mission for God?"

GET YOUR BEARINGS

Beginning with a formal planning agenda is *not* the next step. Instead, the informality of the smaller congregation can allow you to talk to people and groups about what the church is like and what it ought to be doing to fulfill its calling from God.

Your emphasis is that as pastor you want to lead the church to be what God intends for it to be and to help its members grow. After all, the church has chosen you because it believed you were right for the church. You can ask for suggestions concerning how to be the most effective pastor you can be.

TAKE A BASIC APPROACH

As people make suggestions concerning your leadership, you must listen without comment. There will be time for you to have your say. You could schedule a meeting with a group or the entire congregation and have a chalkboard set up or large sheets of paper attached to the wall where the suggestions can be written in brief form. At this point, every suggestion should be received as though it has equal value with all the others. This will encourage people to believe that you want to hear what they have to say.

When suggestions cease, you may want to mention any items omitted which you think are important for consideration. Then you can look at the list and say something like, "Thank you. It looks like we have several things that you feel are important, more than we can get done anytime soon. We will need to decide which ones we do first."

How the various items relate to the church's ministry is then discussed. It may be appropriate to ask the group to choose the top two or three items for priority attention. Or it may be better to find out if one need seems to have stronger support and can serve as a lead emphasis (for example, children's ministry).

To lead with one emphasis does not mean that others will not get attention. It simply means that the church will address other ministries as they relate to the lead ministry. Because of the focus on a point of strong agreement, this approach may be especially helpful in churches where unhealthy conflict or other troubles have occurred.

During this activity it is appropriate to introduce the concept of *dreaming*. The people should be encouraged to think back to the original dream of the founders, if it is an older church, and to redream that dream in the context of today's ministry. With this informal approach to planning, clergy can take members a step at a time toward longer-range planning.

In the beginning stages, the leader can focus on the church's self-image. One way to do this is to ask the people to respond to questions such as What does our church do well? What are our strengths? What are the good things about our church that are on the community grapevine? What things about our church would you like to be on the community grapevine?

You should avoid conducting a "strengths versus weaknesses" assessment. People too easily know the weaknesses. If you focus on the strengths, the weaknesses will be addressed. When a congregation expands its strengths, the church becomes more effective in mission. The companion truth is that when a church becomes taken up with weaknesses, the church begins to lose the strengths it has.

You should retain the information you have gathered for future use. As this material comes alive for you, it will help tell the story of the church. You can study it for your own ideas about which steps should be taken next, and use it in preaching to show the strengths and challenges of the church.

MOVING AHEAD

Moving ahead means staying connected to the church's past. Indeed, in many single-staff churches, people are much more attached to the past than pointed to the future. Ignoring or fighting this attachment always means trouble for pastoral leaders. To overcome a preoccupation with the past and to use it for good, you must celebrate it and learn to tie new ministries to the helpful aspects of that past. Where possible, you also show how changes are true to traditions of the church.

USE A LEADERS' GROUP

If the church already has a council or cabinet consisting of leaders of programs and major committees, you can use it as the base of planning and support for educational ministry. If no such group exists, you can either organize one with church approval or simply meet with such people on an informal basis.

In a very small church where few qualified people are available for council and committee assignments, you should form *one* group. A leader from each major area of ministry in your church (such as worship, Bible study, youth ministry, stewardship, and missions) should be enlisted. The leadership and purpose of the group depend on the matters to be discussed. When Bible study is the focus, then the Bible study leader is the chair, and everyone else serves on the Bible study committee. The same would be true for the other major areas. This group, under the leadership of the pastor, could serve as a church council to coordinate the entire ministry of the church.

CHOOSE THE CURRICULUM RESOURCES

Remember, curriculum is all that the church does to carry out its commission to be the church. Curriculum *resources* are the Bible, lesson guides, audiovisual materials, and other items used in the various activities.

As the pastoral leader you will need to be involved in selecting curriculum resources, even as you are involved in helping the church to determine its curriculum. This will occur as you study what the church says it wants to be and do, gather information from denominational offices and other desirable sources about curriculum materials that fit your church, and ask for samples for this study.

The *leaders' group* mentioned above (or other appropriate group) will help you assess current needs and curriculum materials that are being used. If changes are wanted, recommendations can be made through the church's regular decision-making process. Once adopted for use, interpretation sessions will show how to use curriculum materials. You should keep reading the materials regularly to ensure their relevance to the church's needs.

MOBILIZE THE WORKERS

Remember the pithy words of the person who said, "Pastor, we will do anything you can get us to do." Like it or not, this statement places the burden of leadership on the single-staff minister. It also implies that there are people who will share ministry responsibilities if they are properly recruited, trained, and supported.

People want to know where they are being led. Therefore, leaders should know what is to be accomplished and how. Once these issues are established, it is time to recruit persons for ministry positions.

Recruiting. Sometimes the pastor is the person best suited to recruit workers. Recruiting requires special skills as well as prayer and patience.

You must be sensitive to each person's needs. Some nominees need all the facts about the potential ministry you are asking them to consider. Others are attracted by the challenge of the task or interested in how it will help people. Then there are those who like to be part of a team effort.

With appropriate sensitivity to personal preferences, use the following steps for face-to-face contact with persons to be recruited.

1. Schedule a time convenient to the person. Someone should not be asked to make a serious decision hurriedly or in a place that is not conducive to thoughtful consideration of your request.

2. Recruit in the atmosphere of prayer. You should pray for the person to be asked to serve and for yourself, especially for yourself if the person does not respond positively.

3. Explain clearly the ministry task you are asking the person to accept. You must include what is expected, the potential joys and heartaches, the resources available, the names of others with whom the person will work closely, and the potential for personal growth.

4. Furnish printed information to leave with the person. This may include a brief list of duties, resources available, copies of curriculum materials (if applicable), and any pertinent church document.

5. Allow the person enough time to think and pray before giving a decision. The potential leader should be asked if a week is enough time to make a decision. You can suggest that you will call in a few days to make another appointment to receive the decision.

6. Complete the task as promised. In a few days you should call to see if additional information is needed and to make an appointment to receive the decision. If the answer is negative, you thank the person for his or her consideration and leave open the possibility of other service. If the person responds positively, then you provide any further information needed and review information given earlier.

Developing workers. The pastor may get some help from outside sources, such as denominational training events, but most of the development of volunteer workers will be the responsibility of the pastor. This is a biblical role, as indicated in Ephesians 4:11–12. Pastors and teachers are to equip the saints for the work of ministry.

First Peter 2:9 describes all Christians as ministers, or priests. Every member of the faith family through Jesus Christ is to do the work of the church. A primary task for the equipping pastor is to ingrain this biblical role of ministry in the minds of the people.

Also, the concept of 1 Peter 4:10 is vital to the worker's identity. This verse reminds us that all spiritual gifts are to be used in serving one another, not to be exploited for self. For many people, the best use of their gifts does not always parallel the way they earn their paychecks. The most creative expression of their gifts may be in and through volunteer ministry.

As pastoral leader, you probably have more training in Bible knowledge than do the volunteers with whom you work. Helping them to grow in such knowledge can be one of your most challenging and rewarding tasks. Systematic Bible study can deal with the knotty theological and biblical problems as well as with biblical material that is easier to interpret. If such study is led by someone the workers trust, they can handle more than one might suppose. That means you make sure you are trustworthy and then go for it!

Workers need someone to walk with them and be available to provide guidance as they do their tasks. As the pastor, you may even have to take the leadership in a ministry for a time while providing in-service training for a newly recruited worker and potential leader.

Take the youth ministry as an example. As a younger minister you may have served as a youth leader and can offer expertise no one else in the church possesses. You may find that the best way you can spend some of your time is to work in the youth ministry until you can train someone to take the leadership.

Workers need to know how to handle problems and conflict. You can offer classes or seminars on these topics before conflicts arise. People need to know that problems will arise and conflict will occur. They must know that not all conflict is bad and that it may occur because of a difference over how the church can best do its work. When people care deeply, they will disagree about what is best. You have to sharpen your own skills and knowledge about problem solving and conflict management before you can share with others.

Volunteers want to know how they are doing with their work. There should be some specific time for workers to tell how they are feeling about it. You must encourage questions, ask questions, offer assistance, and give encouragement. At the same time, you watch for signs of stress and/or dropout, do prevention, and show that you genuinely care for them. A follow-up note in which you can give substantive evaluation and encouragement is always fitting.

Recognition. How do you show recognition as the single-staff minister? It is best to be specific. Handwritten notes are effective. Praise in front of others when possible is also appropriate. Recognition of achievement and service can be done during a worship service or at another church gathering. You should be consistent, factual, and Christian in the practice of public praise.

Celebration. Memorable accomplishments, both small and large, can be celebrated with great profit for the entire church and also for individual workers. You and your church should know how best to celebrate everything from homecoming to a fiftieth wedding anniversary. There should be specific guidelines for celebration events when you plan for ministry with a council or committee. However you decide to celebrate, it should be intentional and consistent, but not superficial.

CONCLUDE A MINISTRY

Concluding a ministry depends to a large extent on the conditions present. In the usual closure, celebration and a focus on the future can be mixed with the tears of departure to help strengthen all involved. If conditions are unpleasant, negotiation may be the best approach.

As the departing minister, you seek to leave the church poised for life and ministry without you. That means you either do not start ministries that cannot survive without you, or you make sure new ministries have leaders in place and can succeed after you are gone (this usually requires a few years). All the aspects of the church ideally should be in a healthier state than when you arrived. Remember that the church belongs to God, and you are a steward of the local expression of that divinely ordained institution.

FOR THE ENTIRE JOURNEY

Certain matters are vital all along the way. Remember, people do not want to be managed; they want to be led. If you want to manage someone, you manage yourself.

You must manage your time and resources. A pocket calendar or notebook is a necessity. There you record major events first, such as revival meetings and family commitments; then you schedule other events and appointments according to priority. Jotting down specifics is vital. There is a Chinese proverb that says, "The faintest ink endures longer than the strongest memory." Learning to impose a disciplined approach to memoranda will offend fewer people and accomplish more.

Other suggestions that will guide you along the way are listed in "Tips for the Journey," figure 14.1.

BE SECURE IN YOUR CALLING

The calling to be the only paid staff person is a challenging one. It is not impossible, however. Success depends on many things. Be as wise as a serpent and as harmless as a dove.

Remember that according to Romans 8:28, God is at work in everything, both good and bad (though God does not author the bad) to bring about good for those called for God's purpose. You are linked with a powerful partner in your ministry—and that ensures the foundation for ministry.

Figure 14.1

TIPS FOR THE JOURNEY

1. Communicate clearly and persistently.
2. Learn what needs to be accomplished and pursue that.
3. Make your agenda decent and open.
4. Be willing to take risks because success is not assured.
5. Keep a calendar and publicize events well ahead.
6. Follow good business practices consistent with Christian principles.
7. Communicate clearly and persistently.
8. Know the difference between leading and pushing, and practice leading.
9. Be willing to share the power.
10. Develop your own ministry so as to be more than just a "professional" minister.
11. Learn and use good telephone manners.
12. Guard study and prayer times, and let the people know when they are.
13. Guard and practice quality family time, even if you are a family of one.
14. Practice good communication.
15. Relate to other ministers in mutually helpful ways; form a support group for study/counsel.
16. View every person as one for whom Christ died, and as the object of the church's ministry.
17. Ask for specific help from people who can provide it.
18. Make prayer, Bible study, and spiritual direction priorities in your ministry.
19. Discover, reinforce, and practice the importance of Christian education in the congregation.
20. Learn good writing skills and practice them.
21. Practice good communication.
22. Keep your promises.
23. Make a lifetime goal of being a skilled servant leader after the pattern of Jesus Christ.

CHAPTER 15

The Role of the Pastor
in Christian Education

C. Ferris Jordan

Every church has a pastor or is in search of a pastor. These facts reveal the perceived significance of pastoral leadership in contemporary churches. This perception is biblical, for Paul and his missionary associates were very careful to lead in the selection of elders or mature believers to lead the new congregations (see Acts 14:23).

Titus was left in Crete to complete work that Paul had to leave as he moved to other assignments. Among the tasks given to Titus was the responsibility to see that leaders were appointed (called "elders" in Titus 1:5 and "bishops" or "overseers" in Titus 1:7).

Predominantly Jewish communities in the New Testament church were inclined to use the term "elders," while Greek communities more often used "bishop" to refer to these church leaders. From these early elected leaders evolved the New Testament office of pastor.

Just as surely as pastoral leadership was significant in the New Testament church, the ministry of Christian education was integral to New Testament church life and mission. The pastoral office and the church's educational function were vitally related.

Christian education is not presented in the New Testament as an option in either the church's mission or the pastor's role. Giving attention to Christian education is indispensable to the church's very life, for a church is always only one or two generations away from loss of vitality or even extinction. Pastoral effectiveness demands that appropriate attention be given by the pastor to the ministry of Christian education.

The pastor's work is multifaceted and demanding. How can the pastor appropriately relate to educational ministry so that its vital role in the work of the church is not diminished and so that other areas of pastoral work are not ignored?

THE MISSION OF THE CHURCH
AND THE ROLE OF THE PASTOR

The pastor's role in Christian education and commitment to that ministry will be understood best when the mission of the New Testament church is grasped. Moreover, the Christian education dimension of the church's mission will be given its proper priority only as pastors are able to interpret that mission to the congregation.

The commission given by Jesus to his earliest followers (see Matt. 28:18–20) still stands as the divine blueprint for the mission of New Testament churches. Careful study and interpretation of this passage reveal two primary concerns, evangelism and nurturing. Every investment of a congregation's resources must make its proper contribution to these two objectives. Activities and allocations of resources not properly related to this two-pronged mission are luxuries the church cannot afford.

The mission is marked by urgency. The needs are great. The time is short. Each person among the world's lost multitudes must be brought to Christ, who alone can forgive sin and give a new nature. Then each believer must learn to obey Christ and be shaped in Christ's image through a lifelong process of discipling.

As noted in an earlier chapter, one function of a New Testament church is to educate. This function is indispensable to achieving the church's mission. In the command of Jesus in Matthew 28:19, the focus is on making disciples. *Disciple* is from a Greek word that means "learner" or "pupil." The meaning of Jesus' command to make disciples requires, then, that the commission be interpreted as a command to teach or to instruct.

This mandate also makes it clear that teaching is associated not only with the beginning of teacher-pupil relationships but also with the lifelong relationship the disciple has with Jesus. The mission of the church is to "keep on teaching," and the goal of instruction is producing disciples who obey everything Jesus commanded (see Matt. 28:20).

The word *disciple* goes beyond "convert," but it most definitely includes the transforming conversion that occurs when a person yields life to Jesus as Savior and Lord and is born again. The discipleship journey never begins until a lost person has been redeemed through faith in Jesus. That is why evangelism is one of the two prongs of the church's mission. The mandate to make disciples will be accomplished as believers are going into all the world geographically—and into their personal worlds of family, vocation, and social interaction—giving witness to Jesus Christ.

But the Lord makes it clear that conversion is only the beginning. Jesus is vitally concerned also about the church's faithfulness in nurturing the saved. Many churches function far beneath their potential because they do not give enough attention to growing disciples beyond spiritual infancy and to helping them discover and use their spiritual gifts for the growth of the church. Education is vital to the church's effectiveness in evangelism and discipling.

The education function of the church is biblically based. Obeying the Lord's command is not optional. Pastors must allow these truths to burn themselves deep within their very hearts and must continuously preach and teach these biblical insights to their congregations with conviction and passion.

How do pastors build on this biblical foundation? Some pastors will be privileged to work with staff ministers to lead the laity in achieving the church's educational function. However, most pastors will serve churches without the benefit of ministerial staff. The rest of this chapter introduces pastors in both types of churches to the pastoral office as it relates to the educational dimension of ministry.

PREACHER

The pastor is preacher. In this phase of ministry, the pastor proclaims the good news of Jesus Christ's redemptive work and interprets the whole counsel of God. Thus, the pastor's preaching task encompasses messages that are both evangelistic and edifying to the church. In both dimensions of preaching, the pastor has opportunity to undergird the educational function of the church.

As evangelistic preacher, the pastor tells about the way of life in Christ and invites the lost to public decision. This process often begins with the outreach of educational programs and continues after conversion with the teaching and nurturing of converts.

As edifier of the body, the pastor's pulpit ministry clarifies the church's educational function, encourages lay leaders in the educational ministry, and challenges each member of the body to grow toward Christlikeness.

No church will have a strong educational ministry without pastoral support from the pulpit. Without strong conviction from the pulpit concerning the educational function of the church, pastors soon have a congregation that is lukewarm in an arena where Jesus spoke with urgency.

SHEPHERD

The pastoral office includes also the role of shepherd of the flock (see Acts 20:28; 1 Pet. 5:2). As shepherd, the pastor guides, feeds, protects, and nurtures. Shepherding requires attention to the educational ministry of the church, through Bible teaching, training in discipleship, missions education, and family development. In that way the flock can receive a well-balanced diet, be protected against false teaching, be directed in pathways of righteous living, and receive strength for the daily journey.

TEACHER

In a sense, to become a member of a church is to enroll in Christ's school. The pastor is the primary teacher of the church and must be unswerving in allegiance to the sure word that is to be taught. Among the qualifications Paul listed for the pastoral office is an aptitude for teaching, ("able to teach," 1 Tim. 3:2, NIV). As chief teacher in the congregation, the pastor ought to be a model of good teaching for others chosen by the congregation for the teaching task.

Paul not only instructed Timothy, Titus, and all pastors to teach but also gave strong emphasis to teaching in his own ministry. He stayed in Corinth "for a year and a half, teaching them the word of God" (Acts 18:11, NIV). More than once he "reasoned with" his hearers in the synagogues (Acts 17:2; 18:19). The Greek word translated "reasoned" is from a verb form which means to converse, to discourse with others, to discuss. It is the word from which the English word "dialogue" derives. Paul used monologues effectively, but he also was adept with a dialogical teaching style.

The contemporary pastor's role includes teaching by proclamation from the pulpit, teaching through one-on-one and small-group dialogue, and encouraging church members to participate in small groups or classes. The pastor is teacher. The Master's mandate requires it. New Testament qualifications for the pastoral office undergird it.

EQUIPPER

Paul made it clear in Ephesians that pastors are "to prepare God's people for works of service, so that the body of Christ may be built up until we all reach unity in the faith and in the knowledge of the Son of God and become mature, attaining to the whole measure of the fullness of Christ" (Eph. 4:12–13, NIV). The pastor is an equipper.

Comparing several translations gives insight into Paul's instruction. In the King James Version, pastors are to be "perfecting the saints" for every good work. The Berkeley version suggests the reading "to make the saints fit for the task of ministering" and offers a footnote suggesting that the reference is to "adjusting as a medical term is implied, as when muscles or bones were dislocated."[1] *The New English Bible* renders it simply, "to equip God's people for work in his service."

What a challenge! Pastors are to help believers discover their spiritual gifts and then equip them to use these gifts so that the whole church is edified. A pastor has the delicate task of fitting all the gifts together much as an orthopedic surgeon does when setting broken bones or a neurosurgeon does when reconnecting severed nerves. This is a primary responsibility of pastors, under the guidance of the Holy Spirit.

The C. B. Williams translation, *The New Testament in the Language of the People*, catches the urgency of the task, for Ephesians 4:12 is rendered "for the immediate equipment of God's people for the work of service," picking up on a note of urgency suggested by two Greek prepositions in the text.

Wise pastors will recognize that their energies will be used best as they equip leaders who in turn will equip others. Such an arrangement suggests the need for a well-organized educational ministry as a vehicle.

ADMINISTRATOR

To administer means to manage or direct the execution or application of the affairs of the church.

The pastor administers by

- serving as resource person;

- enlisting the aid of staff and lay leaders in planning, implementing and evaluating;

- eliciting the participation of the maximum number of members of the congregation;

- delegating responsibilities; and

- overseeing the allocation of finances, space and equipment, personnel, and other resources according to the church's Bible-based priorities.

Administering is an integral part of the pastor's relationship to the educational ministry of the church. Some pastors see it as purely secular and hesitate to devote time to administration. Yet the Bible says, "If God has given you . . . administrative ability . . . take the responsibility seriously" (Rom. 12:8, TLB).

The truth is that pastors cannot fail to administer. They will either do it effectively or poorly. To be a poor administrator is to weaken the congregation's potential as a viable force for godliness in an ungodly world. Poor pastoral administration will certainly produce an educational ministry that is disconnected, aimless, and lacking in vitality.

LEADER

The church is the body of Christ, a living organism composed of believers who function under his headship. As a living organism, the body has organizational structure essential to its functioning similar to the human body's need for structure. For the church body to achieve its mission, Jesus has ordained that it have a leader who serves as undershepherd to the Great Shepherd (1 Pet. 5:2–4). The pastor must be a leader.

A church needs such a leader. The Lord has provided a pastoral leader. Leaders must have followers, so the congregation looks to the pastor for leadership. Pastors must always remember, however, that they hold their office by virtue of the call of God and the congregation. They earn the right to lead as they build relationships, develop trust, and communicate a vision for the church in which the congregation can share ownership.

In a sense, "leader" involves all five of the dimensions already cited, with specific emphasis upon *vision* and *direction*. Whereas the "administrator" focuses on management, the leader must have a dream, share the dream, and elicit support for the dream.

The dream may originate with the pastor, may be suggested by a member of the congregation, or may be born in a lay leadership group such as the deacon fellowship or the church council. In any event, the pastor must support the dream and allow time for it to be expressed, nurtured, and owned by the church until the congregation senses God's leadership for the future.

Then the pastor leads through prayer support, enthusiastic promotion, and organizational structures to achieve the desired result. A good leader has a contagious passion for the dream, exposes the congregation to that burden, and seeks through the Holy Spirit's leadership to keep the church focused on its dream.

Effectiveness is a greater concern for the pastor-leader than efficiency. Efficiency focuses primarily on time management and use of resources. Effectiveness gives priority to relationships. Effective leaders avoid manipulation, pressure, intimidation, and immediate gratification. They lead by example and value long-term consequences over achieving immediate goals.

Being an effective leader is vitally related to the pastor's role in educational ministry. Education is about the process of developing believers toward personal Christian maturity and toward church unity. Key leaders who serve on the church council and the education program councils are prominent in dreaming the dream and in its implementation. Effective pastors cultivate relationships with these lay leaders, use their Spirit-endowed gifts, and affirm them in their endeavors.

Pastoral leaders must look to Jesus, who set the example and instructed his followers to live a servant style of leadership. He had a passion for the mission given him by the Father (see John 9:4). Whatever the obstacles and opposition, he refused to be distracted from his mission (see Luke 9:51).

Not only his vision, his passion for the vision, and his focused ministry, but also his manner and attitude are models for pastoral leaders. With humility he washed his apostles' feet and said he was among them as one who serves (see Luke 22:27). He taught with great patience when they were slow to learn (see Luke 9:46–48; 22:24–27) and confronted them with tough love (Matt. 16:15–21; Luke 22:31–34). The pastor who leads in a manner modeled by the Lord of the church will be an effective leader in the educational ministry.

As pastors consider their role, they often fail to grasp the full scope of their assignment and, thus, limit their effectiveness. Every pastor will be more skilled in some dimensions than others, but none can afford to ignore the fact that the pastoral office includes at least the roles of preacher, shepherd, teacher, equipper, administrator, and leader. All these dimensions have potential for giving good input into the divinely mandated ministry of education.

FOSTERING A TOTAL LEARNING ENVIRONMENT

Pastors need to recognize that learning in the church is not limited to formal study groups. Learning lasts longest when it comes from believers' participation in the total life of the church. The church is a dynamic fellowship. What a new convert experiences through participating in the total body life is a powerful dimension of the church's educational ministry. What children growing up in the church family hear and observe in congregational interaction is highly significant. If a congregation's attitudes and actions are not in harmony with material taught in Bible study groups, the ambiguity will create confusion and result in deficient learning. Acts 2:42–47 provides a model in the interdependent spirit described.

The pastor cannot singlehandedly monitor and fashion the congregational life after the New Testament model. The pastor, more than any other church leader, sets the tone for a body life that provides a healthy total learning environment. Pastors can do nothing more significant for the church educationally than to set an example in the same manner in which Paul did (see 1 Cor. 11:1).

Saying the right words in classes, maintaining orthodoxy in the pulpit, and providing the best classroom learning environment (such as group size, space, and equipment) are important.

But excellence in those areas is not enough if there is low commitment, miserly giving, lack of mission and evangelistic concern—or worship services that exalt pleasing the people above reverence for God and business meetings that are more like a tug-of-war between immature children than a time for prayerful decision-making. Pastors who are intentional about fostering a quality of church life that provides a healthy, total learning environment will make a significant contribution to the educational ministry of the church.

BECOMING PERSONALLY QUALIFIED

Another important step is to become personally qualified for the pastor's role in the education ministry. Pastors are divinely called and endowed by the Holy Spirit with resources to fulfill their calling. This does not, however, relieve them of responsibility for becoming increasingly qualified for educational ministry. The following are ways to enhance your understanding of and contribution as a pastoral educator.

NURTURE YOUR RELATIONSHIP WITH GOD

The place to begin is with the pastor's personal walk with the Lord. The highest rank in a minister's priority system ought to be on *becoming*, with *doing* following in proper sequence. How easily routine tasks can get in the way and detract from one's spiritual life. Love relationships must be nurtured or they will stagnate. The pastor who neglects abiding in Christ will become unfruitful (see John 15:4–6). Fruits of the Spirit can only be produced when there is continuous submission to him.

A pastor whose life does not manifest love, joy, peace, patience, kindness, goodness, faithfulness, gentleness, and self-control will be seriously hindered as a leader. The disciplines of the Christian life must have high priority. Only then will the spirit of Caleb (see Num. 14:24) dominate the pastor and become a contagious spirit within the congregation.

Pastors growing spiritually are marked by integrity, a characteristic that means "wholeness" in the sense that the pastor's belief and behavior are in harmony. The author of Proverbs wisely counsels, "The integrity of the upright guides them, but the unfaithful are destroyed by their duplicity" (Prov. 11:3, NIV). Acting with integrity means that pastors accept failures as a basis for learning and growth. It means that others and their views are treated with respect.

DEVELOP YOUR LEADERSHIP POTENTIAL

Leadership is both a learned skill and an art. Pastors can always develop their leadership potential more fully. How can this be done?

Through prayer, potential will be discovered and weaknesses identified. The Holy Spirit will mold, shape, and renew daily as the pastor yields to divine leadership.

Experience will help the pastor grow as leader. Good experience is an excellent teacher. Poor experience provides opportunity for evaluation, correction, and improvement.

Being open to the evaluation of others can lead to growth in leadership. Not all criticism is destructive. Even that which is intended to be negative can be used positively. Moreover, pastors who have valued relationships with fellow ministers can seek their evaluations and recommendations concerning their leadership style and skill. Written, unsigned evaluations solicited by the pastor from responsible lay leaders may also offer insight.

Finally, leadership potential can be developed by attending seminars and by reading books on leadership. Denominational leaders often provide such training and suggest resources. Leadership workshops and reading materials derived from secular sources may also prove helpful. However, the latter should be used with full knowledge that the church is more than an institution or organizational structure. The nature and ministry of the church have spiritual dimensions that are not adequately addressed by business principles, chief-executive-officer mindsets, or worldly standards of success.

MAINTAIN A READING PROGRAM

Another responsible action is to maintain a reading program. Topping that list should be consistent devotional Bible reading. Reading regularly from a variety of sources ranging from the newspaper and news magazines to current best-selling books will keep you in touch with world events and with the needs, interests, and problems of people. Studying commentaries and other Bible study aids will enhance your growth in biblical under-standing and ability to interpret the Word. Including current works on theology, Christian ethics, church growth, pastoral care, preaching, church history, and church administration will ensure balance in the reading program.

Often overlooked are reading resources related to Christian education. However, attention given to items in the following categories can enhance the pastor's qualifications for leading in Christian education ministry: (1) educational philosophy and principles; (2) historical foundations of Christian education; (3) developmental psychology; (4) teaching/learning theory; (5) administration of Bible teaching, discipleship, and missions education programs; (6) dated periodicals related to the administration of education programs in the church.

ATTEND TRAINING SESSIONS

A final action that will enhance personal qualifications is attending training sessions related to Christian education. The pastor who expects lay leaders to reserve time and money for these occasions must set an example through personal attendance.

When attending such events, the pastor will usually select conferences designed for the pastor. However, occasionally he or she should choose conferences related to administration of preschool, children, youth, and adult educational programs; conferences related to reaching and teaching persons in each of those groups; and conferences related to developing and maintaining specialized ministries with groups like senior adults, single adults, and families.

No pastor can be an expert in all dimensions of Christian education nor in every age grouping, but all pastors can seek to become increasingly qualified. In so doing, they gain confidence, earn credibility with their people, and do a better job.

At the outset of this chapter, two types of churches were mentioned: those served by an education staff and those served by a pastor only. The remaining parts of this chapter will focus on the pastor's educational duties in each of those types of churches.

WORKING WITH AN EDUCATIONAL STAFF

In larger churches the pastor and one or more staff ministers provide the leadership for Christian education. Sometimes, a church will call a minister with combined responsibilities, such as music and education, or education and youth. Other churches have ministers with singular responsibilities, like education, youth, single adults, senior adults, or children. Churches choose various staff patterns and titles according to their circumstances. How the pastor relates to the educational staff will be dependent upon the number of people, level of experience, church size, gifts of the pastor, and the level of supervision and interaction needed.

The following suggestions provide ways for pastors to relate responsibly to other staff ministers and to the church's educational ministry. Generally, this will be as the team coach.

Having a multiple staff does not guarantee a staff team. Teams are built by intentional effort, patience, and cooperative endeavor. In building a church staff team and guiding its plays, the pastor is the player-coach.

VALUE THE TEAM CONCEPT

A prerequisite to the pastor's effectiveness in team building is a conviction that the team approach is important. A paraphrase of an Ecclesiastes passage offers thoughts to ponder: "Two can accomplish more than twice as much as one, for the results can be much better. If one falls, the other pulls him up; but if a man falls when he is alone, he's in trouble" (Eccles. 4:9–10, TLB). Of course, the assumption here is that the two are working together, not against or in competition with each other.

Biblical models of ministry teams can be cited. Moses' work with designated judges (see Exod. 18), Jesus' decision to work with a team of apostles, and the various missionary teams of Paul and associates are examples. These teams were not perfect. One of the Twelve was a traitor. Conflicts about greatness and methodology, as well as personality conflicts, existed on the apostolic and missionary teams. Church staff teams are not perfect either, but they have potential for working together and serving the Lord well.

Teamwork means working together. Building a staff team requires that pastors be clear in their own identity, comfortable in their roles, and not threatened by the gifts and achievements of other staff members. They must have a high level of respect for and trust in each staff minister, and engender respect and trust among the other team players.

NURTURE HEALTHY STAFF RELATIONSHIPS

In building and guiding a team, the pastor must give constant attention to relationships. As coach, the pastor must teach and model principles of interpersonal relationships that Paul taught the whole congregation in Romans 12 (NIV): "Do not think of yourself more highly than you ought" (v. 3); "love with sincerity" (v. 9); "be devoted to one another in brotherly love" (v. 10); "honor one another above yourselves" (v. 10); "never be lacking in zeal, but keep your spiritual fervor, serving the Lord" (v. 11); "be joyful in hope, patient in affliction, faithful in prayer" (v. 12); "bless those who persecute you" (v. 14); "rejoice with those who rejoice" (v. 15); "mourn with those who mourn" (v. 15); "live in harmony with one another" (v. 16); "do not be proud . . . do not be conceited" (v. 16); "do not repay anyone evil for evil" (v. 17); "be careful to do what is right in the eyes of everybody" (v. 17) and "If it is possible, as far as it depends on you, live at peace with everyone" (v. 18).

Teams are fragile. They are either changing and maturing or becoming stagnant. Teams can break apart easily. They may do so for several reasons, but most often the root is lack of humility and need for spiritual maturity by each player. Submitting to the Holy Spirit for renewal and practicing the principles of Romans 12 will bond team members. Staffs that practice New Testament teachings will work as a team, and they will model for the congregation how to relate as God's people on mission.

Besides working on healthy interpersonal relationships, a pastor must give attention to other aspects of a coach's job: teach the basics of the game, design team strategy, serve as keeper of the vision, dream a new dream as appropriate, discover hidden potential and put it to use, encourage teamwork, provide inspiration, give credit for success, and take responsibility for failure. Effective pastors will find ways to accomplish these tasks, common to all coach/team relationships, in relating to staff colleagues.

CONDUCT REGULAR STAFF MEETINGS

Openness to new ideas and freedom of expression is encouraged in regular staff meetings! Full communication is the goal. Negotiation leads toward consensus decision-making. The staff stays focused on the mission of the church and the priorities essential to that mission. There is adequate time in staff planning retreats and in regular staff meetings for projecting plans, goals, and strategies related to the education ministry of the church.

CLARIFY RESPONSIBILITIES

The church personnel committee works to provide well-formulated job description statements for each educational staff person. The pastor's participation with that committee in interviews with potential staff persons ensures clear communication of expectations.

RESPECT LINES OF SUPERVISION

When pastors serve with a minister of education and other staff ministers, making the minister of education directly responsible to the pastor and then allowing him/her to oversee the work of the other education staff will be helpful. Such an arrangement, when approved by the personnel committee or other appropriate body, will clarify lines of responsibility and give the minister of education the authority and leadership opportunity needed to provide effective ministry.

Conducting annual or semiannual evaluations of the minister of education's work will allow the pastor to offer affirmation of strengths and to offer assistance in areas of weakness. The minister of education can conduct similar reviews with other staff members.

PROVIDE SUPPORT

As the team coach, the pastor should represent the educational staff and their concerns in every appropriate arena. Giving public recognition and affirmation, sharing the platform in worship services, and giving support for education needs in budget-planning meetings are examples of strong pastoral support. In addition, the pastor can interpret the education ministry to deacons and other leaders, encourage their support with prayers and attendance, and challenge them to stimulate congregational support for the educational programs and ministries.

Leading an annual worship service for recognizing and commissioning volunteer teachers and leaders is another positive contribution to team ministry. Pastoral presence at educational events will also reinforce the priority of Christian teaching and learning.

THE PASTOR AS MINISTER OF EDUCATION

In smaller churches and in mission settings, the pastor (or evangelist) often is the only minister and must fulfill the duties of a minister of education. Ministerial students must recognize this fact and choose a degree program and course electives that will prepare them for this possibility.

Suggestions offered above for the pastor in larger churches have application for the single-staff church pastor. Some emphases presented in this section are applicable to the multiple-staff church pastor, too. However, in a single-staff situation the pastor must work more directly with lay volunteers.

ENLIST LEADERS

The educational ministry of the church is only as effective as those who lead. Whatever prayer and thought are given to the selection of lay leaders for educational programs are efforts well worth it.

Use the nominating committee. Nominating committees can coordinate selection and enlistment in the best interest of the total church program. Pastors do well to guide in the choice of persons to serve on the committee, seeking persons of a spiritual maturity level who have a good knowledge of the church. Members must respect confidentiality, be keenly aware of spiritual giftedness of potential workers, and avoid decisions that honor personal feelings and preferences above the well-being of the whole church. Directors of educational programs may be added to the committee as they are elected.

Once the nominating committee has been selected, the pastor has responsibility for training the members. These topics should be included in an orientation session: the role of the laity and God's plan concerning spiritual gifts; the role of prayer in seeking workers; ways to solicit member preferences for positions; church-adopted qualifications for service; and any information about positions (workers covenants, job descriptions, and similar documents).

It is important to explain the need for forthrightness in discussion and confidentiality about committee deliberations. All should realize that continuity will be important but that at times changes will be necessary for the good of all involved. The training can conclude with discussion of the enlistment process to be used.

Follow a well-designed enlistment process. Faulty enlistment will contribute to mediocrity, frustration, and perhaps failure in the service rendered by volunteer leaders. But sound enlistment procedures will enable wise selection and generate a high level of commitment. This process begins by involving leaders in recommending and enlisting those with whom they will work.

The process continues, as noted in chapter 14, through these steps:

1. Ask the potential worker for an appointment at a time and place conducive to serious discussion.

2. During the visit, review information about the job (use a job description and/or workers covenant if available), current curriculum resources, and other related documents.

3. Allow time for questions, answers, and discussion.

4. Close with prayer.

5. Set a date for follow-up contact with an appropriate time lapse for prayerful decision-making.

6. Make the contact and receive the response. In case of a negative answer, the pastor avoids use of pressure, manipulation, or guilt tactics. The person is thanked for the time spent and asked if there is another place of service that would hold interest.

Commission the leaders. A careful enlistment process takes work, but it is time well invested. When that enlistment is reinforced by a public commissioning service, the likelihood that leaders will take their roles seriously and serve faithfully is increased.

Carefully selected congregational hymns and special music, well-chosen biblical passages, a sermon focused on leadership commitment and congregational support, and meaningful responsive reading can combine to provide a dynamic worship experience. Leaders will be affirmed and congregational responsibility will be enhanced. Accountability to the Lord among ministerial staff, lay leaders, and congregation will be established.

TRAIN LEADERS

As important as careful enlistment and meaningful commissioning are, training the leaders is essential. To ask a person to fill a leadership position and to fail to provide training and adequate resources is unfair to the leader and detrimental to the mission of the church.

Preservice training. The training begins with preservice efforts. These endeavors may include potential leader training, which is focused on members of the congregation having leadership potential but not yet serving in an elected role. One-on-one enlistment of enrollees, a high level of commitment, a system of accountability, and a public graduation ceremony are components that will strengthen potential leader training.

Inservice training. Once persons are in office, periodic training will make their work more effective and enjoyable as well as diminish the likelihood of frustration, discouragement, and resignation. A balanced training program will include biblical and doctrinal components, leadership skill development in the required areas of expertise, and personal Christian growth studies.[2]

PLAN WITH THE LAITY

Planning is a vital but often neglected dimension in Christian education ministry. Believers' progress toward spiritual maturity is hindered and church effectiveness in achieving its mission is limited because efforts lack clear objectives, goals, and strategies. Pastors who recognize the value of planning and involve lay leaders in that process are wise leaders in Christian education. Such planning usually occurs in a church (or coordinating) council and program councils, or committees.[3]

On the church council, recognized lay leaders represent both the interests of the congregation at large and the concerns of their assigned leadership areas. As the pastor works with key leaders in planning, coordinating, and evaluating the total church program, a total approach to the church's ministry and a balanced educational program are much more likely. A valuable secondary benefit is the development of the laity and the enhancement of the shared leadership concept in the church.

Program councils are led by the lay leader of each educational program and consist of lay persons responsible for various levels of work within the lay leader's unit. Each council focuses on setting goals, planning strategies, allocating resources, coordinating activities, and evaluating progress. When these functions are performed well, each program not only is strengthened but also contributes more effectively to the total work of the church. Again, the laity is empowered, held accountable, and allowed to function at a level of significance suggested by New Testament teachings.

AFFIRM THE LEADERS

Commitment to effective and continuous service will be deepened when volunteers are appropriately affirmed. Taking lay leaders for granted, neglecting to acknowledge their accomplishments, and failing to express gratitude contribute to low morale and to brief tenure.

The pastor's role in Christian education includes offering affirmation in every appropriate way. Public acknowledgments, words of thanks in church publications and in personal notes, appreciation spoken to leaders individually and privately, worker appreciation banquets, and public recognitions of persons who have served well with long tenure are among the ways workers can be affirmed.

CELEBRATE VICTORIES

Smaller churches can lose sight of their significance and easily develop a complacent or passive attitude. Wise pastoral leadership in Christian education will lead lay leaders and the whole congregation in celebrating each accomplishment. Such celebrations give glory to the Lord, encourage the laity, reinforce congregational bonding, and offer incentive to continuing effort.

Celebration may take the form of public recognition of organizational units for a job well done, a congregation rejoicing together over the baptism of a new convert reached through the educational ministry, or a specially planned worship service focused on a significant milestone reached.[4]

THE PASTOR'S ROLE

The pastor is the primary leader in the congregation. The success of an enterprise so integral to the church's mission as the educational ministry is directly related to the pastor's interest, personal investment, and appropriate involvement. The pastor's role in Christian education ministry can never be delegated to anyone else. Pastors who accept that role and fill it as good stewards of a divine trust fulfill a significant dimension of their calling and contribute nobly to the mission of the church.

Resources for Further Study

Section One: Foundations for Administration and Leadership

Aleshire, Daniel. *Faithcare*. Philadelphia: The Westminster Press, 1988.

Benson, Peter L., and Carolyn H. Eklin. *Effective Christian Education: A National Study of Protestant Congregations*. Minneapolis: Search Institute, 1990.

Downs, Perry G. *Teaching for Spiritual Growth*. Grand Rapids: Zondervan, 1994.

Edge, Findley B. *A Quest for Vitality in Religion*. Second edition. Macon: Smyth and Helwys Publishers, 1993.

Foster, Charles R. *Educating Congregations*. Nashville: Abingdon Press, 1994.

Little, Sara. *To Set One's Heart*. Atlanta: John Knox Press, 1983.

Malphurs, Aubrey. *Pouring New Wine into Old Wineskins*. Grand Rapids: Baker Books, 1993.

Mims, Gene. *Kingdom Principles for Church Growth*. Nashville: Convention Press, 1994.

Pazmino, Robert W. *By What Authority Do We Teach?* Grand Rapids: Baker Books, 1994.

———. *Principles and Practices of Christian Education*. Grand Rapids: Baker Books, 1992.

Roehlkepartain, Eugene C. *Exploring Christian Education Effectiveness*. Minneapolis: Search Institute, 1990.

———. *The Teaching Church: Moving Christian Education to Center Stage*. Nashville: Abingdon Press, 1993.

Seymour, Jack L., Margaret Ann Crain, and Joseph V. Crockett. *Educating Christians*. Nashville: Abingdon Press, 1993.

Wilhoit, Jim. *Christian Education and the Search for Meaning*. Second edition. Grand Rapids: Baker Books, 1991.

Section Two: Administrative Principles and Procedures

Anderson, Leith. *Dying for Change*. Minneapolis, Minn.: Bethany House Publishers, 1990.

Barna, George. *Turn-Around Churches*. Ventura, Calif.: Regal Books, 1993.

Bellman, Geoffrey M. *Getting Things Done When You Are Not in Charge: How to Succeed from a Support Position*. San Francisco: Berrett Koehler, 1992.

Cosgrove, Charles H., and Dennis D. Hatfield. *Church Conflict*. Nashville: Abingdon, 1994.

Dudley, Carl S. *Energizing the Congregation*. Louisville: Westminster/John Knox Press, 1993.

Fischer, James C., and Kathleen M. Cole. *Leadership and Management of Volunteer Programs*. San Francisco: Josey-Bass, 1993.

Foltz, Nancy, ed. *Christian Education in the Small Membership Church*. Birmingham, Ala.: Religious Education Press, 1990.

Gangel, Kenneth O., and James C. Wilhoit. *The Christian Educator's Handbook on Spiritual Formation*. Wheaton, Ill.: Victor Books, 1994.

Gangel, Kenneth O., and Samuel L. Canine. *Communication and Conflict Management*. Nashville: Broadman Press, 1992.

Griggs, Donald L., and Judy McKay Walther. *Christian Education in the Small Church*. Valley Forge: Judson Press, 1988

Habermas, Ronald, and Klaus Issler. *Teaching for Reconciliation*. Grand Rapids: Baker Books, 1992.

Harris, Maria. *Fashion Me a People*. Louisville: Westminster/John Knox Press, 1989.

Heath, Daryl, comp. *BreakThrough Small Sunday School Work*. Nashville: Convention Press, 1990.

Kowalski, Theodore J. *The Organization and Planning of Adult Education*. Albany: State University of New York Press, 1988.

Leas, Speed. *Leadership and Conflict*. Nashville: Abingdon, 1982.

Lowry, Robert N., comp. *Designing Educational Buildings*. Nashville: Convention Press, 1990

McCormick, Gwen E. *Planning and Building Church Facilities*. Nashville: Broadman Press, 1992.

Piland, Harry M. *Going One on One: A Comprehensive Guide for Making Personal Visits*. Nashville: Convention Press, 1994.

Powers, Bruce P., ed. *Church Administration Handbook*. Nashville: Broadman Press, 1985.

Ratcliff, Donald, and Blake J. Neff. *The Complete Guide to Religious Education Volunteers*. Birmingham, Ala.: Religious Education Press, 1993.

Roozen, David A., and Kirk C. Hadaway. *Church and Denominational Growth*. Nashville: Abingdon, 1993.

Schaller, Lyle E. *44 Steps Up Off the Plateau*. Nashville: Abingdon, 1993.

———. *21 Bridges to the 21st Century*. Nashville: Abingdon, 1994.

Schein, Edgar. *Organizational Culture and Leadership*. San Francisco: Josey-Bass, 1992.

Schuller, David S., ed. *Rethinking Christian Education*. St. Louis: Chalice Press, 1993.

Stubblefield, Jerry M. *A Church Ministering to Adults*. Nashville: Broadman Press, 1986.

Wilhoit, Jim, and Leland Ryken. *Effective Bible Teaching*. Grand Rapids: Baker Books, 1988.

Williams, Dennis E., and Kenneth O. Gangel. *Volunteers for Today's Church*. Chicago: Baker Books, 1993.

311

Section Three: Educational Leadership in the Local Church

Brown, Carolyn C. *Developing Christian Education in the Smaller Church*. Nashville: Abingdon, 1982.

Bryce, Herrington J. *Financial and Strategic Management for Nonprofit Organizations*. New Jersey: Prentice-Hall, 1987.

Burt, Steven E., and Hazel A. Roper. *Raising Small Church Esteem*. Washington, D.C.: Alban Institute, 1992.

Coote, Robert E., ed. *Mustard Seed Churches: Ministries in Small Churches*. Minneapolis: Fortress Press, 1990.

Foltz, Nancy T., ed. *Religious Education in the Small Membership Church*. Birmingham: Religious Education Press, 1990.

Grenz, Arlo. *The Confident Leader*. Nashville: Broadman & Holman Publishers, 1994

Hassinger, Edward W., John S. Holik, and J. Kenneth Benson. *The Rural Church: Learning from Three Decades of Change*. Nashville: Abingdon, 1988.

Hersey, Paul, and Kenneth H. Blanchard. *Management of Organizational Behavior: Utilizing Human Resources*. New Jersey: Prentice Hall, 1988.

Martin, Glen, and Gary McIntosh. *The Issachar Factor*. Nashville: Broadman & Holman Publishers, 1993.

Means, James. *Effective Pastors for a New Century*. Grand Rapids, Mich.: Baker Books, 1993.

Randolph, W. Alan, and Barry Z. Posner. *Effective Project Planning and Management: Getting the Job Done*. New Jersey: Prentice Hall, 1988.

Weisbord, Marvin R. *Organizational Diagnosis: A Workbook of Theory and Practice*. New York: Addison-Wesley Publishing Company, 1990.

McCoury, D. G., comp. *Pastoring the Single-Staff Church*. Nashville: Convention Press, 1990.

Pappas, Anthony G. *Money, Motivation, and Mission in the Small Church*. Valley Forge: Judson Press, 1989.

_____, and Scott Planting. *Mission: The Small Church Reaches Out*. Valley Forge: Judson Press, 1993.

Stevens, R. Paul, and Collins, Phil. *The Equipping Pastor*. Washington D.C.: Alban Institute, 1993.

Stubblefield, Jerry M. *The Effective Minister of Education*. Nashville: Broadman Press, 1993.

Resources for Specialized Educational Activities

Preschoolers

Carey, Geraldine Addison, and Kay Vandevier Henry. *Teaching in Church Weekday Education*. Nashville: Convention Press, 1988.

Couch, Robert A. *Church Weekday Early Education Administrative Guide*. Nashville: Convention Press, 1980.

Halbert, William A. *Church Weekday Early Education Director's Guide*. Nashville: Convention Press, 1972.

_____. *The Ministry of Church Weekday Early Education*. Nashville: Convention Press, 1977.

Ratliff, Donald, ed. *Handbook of Preschool Religious Education*. Birmingham: Religious Education Press, 1988.

Children

Beaty, Willie R., comp. *New Horizons in Vacation Bible School*. Nashville: Convention Press, 1993.

Christian Day School Administrative Guide. Nashville: Convention Press, 1978.

Couch, Bob, comp. *The Ministry of Childhood Education*. Revised. Nashville: Convention Press, 1995.

LaNoue, John. *Day Camping Director's Guide*. Nashville: Convention Press, 1985.

———. *A Guide to Church Camping*. Nashville: Convention Press, 1976.

———. *A Notebook for the Christian Camp Counselor*. Nashville: Convention Press, 1978.

Ratliff, Donald, ed. *Handbook of Children's Religious Education*. Birmingham: Religious Education Press, 1992.

Roehlkepartain, Jolene L., ed. *Children's Ministry That Works!* Loveland, Colo.: Group Books, 1991.

Youth

Borthwick, Paul. *Organizing Your Youth Ministry*. Grand Rapids: Zondervan Publishing Company, 1988.

Richards, Lawrence O. *Youth Ministry—Its Renewal in the Local Church*. Revised edition. Grand Rapids: Zondervan Publishing House, 1985.

Ross, Richard. *Youth Ministry Council Guidebook*. Nashville: Convention Press, 1987.

Taylor, Bob R., comp. *The Youth Ministry Planbook*. Nashville: Convention Press, 1977.

Single Adults

Allbritton, Cliff, Tim Cleary, Ann Gardner, and Horace Kerr. *Single Adult Ministry in Your Church*. Nashville: Convention Press, 1988.

Fagerstrom, Douglas L., ed. *Singles Ministry Handbook*. Wheaton: Victor Books, 1988.

Koons, Carolyn A., and Michael J. Anthony. *Single Adult Passages: Uncharted Territories*. Grand Rapids: Baker Book House, 1991.

Wood, Britton. *Single Adults Want to Be the Church, Too*. Nashville: Broadman Press, 1977.

Senior Adults

Kerr, Horace L. *How to Minister to Senior Adults in Your Church*. Nashville: Broadman Press, 1980.

Family Ministry

Garland, Diana S. Richmond, and Diane L. Pancoast. *The Church's Ministry with Families: A Practical Guide*. Dallas: Word Publishing, 1990.

Sell, Charles M. *Family Ministry*. Grand Rapids: Zondervan Publishing House. 1981.

Notes

CHAPTER ONE

1. I realize that many scholars and theologians in my formative years were rediscovering the role of family in Christian education. Roger Shinn, however, first captured my attention through his writing. This particular idea came from Roger Shinn, "The Educational Ministry of the Church," in *An Introduction to Christian Education*, ed. Marvin J. Taylor (Nashville: Abingdon Press, l966), 12.

2. Ibid.

3. For additional information, see chapter 4, "How to Plan and Evaluate."

4. James D. Smart, *The Teaching Ministry of the Church* (Philadelphia: Westminster Press, 1954), 107.

CHAPTER TWO

1. W. O. Carver, "Introduction," *What Is the Church?* ed. Duke K. McCall (Nashville: Broadman Press, 1958), 3.

2. E. Glenn Hinson, *The Integrity of the Church* (Nashville: Broadman Press, 1978), 47.

3. Ibid., 44.

4. H. Richard Niebuhr, *The Purpose of the Church and Its Ministry* (New York: Harper and Row, 1956), 19.

5. Ibid., 31.

6. Albert McClellan, comp., A *Basic Understanding of Southern Baptist Missions Coordination* (Nashville: Inter-Agency Council, SBC, 1972), 10.

7. James Smart, *The Teaching Ministry of the Church* (Philadelphia: Westminster Press, 1954), 85.

8. Randolph Crump Miller, *The Clue to Christian Education* (New York: Charles Scribner's, 1950), 37.

9. John Westerhoff, *Will Our Children Have Faith?* (New York: Seabury Press, 1976), 38.

10. Ibid., 39.

11. Miller, *Clue to Christian Education*, 37.

12. *The Oxford English Dictionary*, I (Oxford: The Oxford University Press).

13. Blaise Pascal, *Pensees*, trans. H. F. Stewart (New York: The Modern Library), 13.

14. Ibid., 31.

15. Benjamin Jacob in Westerhoff, *Will Our Children?* 83.

16. Westerhoff, *Will Our Children?* 83.

17. Roger Shinn, "Education Is a Mystery," *Colloquy on Christian Education*, John Westerhoff, ed. (Philadelphia: Pilgrim Press, 1972), 19.

18. Maria Harris, *Fashion Me a People* (Louisville, Kentucky: Westminster/John Knox Press, 1989), 68ff.

19. Arthur Adams, *Effective Leadership for Today's Church* (Philadelphia: Westminster Press, 1978), 5.

CHAPTER SIX

1. Carolyn C. Brown, *Developing Christian Education in the Smaller Church,* (Nashville: Abingdon, 1982), 47.

2. Ibid., 56.

3. Philip Kotler, *Marketing for Non-profit Organizations* (Englewood Cliffs: Prentice-Hall, Inc., 1975), 55.

4. Stephen R. Covey, *The 7 Habits of Highly Effective People: Powerful Lessons in Personal Change* (New York: Simon & Schuster, 1989), 178.

5. Ibid., 188.

6. Ibid., 195–197.

7. Ibid., 199.

8. Ibid., 221.

9. James K. Van Fleet, *Power with People* (West Nyack, N. Y.: Parker Publishing Co., Inc., 1970), 73.

10. Ibid., 108–10.

11. Reginald M. McDonough, *Working With Volunteer Leaders* (Nashville: Broadman Press, 1976), 58.

12. Van Fleet, 145–58.

13. Reginald M. McDonough, *Keys to Effective Motivation* (Nashville: Broadman Press, 1979), 80.

14. McDonough, *Working with Volunteer Leaders*, 59–60.

15. Ibid., 63.

16. Ibid., 58–65.

17. McDonough, *Keys to Effective Motivation*, 125–28.

CHAPTER SEVEN

1. This is an assumption that frequently exists only as an ideal. Church leaders are prone to become positioned as either job- or person-oriented. This author views the ideal as workable and practical in churches in which evaluation and adjustment are normal parts of educational administration.

2. For assistance, see chapter 11, "Guiding Outreach and Enlistment."

3. Portions of the information in this section are adapted from the first edition. The editor expresses appreciation to Charles A. Tidwell for his ideas on the topic.

4. Ibid.

5. For specific information and guidance related to a program or organization, consult your denominational office or religious publisher for recommended resources.

CHAPTER EIGHT

1. Resources for each of the following categories are listed in the "Resources For Additional Study" section at the end of the book.

2. Willian H. Halbert, Jr., *The Ministry of Church Weekday Early Education* (Nashville:

Convention Press, 1977), 9–11. This book was one of the first resources for churches in this area of ministry.

3. Ibid.,12–14.

4. Halbert's book provides information relating to these questions. Additional information is available in William H. Halbert Jr., *Church Weekday Early Educaiton Director's Guide* (Nashville: Convention Press, 1972); and Robert A. Couch, *Church Weekday Early Education Administrative Guide* (Nashville: Convention Press, 1980).

5. John LaNoue, *Day Camping Director's Guide* (Nashville: Convention Press, 1985), 1.

6. Richard Ross, *Youth Ministry Council Guidebook* (Nashville: Convention Press, 1987). This booklet provides practical information related to the youth council.

7. Ann Alexander Smith, *How to Start a Single Adult Ministry* (Nashville: The Sunday School Board of the Southern Baptist Convention, 1980), 23-24.

CHAPTER NINE

1. Nancy T. Foltz, "Overview of Religious Education in the Small Membership Church," in *Religious Education in the Small Membership Church* (Birmingham: Religious Education Press, 1990), 8.

2. Ibid., 17.

3. Donald L. Griggs and Judy McKay Walter, *Christian Education in the Small Church* (Valley Forge: Judson Press, 1988), 17.

4. D. Campbell Wyckoff, "Curriculum in the Small Membership Church," in Foltz, *Religious Education*, 181.

5. Carolyn C. Brown, *Developing Christian Education in the Smaller Church* (Nashville: Abingdon, 1982), 91.

6. Ibid., 33.

7. Griggs and Walther, *Christian Education*, 27.

8. Pamela Mitchell, "Educational Ministry, the CCD, and the Sunday School," in Foltz, *Religious Education*, 83.

9. Ibid.

10. Bob I. Johnson, "Lay Religious Leadership and the Planning Process: Volunteers," in Foltz, *Religious Education*, 139.

11. Foltz, *Religious Education*, 14.

12. Brown, *Developing Christian Education*, 37.

13. Ibid., 37–38.

14. Lyle E. Schaller, in Douglas V. Johnson's *The Care & Feeding of Volunteers* (Nashville: Abingdon Press, 1978), 8. (Also Bob I. Johnson, "Lay Religious Leadership," in Foltz, *Religious Education*, 142.

15. Brown, *Developing Christian Education*, 47.

16. Ibid., 51.

17. Ibid., 54.

18. Ibid.

19. Ibid., 40.

20. A checklist for evaluating curriculum materials is included in chapter 7, "Administering Church Educational Organizations."

21. Griggs and Walther, *Christian Education*, 78.

22. Brown, *Developing Christian Education*, 43.

23. Wyckoff, "Curriculum," in Foltz, *Religious Education*, 182.

24. Ibid., 182.

25. Ibid.

26. David R. Ray, *The Big Small Church Book* (Cleveland: The Pilgrim Press, 1992), 87.

27. Griggs and Walther, *Christian Education*, 70.

CHAPTER TEN

1. See Robert J. Havighurst, *Developmental Tasks and Education* (New York: Longmans, Green and Company, 1952), 5.

2. The current Church Study Course Catalog may be obtained by writing to Church Study Course, MSN 117, 127 Ninth Avenue North, Nashville, TN 37234.

CHAPTER TWELVE

1. See *The Ante-Nicene Fathers, Translations of the Writings of the Fathers down to A.D. 325*, A. Roberts and J. Donaldson, ed. (Grand Rapids, Mich.: Wm. B. Eerdmans Publishing Company, reprinted 1979–1989), vols. 1–10.

2. *Luther's Large Catechism*, J. N. Lenker, trans. (Minneapolis, Minn.: Augsburg Publishing House, 1967).

3. Elizabeth O'Connor, *Journey Inward, Journey Outward.* (New York: Harper and Row, 1968).

CHAPTER THIRTEEN

1. Adapted from Henry Mintzberg, *The Structuring of Organizations* (Englewood Cliffs, N.J.: Prentice Hall, 1979).

2. Adapted from Alan C. Filley, *Inter-personal Conflict Resolution* (Glenview, Ill.: Scott, Foresman, 1975).

CHAPTER FIFTEEN

1. *The Holy Bible: the Berkeley Version in Modern English* (Zondervan Publishing House, 1960).

2. Leadership development materials are available through religious book stores and denominational publishers. For additional guidance in leadership training, see chapter 10, "Training Teachers and Leaders."

3. For additional information, see chapter 5, "How to Organize and Coordinate."

4. See the biblical precedents for such corporate celebrations (1 Chron. 29:9–20; 2 Chron. 6:1–7:10; Acts 11:1–18; 21:17–20a).